D0572473

Top Ten Tips for Parenting Your Teen

1. With privilege comes responsibility. If your teen receives a privilege (a later curfew, permission to use the car, a chance to throw a party at your home, etc.), he must take full responsibility for his actions.

2. Get your facts straight. Nothing kills your credibility with a teen faster than turning out to be wrong.

3. Pick your battles. Don't fight over the insignificant; save your strong words for major issues.

4. Be as nonjudgmental as possible about your teen's friends. If you've communicated your values, your teen will make the right decision in the long run.

5. Teenagers need consistent limits. Don't be afraid to set them.

6. Protect your teen from making mistakes that can last forever. If your teen is doing something that is dangerous to herself or anyone else, get involved.

7. Keep your teen closely tied to the family. She wants and needs to be surrounded by the people who love her best.

8. On the other hand, be prepared to turn in your "being in charge" card. Over time, your teen should be making more and more of her own decisions.

9. Listen before you speak. You may change your mind once you hear what your teen has to say.

10. Always believe in your teen. Believing that your child is good can be a self-fulfilling prophecy.

alpha
books

Top Ten Signs of Possible Trouble

1. If your teen has chosen a friend who is bad news, he may be signaling for help.

2. Loss of body weight, distortion of body image, fear of weight gain, or a preoccupation with food may signal an eating disorder.

3. If your teen isn't keeping up with his peers in school and shows a consistent pattern of difficulty with some aspect of his studies, he may have an undetected learning disability.

4. A teen who "just isn't trying" in school may be an underachiever in need of some attention.

5. A teen who has taken up smoking should be urged to quit before it becomes addictive. Stress that smoking causes several kinds of cancers, makes her unattractive (smokers have early wrinkles and bad breath), and is an expensive habit.

6. Painful or burning urine, an unusual discharge from the penis or vagina, or soreness or a persistent pimple in the genital area of a sexually active teen may be a sign of infection.

7. A teen who threatens to run away may actually do it. Take him seriously.

8. Overwhelming sadness or any type of change in behavior may signal a teen who is suffering from depression.

9. A teen who threatens to commit suicide or gives away her possessions should be taken seriously.

10. Marked changes in behavior such as a shift in friends, a lack of interest in activities he formerly enjoyed, or frequent signs of illness may signal emotional problems or substance abuse.

Don't give up on your teenager. No matter what he has gotten into, he still needs a parent. Get professional help if you need it, but don't ever give up.

The COMPLETE

IDIOT'S

GUIDE TO

Parenting a Teenager

by Kate Kelly

alpha
books

A Division of Macmillan General Reference
A Simon & Schuster Macmillan Company
1633 Broadway, New York, NY 10019

International Standard Book Number: 0-02-861277-9
Library of Congress Catalog Card Number: 96-085367

98 97   8 7 6 5 4 3 2

Interpretation of the printing code: the rightmost number of the first series of numbers is the year of the book's printing; the rightmost number of the second series of numbers is the number of the book's printing. For example, a printing code of 96-1 shows that the first printing occurred in 1996.

Printed in the United States of America

Publisher
Theresa Murtha

Editor
Jennifer Perillo

Production Editor
Lynn Northrup

Copy Editor
Theresa Mathias

Cover Designer
Mike Freeland

Illustrator
Judd Winick

Designer
Kim Scott

Indexers
Ginny Bess
Gina Brown

Production Team
Angela Calvert
Kim Cofer
Aleata Howard
Erich Richter

Contents at a Glance

Contents

Foreword

Congratulations! You are reading a book that will help you help your teen. Kate Kelly, author and mother of three, has researched adolescence thoroughly and offers a warm and friendly reference guide that is full of vital information. Her advice is right on target, whether your teen is a perfectionist or an underachiever, whether she's about to get her driver's license or is seeking a college scholarship, whether he is surviving a breakup or on the verge of becoming sexually serious. Kate tackles everything from learning disabilities to checking accounts. She provides safety tips for when your teen is behind the wheel, in the back seat, on the ball field, and even online in cyberspace.

Kate is funny, smart, and sensible. You want to have a meaningful talk with your teen? Do it in the car, she says, so your son or daughter can avoid eye contact—it's easier to have a heart to heart when you're not face to face. You want your teen to be a reader? Don't just talk up Shakespeare. Sprinkle your home with *People*, teen magazines, and current thrillers (and pssst…if your teen hones his reading skills with Stephen King, don't call it junk).

I'm a mother and the author of *Girltalk: All the Stuff Your Sister Never Told You*. I've answered thousands of letters from teen girls, I write a question-and-answer column for *Girl's Life*, and I have appeared as a Voice of Reason on more than one hundred television talk shows. I do my best to help teens. But by the time I meet the young guests on programs such as "Underaged, Oversexed, and Out of Control," "My Little Girl Has Big Problems," or "Teen Pregnancy Can Ruin Your Life," their troubles have gotten pretty out of hand. These teenagers need advice, sure, but what many needed and didn't have were loving parents who cared enough to act as both advocates and role models.

You are trying to be there for your child. Deep down he or she undoubtedly knows this. And he or she is lucky. But since your own days are probably full, you may not have enough time to become an expert on AIDS, alcohol abuse, video games, computer literacy, or teen money management. That's where *The Complete Idiot's Guide to Parenting a Teenager* comes in. Kate's book can make a big difference in your family's harmony and in your teen's success and self-esteem. She can lead the way through the rocky terrain ahead.

Oh, and next time you bring up a sensitive subject, and your teen's response is "Moooooooom, I know that already!" or "Daaaaaad, give me a break!" don't be discouraged. One of your jobs as a parent is to arm your child with information—and one of his jobs as a teen is to disdainfully imply that he's been there, done that. He probably hasn't. Let him save face, but never stop trying. Your children need to know that you are on their side. Your support, interest, praise, and love will give them the fuel they need to grow up, up, and away.

Enjoy these moody and tumultuous years. Your teens may be tying up the phone lines and leaving trails of clothes, books, and CDs in their wakes. But all too soon, they'll fly from the nest. You'll miss them, you'll welcome them home when they visit, and most important, you'll want to know that you did all you could to ensure your future friendship and to launch their lives as independent individuals. The task is great—the rewards, greater still.

Carol Weston

Carol Weston is the author of *Girltalk: All the Stuff Your Sister Never Told You.*

Introduction

"Little kids, little problems. Big kids, big problems." You may have heard this when your children were babies and kept you up all night, but who would have ever believed it was true?

The issues parents of teenagers must face really are the more serious ones—and even more serious than when you and I were teens. Whether the issue is sex or drugs or cigarettes, today's parents certainly have their work cut out for them when it comes to the serious problems.

Yet the day-to-day issues are just as vital. Despite the occasional walls your teen will build around himself, you have to keep the "two-way communication system" turned on. You have to keep the channel open, not only so you can share good times with your teen, but also so you have a method for providing helpful warnings and information when he's headed for trouble.

If you're like most parents, the two issues that drive you absolutely *crazy* are the state of your teen's room and her nonstop use of the telephone. Well, this book offers plenty of good advice to help you come up with a parent- and teen-friendly solution.

All the pieces are here to guide you through the hills and valleys of parenting a teen. If I've done my job, this book has the underpinnings of the phrase that has guided my parenting:

"You have to give your children both roots and wings"

A lot of this book is about "roots"—the importance of the family, the household, and raising kids who feel positively about themselves, which will help them grow into strong and good men and women.

But another part of this book is about "wings"—showing your teen how to do something and then stepping back and letting her succeed or fail based on her own merits. If she can try her wings while still under your (broader) wing, it is ever so much easier.

Keep nourishing your teen's roots (she is too young to let go), but give her the space she needs to test her wings on her own. This book will help you do both.

It's a challenging job, but someone has to do it. You'll need to take a deep breath now and then, but have fun!

How the Book is Organized

This book is organized to make it easy for you to find what you need when you need it:

Part 1: Home and Family. The family is the first to suffer when your child becomes a teen. (What better place than home to air a really bad mood?) The first and most important step in coping with your teenager is maintaining communication. After that there is advice on keeping your teen tied to the family, and working with her to maintain a room where you don't need wading boots just to get through the clutter. You learn how to create a home and family life that is both teen- and parent-friendly.

Part 2: Teens Inside and Out. What makes teenagers tick? If you're reminded of what it's like to live in a body that grows so quickly you hardly recognize it, and if you gain additional insight into the emotional life of teens, you'll be a more understanding parent. This part also talks about ways to maintain your teen's self-esteem, the single most critical factor to getting her through these challenging years. There's help for you, too, such as what to say when your teen comes home sporting purple hair!

Part 3: School Life. You got your child through elementary school, so your job is finished, right? Wrong. As teens make the transition into middle school and then into high school, they can use some guidance. This part shares some tricks on homework management, explains the possibility of undetected learning problems, and talks about guiding your teen toward extracurricular activities that will lead to a social life of which even a parent will approve. The final chapter looks ahead to college; read this when your teen starts high school. There's plenty of information on building a good school record, and the longer you have to think about this "big decision," the easier your teen's choice will be.

Part 4: Special Interests, Special Privileges. This part tells you all you need to know to become current with the issues that are important to your teen. Do you really need a computer? What does "online" mean? What are reasonable telephone rules? How can you keep a young driver as safe as possible (other than not letting her drive)? And turn to the sports chapter when your teen spends six days a week at practice, and read it, too, when he doesn't make the team. There are lots of suggestions on how both of you can cope.

Part 5: Healthy Body, Healthy Mind. The saying "You can lead a horse to water, but you can't make him drink" might apply here. Much of what your teen does is out of your control—she's the boss of her own being now. However, this part contains solid information about creating an atmosphere that will promote good health. Not only do you want her to learn to eat right, but you want her to think a lot more than twice about drugs or premarital sex. In this part, you get the vital information every parent should know about drinking, drugs, smoking, and sex. The part concludes with what to watch for if your teen is in trouble.

Part 6: Practically Speaking. Schools should teach a class on Money Management 101, but they didn't when we were kids and they don't now. That's why it's very important for parents to give serious thought to what they can teach their teens about managing their money—a subject that, when mastered, can make all the difference in how a young person starts out in the world. Turn to this part, too, for some excellent information on finding scholarships and financial aid money. There's plenty out there, but you do need to know where to find it. Teen employment is also covered here.

If you need more information on any topic, turn to the Resource Directory in the back of the book. Here you'll find a list of places to contact for information on a myriad of teen-related topics. Pick up the phone or write a letter and the material is yours for the asking.

Extras

In addition to the main narrative of *The Complete Idiot's Guide to Parenting a Teenager,* you'll find other types of useful information, including statistical information proving that your family isn't the only one going through this particular experience, side "chats" with suggestions on how you can better relate to your teen, and danger signs that may mean your teen is headed for trouble. Look for these features:

Info Flash

Here you'll read about hard facts or recent statistics concerning the issues discussed in each chapter. You've got to know the facts when you talk to your teen, and you may find the statistics reassuring—hardly anything your teen does is something another teen hasn't tried before.

Tuning In
This feature shows you what a particular topic or problem really means to your family, or what will help you connect with your teen. Read these tips for additional insight.

Danger Zone
This feature provides warning signals, ranging from lists of symptoms that signal possible trouble to alarming trends that are taking place in our society.

Acknowledgments

While many people offered helpful advice (and lived through experiences with their teens, from which I benefited!), there are some special individuals whom I'd like to thank.

Tops on the list is my own teenager, Mandi Schweitzer, who has blazed the "teen trail" in our family for her two sisters, Bibi and Callie. (Every eldest deserves special recognition for "parent training.") The day she looked at me like I was a space alien was the day I knew I had to write this book because I did, indeed, feel like a complete idiot. Once the book was underway, she helped with research, contributed greatly to the chapter on computers and video games, and read every word, telling me when I was off-base about something. Throughout all this, she kept right on being a teenager, which, of course, was invaluable to me.

I'd also like to thank the many teenagers who answered my online questions. I only know your screen names, but if you should find this book around your house, I hope that your life is the better for it. My book is certainly better for the fact that you took time to answer me. May each of you have a smooth entry into adulthood.

Next, I'd like to thank Marian Edelman Borden and Dr. Suad Noah. Marian, a writer and mother of four, not only read chapters and provided feedback, but she has always been there as a sounding board for my many parental issues and questions. Suad Noah provided background suggestions for the book, and she, too, has been instrumental in helping me recognize the importance of believing in your child.

Nutritionist Michelle Daum and her husband, pediatric gastroenterologist Dr. Fred Daum, were very generous with their time. Both read selected material for accuracy and not only gave feedback but checked facts on their own so the material could be as current as possible.

The financial aid chapter covers very complex material, and Elinor Fredston, director of the college information office at Mamaroneck High School in Mamaroneck, New York, was kind enough to go through the material to be certain that it was clear—and as up-to-date as possible for a subject that is constantly changing.

For help with the ins and outs of applying to college, Joan Davis, a college admissions counselor in Seattle, Washington, provided insight and perspective.

Dr. Ann Engelland deserves special thanks, not only for providing perspective for the book, but for going through her library and providing invaluable resources for me to use.

I called Sandra Lovell, a trainer for Planned Parenthood of Northern New England, looking for advice on teenagers and sexuality, and in addition to that, what I found was supportive, loving advice for many aspects of dealing with teens.

Jennifer Perillo at Macmillan Consumer Information Group offered reassuring support as I worked my way slowly through my quite thick files. Thank you, Jennifer, for your patience and understanding.

No list of thank-you's would be complete without acknowledging my husband, George, who not only is my partner in parenting, but who has always supported my "mother's intuition." And because I was at school or driving the kids around on many days when I needed to be at my computer, he was a major contributor to this book for his weekend entertainment plans. Thank you for your love and most of all for your support, George.

Special Thanks from the Publisher to the Technical Reviewer

The Complete Idiot's Guide to Parenting a Teenager was reviewed by an expert in the field who not only checked the technical accuracy of what you'll learn here, but also provided insight to help us ensure that this book tells you everything you need to know to raise a happy, healthy teen. Our special thanks are extended to Dr. Edward Levin.

A Diplomate in Clinical Psychology, Dr. Levin has worked with children, adolescents, adults, and families for many years. He is the author of "Help!"—an advice column for teenagers, teachers, and parents, which appears in Scholastic *Choices* Magazine. Dr. Levin is a supervising and training psychoanalyst at the New York Freudian Society, an affiliate of the International Psychoanalytic Association.

Part 1
Home and Family

Where is that kid you love like crazy?

She's there, but she's hiding. She thinks it's time to start being more independent, and she's not sure it's "cool" to show that she loves her mom and dad and siblings. She does, though, and the key to a pleasant home and family life is to always remember that.

Remember it when she's rude to you in front of your friends.

Remember it when she forgets to do her chores.

Remember it when you open her bedroom door and are afraid to enter.

This part of the book offers advice on creating a home and family life that is both teen- and parent-friendly. With a good sense of humor and realistic expectations, the seemingly impossible is totally possible—and even fun!

Chapter 1

Communicating with Your Teen

In This Chapter

➤ Talking (and listening) to your teen

➤ The noncommunicative teen: turning a grunt into a paragraph

➤ Repairing communication break-downs

Parenting a teen is a lot like being an air traffic controller. Some of the following rules could apply equally to either job:

1. You have to keep the aircraft (teenager) on your radar screen at all times.

2. When you bring the aircraft (teenager) in and something is wrong, you have to do your best to fix it up and get it ready for the next scheduled flight.

3. You cannot leave your post without arranging for a "sub" to work your shift.

4. When the aircraft (teenager) hits air turbulence and the ride gets rough, you have to stick with your job. There's no more important time to be there.

5. You have to keep the traffic moving evenly, but the pilot (teenager) holds ultimate control.

6. Your greatest danger is losing communication with the pilot (teenager). If that happens, you have to work constantly to reestablish communications.

Parents, like air traffic controllers, hold high-stress jobs, and the number of people who give up is high.

So often teens say, "Back off," and parents do, thinking that they're giving their child space to grow. In fact, they're leaving their kid with an uncertain flight path.

The next time your teen is moody, and you're tired of him grumping around, consider this: instead of hearing the whiny, complaining voice of adolescence, think back to a time when your three-year-old shouted, "Mommy, look at me! I can do it!" or your ten-year-old called out, "Hey Dad, did you see that catch?" or your pre-adolescent lifted her eyes when performing in the school play just to make sure you were watching her. Your teen is doing the same thing; he's just gotten better at watching secretly for your reaction.

So no matter how disinterested your teen may *seem,* she's actually there watching very carefully for how you react, what you say, and what you do. And she desperately wants to communicate with you—but on her terms.

Because communication is *the* most vital issue in parenting an adolescent, I'm going to look at it first. If you can keep your "relationship lines" open, you can conquer just about anything that comes along.

Who Ya Talkin' To?

One challenge of understanding teens is that the term "teenager" covers a broad spectrum of people—anyone from the shy adolescent entering middle school to the independent high school senior who has just gotten into his first-choice college. General guidelines will help you better understand the dynamics of communicating with a teen:

➤ **Young teens** (ages 13-14) are continuing to work at establishing their separate identities, and they express this in more obvious ways than they have before. Their attitude at home may be one of rebellion (though they aren't likely to be quite so outspoken or outrageous away from home). They may be dismissive of your thoughts and opinions, but they're still absorbing what you say. Not wanting to be seen with you in public is part of this early stage of differentiating who they are.

➤ **Middle teens** (ages 14-16) are beginning to take more risks. They often make decisions based on what's happening at the moment without regard for how it may affect themselves, their family, or the world around them. (This thinking will change as they continue to develop.) They will begin to experiment with alcohol, drugs, and sex, and it's more important than ever that you continue to communicate your values on these subjects.

➤ **Older teens** (17-up) are coming around and if you've maintained a decent relationship, you may find that suddenly your teen and his friends may alight for a few minutes to talk with you before they go on to something "more important." This can be a rewarding stage, as you begin to get a glimpse of your teenager as a future adult.

An important task of these years is for your teen to become an independent person, free of her reliance on her parents. As a result, teenagers display a certain amount of rebellion, defiance, discontent, turmoil, restlessness, and ambivalence. Emotions usually run high, and mood swings are common. But throughout, they listen. They may choose to ignore you, but don't believe it for a minute when they say, "I didn't hear you." They did.

Info Flash

According to a recent Carnegie Council report, many parents (who admittedly are busy, stressed-out, and confused about their roles) disengage from their teenagers too soon. They believe that hostility from their adolescent is inevitable and that they should get out of the way to let their child become independent.

As a result, kids are left to drift and sometimes get into trouble with nobody nearby to notice.

Setting the Scene

The easiest way to communicate with someone is when you're doing something enjoyable together.

Some families find that ongoing family activities promote communication. (A one-time activity like a day-trip to an amusement park may be fun, but it doesn't provide the regular contact that encourages a relationship to grow over time.) Some family activities might include:

➤ Keeping a jigsaw puzzle in the living room that family members (two or three together) work on at odd points during the week.

➤ Having a television show that two or more of you enjoy watching together.

➤ Preparing and eating Sunday morning breakfasts (or other meals) together.

➤ Making Sunday night "movie night" and going out to a movie together (on Sunday evenings, your teen may be less concerned about being seen in public with you) or renting a movie to watch together at home.

While family activities are very important, you also have to look for activities you can do one-on-one with your teen. (Don't worry, you don't have to take up snowboarding.) However, don't expect the traditions you began when your child was younger to last throughout the teen years—be open to change.

The activity could be as simple as a spur-of-the-moment lunch at the local diner or it could be special tickets for anything from a rock concert or a football game to the ballet. The key to making this work is to follow *her* interests (don't drag her to the opera if you're the only one who likes it). Then she'll be a willing companion, and chances are you'll both have a great time.

Tuning In

A good conversation starter can be as close as your garage. Most kids will open up during a car ride. They're relaxed and they don't have to make eye contact often. (Carpooling is a great time to pick up some "communication information" on your own. The kids will talk about what's going on in their lives and will forget that you're there. Don't remind them by participating!)

Talking to Your Teen

Teens are famous for their noncommittal monosyllabic responses:

➤ "How was school?" "Okay."

➤ "Have you finished your homework?" "Mostly."

➤ "Where are you going?" "Out."

There are ways to try to improve the level of conversation, though it does take some experimenting to find out what works in your household. Here are some ideas:

➤ Remember that your teen is the boss. He can tell you a lot or a little, so accept the fact that you have to ignore the bad moods and accept the good ones. (Occasional bad moods should be ignored; persistent moodiness may be a sign of deeper trouble, and you may want to consult a professional.)

➤ Validate your teen's feelings without going overboard. "I can really understand how you must have felt" will go over better than "Wow! That must have been SO embarrassing!" (If an incident was embarrassing, your teen has already suffered enough!)

➤ Tell your teen what's going on with you. Next time your teen gets in the car and answers "okay" to your question about school, try saying this: "Well, I had *some* day at work. My boss decided she needed something a day earlier than she'd told me, and I had to cancel everything to get it done." Over time, your teen may begin to see that volunteering a report is an acceptable way to communicate.

➤ Share your own memories on specific subjects. Your teen has a tough math teacher? Well, didn't you have one who was absolutely crazy? Tell your teen (sympathetically) how *you* survived the year.

➤ Accentuate the positive. Remember how your mother used to say, "If you don't have something good to say, don't say anything at all." Well, she could have been talking about teens. Realistically, there may be times when you have to have some "tough talks," but they should be few and far between. (You'll learn how and when to handle them in the following chapters.)

➤ Keep things light. If you can get your teen to laugh at you or at herself, your relationship can go far—because it's fun.

There will be days when you could be Oprah and your teen still won't open up to you, but other times, he'll be happy to talk—providing that you listen uncritically, and without too much comment.

Parent-Speak Teenagers Hear

It's easy to talk, but not so easy to make your teens listen. Here are some strategies that can help:

➤ Make statements describing how you feel (use "I" a lot): "I feel worried when you don't come home on time" is much better than the accusatory "You're always late."

➤ If you need to discuss something important, think it through (you can even make notes if you need to). Especially with emotionally charged issues, you want to be clear, and you want to lay the groundwork once. Having to reopen an unpleasant conversation isn't easy.

➤ Be clear and concise in your messages. If you don't approve of teenage drinking, say so. (Refer to Chapter 19 for more information.)

➤ Convey love in all of your messages. "I really love you, but I don't think the plan your friends have for going out of town on Friday is well thought out. I just don't feel comfortable letting you go. I'm sorry." (If this scenario plays out like most, the other friends probably will be denied permission to go, too.)

Tuning In

If emotions are difficult for you to express, try writing them down. "Angry" notes are probably best written and thrown away (but you'll feel better for having blown off steam), "love" notes provide reassurance and inspiration for your teen, and "apology" notes prove that your communication path really is two-way.

Writing notes should not be a substitute for face-to-face conversation (or even a face-to-face apology from you if you blow up at him in front of his friends, for example), but it can fill a gap when you're temporarily at a loss for (spoken) words.

How NOT to Talk to Your Teen

Here's what not do to when you talk to your teen:

➤ Deliver a lecture or a monologue with no opportunity for your teen to respond.

➤ Take an authoritarian approach: "That's how we're doing it because I say so."

➤ Open with an accusation: "Mrs. Smith said she saw a bunch of you in the park in the middle of the school day. You must have cut class."

➤ Fail to take into account your teen's perspective.

➤ Yell to get your point across. If you do lose your temper (and everyone does now and then), apologize later on after you've calmed down. You don't have to apologize for how you feel, just for blowing up. Highly charged anger directed at someone is inappropriate no matter what the situation. There are more effective ways to explain how you feel.

➤ Nag. It doesn't work anyway.

➤ Criticize. Most of the things to which you'll object have to do with trends your teen is following to be one with his peers. If you allow your teen to take charge of himself in areas such as clothing, hairstyles, makeup, music, room decor, speech, and use of money, you're less likely to have difficulties with major issues, such as substance abuse. (Remember, too, the more you complain about strange and untraditional behaviors, the longer they will last.)

There may be occasions when you want to express your opinion, and that's okay, too. Just say how you feel in a non-accusatory way. For example, you might say that you regret that your son got his head shaved and will look forward to when it grows out. Ridiculing his shave-job will only make him angry at you.

Info Flash

Communicating with teens when they're around is tough enough, but it's really difficult to communicate with them when you don't know where they are. Chapter 13 has some innovative ideas for ways to stay in touch via the telephone, but you might also consider a beeper. For a few dollars a month, you have a way to get in touch with them to let them know you need to hear from them.

Listening to Your Teen: Do You Hear What I Hear?

Listening is more than being quiet while someone else talks. Here are some guidelines:

➤ Pay attention to the trivial as well as the important. If your teen realizes that you're a good listener, he's more likely to talk to you about all kinds of subjects.

➤ Give your undivided attention to your teen if he's telling you something that's important to him. Don't read or do dishes or channel-surf.

➤ Teens share intimacies at some of the most awkward times. If you can, try to clear time to listen right then; if you can't, let your teen know that you really do want to talk and suggest another time.

➤ Ask questions to clarify, but not to criticize. There will be times when your teen will interpret any question as criticism. If she does, back off (assuming there is no safety issue involved). You'll get more of the story by staying mum.

Being Unreasonable Is Reasonable for a Teen

Five minutes ago your daughter was bad-mouthing her friend, Jenny. Now she reappears in the kitchen, fresh from a phone call, and says: "I'm going over to Jenny's tonight. Will you drive me?"

What you should *not* do is comment on the fact that five minutes ago she never wanted to see Jenny again. Assuming there is no issue of physical safety involved, the wise parent won't even raise her eyebrows. Your daughter will repeatedly change her mind about Jenny (and many other issues) during the coming years, and she'll make the best decisions as to what's right for her if you just listen but stay uninvolved.

"That was then, this is now" is another phrase that is helpful to remember when speaking to teens. Your son may have just spilled his guts about how difficult chemistry is or how bad he felt about not making the soccer team. Those conversations should be on his terms. Bringing sore subjects up again later on will earn you several black marks in his mental column of "Things I Can't Tell My Parents."

Communicate Belief in Your Child

The surest way to cut off communication with your adolescent is by being critical of your teen or by doubting her behavior. If you're "on her case" all the time, she'll disappear as often as possible. (Wouldn't you?)

Express interest and support in your teen's activities. "It's okay if you can't come to my baseball game," should not be understood as permission for you to stay at home. While you may have to miss some games (or performances or other events), get to as many as you can. In addition to showing your support for your teen, it gives you a brief glimpse into her world. You'll see her friends, know who she's talking about, and you'll probably have the opportunity to meet some of the other parents—contacts that will be important as you weather these years.

Info Flash
Most teens talk to their mothers; fathers need to become part of the communication loop, too. Availability helps any communication equation, so the father looking to be more involved with his teen might offer to fill in on weekend carpooling, or think of a father-teen activity that provides opportunity for conversation.

A sure-fire way to keep communication channels open at all times is to always be open to his opinions. He will be more attentive to your question if the question has something to do with his lifestyle. (His opinion on the presidential debates will only be a good conversation-opener if he's a news or politics junkie.) The opinion could be anything from where the family ought to take Grandma to dinner to whether his school's sports teams are doing well. Some days he'll sit down and chat for 15 minutes; other days you'll get a brief answer, but that's okay. You've treated him like an adult by letting him know that you care what he thinks.

If You're in a Rut with Your Teen

There's no doubt that communicating with a teen is a road filled with ruts. It's easy to get stuck. A few bad months of disagreeing over everything can make it seem doubtful that the two of you will ever speak civilly again. Here's what to do:

➤ If your spouse is still on good terms with your teen, assign him or her the job of prime communicator.

➤ If there is no one to fill this role, then reduce your conversation to the bare necessities. Anything you say should be said civilly and with no sarcasm.

➤ Begin looking for nice things to say, whether it's how good she looks on a given day or the fact that (at last) she remembered to dunk her plate in the sink after dinner. Say nice things with good spirit.

If you're going through a truly horrendous time with your teen, it may seem like you will *never* be able to think of a nice thing to say, but you will. As you cool down, start remembering what you've always liked about your kid, and from one or two good qualities, more will follow.

A business executive was once speaking to a colleague about a coworker whom both of them disliked. The colleague asked the executive, "But you seem to accept him in better spirit than I do. How do you do it?" The business executive said, "In sales, I learned that you always have to find one thing to like, and after a lot of observation, I finally realized I really like Jim's ties. As a matter of fact, he's got truly *great* taste in ties. After that, I could always start a conversation on friendly turf, and we usually do well from there." The same will follow with your teen (although you'll probably have to find something to like besides his taste in ties).

➤ As the tension cools, try to think of something your teen might enjoy doing with you. If the two of you are great basketball fans, splurge on tickets and go. At the event, continue not to nag or say anything negative.

➤ As the hostility drops, take small steps toward asserting a normal relationship: "John, could you please see that your uniform gets into the laundry tonight?" should be taken in the spirit in which you said it; if he stomps around and says it's your fault it isn't in the laundry already, then repeat the above steps for a few more weeks to see if a bond can be built.

Danger Zone CAUTION
If retreating for a time, moving forward with kindness, and then trying to assume a normal relationship doesn't work, consult a professional. Counseling may be able to root out what's troubling your teen.

Final Thoughts on Communication Breakdowns

Here's what teens say cause communication breakdowns:

➤ "My mom always wants to give me solutions to my problems when all I really want is for someone to listen to me. If I can talk it out, I can probably figure it out for myself."—M.W., 16

➤ "My parents always say everything I'm going through is a phase. They never relate to my problems or acknowledge that I have problems—they say it's just a stage."—A.R., 15

➤ "Sometimes I just don't feel like talking, but my parents won't leave me alone. They just keep asking questions."—J.M., 15

➤ "I'm an only child, and my mom reads all these parenting books and is always comparing me to them. She also wants to know too much about my life. I like talking to her most of the time, but when she wants to be the 'expert' about what's going on with me, I don't feel like talking." —K.D., 16

➤ "My mom and her friends gossip about our lives all the time, and she asks me the most embarrassing questions about dating. I've finally had to say, 'Mom, I'm not giving you any more details.'"—H.H., 18

➤ "My mom doesn't realize that while, yes, I've made mistakes, generally I try to be the best person I can be. It bugs me that she totally underestimates me."—S.T., 17

The Least You Need to Know

➤ Though your teen wants to talk on his terms, he does still want to communicate with you.

➤ Find activities you can do together to foster opportunities for talking. (If time is tight, try the car—most kids will talk while you drive.)

➤ Listen more than you talk.

➤ Don't nag, lecture, or criticize. These don't promote two-way conversations.

➤ Try to resist bringing up touchy issues you and your teen spoke about previously. Remember, that was then; this is now.

➤ While you must still be the parent in this relationship, try treating your teen with the respect and tact you would use with a good friend.

Chapter 2

Family Involvement and Obligations

> ### In This Chapter
>
> ➤ Family time
>
> ➤ Obligations are a two-way street
>
> ➤ Planning for the future

Jerry Seinfeld has been quoted as saying, "There is no such thing as fun for the whole family," and this is almost true if you have teens around. You can no longer drag them along to family picnics if there's no one there who interests them; they don't want to be seen going to the movies with you; they have so many activities they're rarely home; and when they *are* home, they can be moody and difficult.

So just when it's looking like a good time to beat a hasty retreat, don't. It's one of the worst things you can do for your teen. Whether you're part of a traditional nuclear family, a single parent family, or a newly blended family, it's important to help your teen feel like he belongs, and—like it or not—it's good for your teen to interact with annoying siblings and parents who think that it *is* reasonable to ask him to take out the trash.

On the other hand, too much togetherness with your teen isn't really healthy either. Teens need their space and an increasing amount of independence. So your teen can bag the picnic, or leave early after dinner at Grandma's. But don't ever let her think the family is a low priority—it isn't. (Deep inside it isn't even a low priority to her. She still needs and wants you very much.)

"You're [Still] in the Family Now": Family Involvement

Family expectations don't always have to do with chores or with grades; some expectations have to do with what kind of family members you are all expected to be. While a parent's obligations involve providing food, shelter, guidance, and safe passage through childhood, children—and adolescents—have obligations, too. These obligations have to do with being thoughtful, kind, reliable, and being there so you can enjoy being a family together.

Family mealtimes are a good time to get together. Realistically, rounding everyone up for a meal may seem like a practically inhuman feat, but keep trying. If Sunday night is the only night when other obligations don't interfere, make that dinner a required one.

Some families like to get together regularly in a family meeting. Topics under discussion can range from division of chores to how to solve the bathroom crush in the morning to where the family should go for vacation. Monthly meetings may be enough, or you may decide to schedule them on an as-needed basis.

(If you have memories of a father or mother who turned family meetings into long lectures, then try a more casual time for discussing family matters, such as over dinner or when you're all in the car.)

Tuning In

One good reason for requiring your teen's presence at certain events (family gatherings or neighborhood block parties) is that you need to keep broadening his network. The African proverb "It takes a village to raise a child" is a true one. The more people you can involve in your child's life, the emotionally richer and safer he'll be.

These situations also provide your teen with experience interacting with adults—a skill that will benefit him as he makes his way in the world. By including your teen in family and community events, you also have the opportunity to set an example. If you're always the one who remembers to call your elderly aunt to ask if she needs a ride to the family dinner, or if you make time to speak with everyone when you go to a community picnic, your teen will eventually notice your behavior.

That said, remember she is a teen with a life of her own. Require that she come to what you consider "priority" events, and let her slide on some of the others.

Having Fun as a Family

Teenagers may be resistant to taking a vacation with the family. Yet family vacations offer you a chance to build relationships and enjoy your time together. All of you are free from at-home distractions, and once your teen is comfortable, she'll probably revert to being "just one of the family" again. A few pointers on planning the ideal family vacation:

➤ Give your teen input into where the family is going. Each family member should specify what they want to do: one may want to visit museums, another may want a theme park, a third may want to take a road trip to see the country. After you've heard everyone's "requirements," chances are good you'll be able to come up with a location that meets everyone's needs.

➤ Most families who travel with teens report that the best trips are ones where the teens have some freedom. (You probably don't want to spend 24/7 with them at home; why would you want to do it on vacation?) Find a way to give everyone some individual space.

➤ Also consider teen-sleep, which isn't like normal-sleep. Because most teens like (and need) to sleep late, plan a family or individual activity that doesn't have to involve your teen in the morning. His eyes will be open by lunch, and you can bring him along after that.

Families who have established a tradition of good family trips report that their college-age kids check on when the family trip is scheduled before booking the rest of their summer plans. Not a bad goal to keep in mind!

House Rules: Family Obligations

Household rules—and the consequences of breaking them—should be spelled out clearly. (Family meetings may be the ideal time to do this.) Writing them out and posting them will avoid confusion. Some of the topics that usually come up involve shut-down times for the telephone; curfews; car rules; use of loud music after a certain hour or during homework time; and so on. (These subjects will be covered in detail in later chapters.)

Consequences for breaking these types of rules are generally best matched to the offense. Breaking a telephone rule might result in no telephone use the following night, for example.

Ask for your teenager's input on all issues discussed at the family meeting—including rules. Your teen may have a perfectly valid reason why he can't fulfill one of your expectations, and working out a solution now will save you both irritation later on.

Taking a Stand

One difficulty about taking a stand is that there is no "teen rule book" you can buy that will tell you how to judge issues of permissions, independence, and control. As you read through this book, you'll find lots of advice that suggests a certain level of acceptable and unacceptable behavior, but you'll have to take responsibility for wrestling with yourself regarding what *your* family rules will be. You'll also have to work out any differences you have with your spouse if you're part of a two-parent household. Who deals with school-related problems? Whose curfew rule holds? Who determines social guidelines? It isn't easy. (But then again, whoever said it would be? If only babies came with notes!)

Parents who are consistent with their rules have an easier time than parents who aren't specific or who are too flexible. (If you've been consistent since your teen was a toddler you'll probably have an easier time now; if you weren't so consistent, it's *never* too late too start.) If a parent says "no" to a particular sleep-over with questionable circumstances, the teen who is used to consistency will understand it as "no." The teen whose parents are inconsistent will simply wheedle, assuming that she will eventually get her way.

To further complicate this, the parents who have spent years saying unreasonable no's to reasonable requests may well find that they raise a teenager who sneaks out of the window at night. Kids know when you're saying no just to say no, and when you're saying no to keep them safe.

One of the most challenging and interesting aspects of parenting today is the fact that our generation has not taken an authoritative approach to parenting, and we're raising a generation who is not afraid to ask questions. We have to be prepared to respond to them.

If your teen has a complaint about something, listen to her. You don't have to give in every time, but give her a hearing, and then make a reasonable decision about what to do.

When Being Reasonable Isn't Enough

No matter how consistent you are, at some point you're going to say, "Please be home by midnight," and she's going to respond with "You're ruining my life. No one else has to be home that early." What should you do? You have some choices:

You can listen to her plea and decide whether there's room for flexibility.

Or

You can decide that a midnight curfew is more than reasonable for tonight. If this is your decision, don't stoop to arguing with her. Just state your case and the consequences if she doesn't meet her obligations.

The best punishments fit the crime. If she swears at you about the midnight curfew, but keeps the curfew, she won't lose any points, but tell her that politeness will earn her additional flexibility in the future; rudeness won't. If she defies you and misses her Friday curfew, restrict her social life on Saturday.

When Your Teen Makes an End Run (Around You)

Kids can get pretty good at "working you over." Here are the most common strategies they use:

➤ *Divide and conquer.* Say that Dad says it's okay when you ask Mom, or vice versa. The same game can be played throughout the neighborhood: "Mary gets to go to the rock concert, so can I?" Good spouse-to-spouse or parent-to-parent communication is the secret to being heads-up on this ploy.

➤ *Everyone else gets to...*This is a good one. Remember that you still have to decide what's right for your child.

➤ *I know what I'm doing.* A statement of independence and autonomy designed to get you off their back. Remember, you're still the parent. You have to decide if they *really* know what they're doing. If they don't, does it matter? (No, if it involves programming the VCR; yes, if he wants to drive out of town to a game when a storm is threatening.)

CAUTION

Danger Zone

If your teen challenges you, try to avoid losing your cool! It's damaging to your relationship with your teen. When you feel yourself getting angry, ask that the discussion be delayed, and then excuse yourself. You may want to consult your spouse or a friend, or simply step outside for a few minutes.

If you do blow up at your teen, apologize later. Out of control anger is never appropriate (and only effective temporarily), so an apology will stand you in good stead.

When there is an underlying problem, try to work it out. If the two of you are head-to-head, ask your spouse or a friend to mediate.

Tuning In

When your teen comes home announcing a good decision she made, reward her. If she tells you that she decided to come home early from a keg party that was getting out of hand, tell her you admire her good judgment.

Another favor you can do your teen (besides noticing when she's wise) is to offer to stick up for her when the going gets rough. Be willing to stand up for your teenager. Teens are a misunderstood group, and it is not unusual for them to be accused of something they didn't do. It's also perfectly possible for a teen to get off on the wrong foot with a teacher. Sometimes your stepping in can make a difference.

If you sense that your teen or his friends are being misunderstood, talk to your teen about whether he would appreciate your stepping in. Often adult interference is unwelcome, but if he is up against a difficult situation, it may help him out, and certainly your belief in him will earn you a lot of respect.

The Buck Stops Here

During these years, your teen has to learn to make decisions in preparation for adulthood. It's your job to gradually increase your level of trust and his level of responsibility.

While you would never agree to a dangerous decision, something that might result in physical harm (to her or to anyone else), it's time to start letting out the rope bit by bit. First decisions for young teens might be inconsequential ones like whether her hair should be short or long; later ones might involve whether to talk to a friend about something that's bothering her or whether she wants to take AP Physics. You can be there as a sounding board, possibly commenting on the pros and cons of a particular decision, but when all is said and done, more and more decisions belong to your child. Making mistakes is part of life, and it's much better for your teen to go through those "learning mistakes" while she's still in the safety net of the family. (Remember, she's the pilot, you're the air traffic controller.)

Get a Life (Your Own)

It's easy to get sucked into your teen's problems as if they were your own. Remember to pay attention to *your* life and let your teen make the ultimate decisions (most of the time) about her own.

Thinking the Unthinkable

Nobody likes to think about dying, but if something were to happen to you, what would happen to your teen? One of the most important things you can do for your teen (and your family) involves a piece of paper—your will. If you're like most people, chances are you haven't thought about it. But it's important to draw up and execute one now. Dying intestate (without a will) means that your assets will be distributed according to state law, not according to your wishes.

Contact a lawyer now, and get your will taken care of. (If you've already written a will, but want to revise it, draw up a new one and make sure your old one is destroyed.)

You may also want to reconsider your choice of guardian. The person or family you selected when your child was little may not be the perfect guardian for your teen. Your teen's guardian may be too old to keep up with teens, or may have moved away.

Parenting of teens requires enormous quantities of mental energy to engage the teenager while "holding the line." Some parents find that family friends make ideal guardians—because they're in the community and are going through similar stages with their own kids.

> **Info Flash**
> You can divide guardianship so there's a "guardian of the person," who will watch your child, and a "guardian of the property," who will manage the inheritance. (Ideally, the two guardians should have a good working relationship.) Consult a lawyer for more information about guardianship.

The Least You Need to Know

➤ Family time should still be a priority, even for teenagers.

➤ You need to provide consistent rules, with some (occasionally) negotiable flexibility. Teens who have guidelines do better than those for whom everything is negotiable.

➤ Begin to let your child make more and more of her own decisions, starting with small things.

➤ When your teen exercises good judgment, be supportive.

➤ Make the time to plan for your child's future, if anything should happen to you and your spouse.

Chapter 3

Pitching In: Household Responsibilities and Chores

In This Chapter

➤ Encouraging your teen to assume some household responsibilities

➤ Determining which chores are appropriate for your teen

➤ Establishing a "chore calendar" of assignments and deadlines

➤ Teaching your teen how to get chores done

Family life features few "performance reviews." Few families take the time to evaluate how things are going and make a new plan based on that evaluation. It seems like only yesterday that your son was six and he needed some help from you when it was time to pick up his room. He's a teenager now, and it is right—and appropriate—to shift an increasing amount of personal and household responsibility to his shoulders.

This chapter shows you how to do it—peacefully.

Life with a Teenager: Teaching Personal Responsibility

The very coupling of the words "household" and "teen" probably makes you sigh. If your family room is typical, chances are that it's normal after-school state features a floor strewn with backpacks and sneakers (for feet bigger than you ever dreamed possible), a couch draped with clothing and open magazines, tables with snack dishes still awaiting a conveyor belt to the kitchen, and at least one body lounging at a computer or sprawled on a chair or the floor doing homework while talking on the phone.

If you were to venture down the hall and through the mist into a typical post-teen bathroom, you would find wet washcloths in the tub and—if you're lucky—a crumpled soggy towel slung over the towel bar. (More likely, the towel would be lying in a damp mound on the floor.)

If you live with a teen who doesn't have a clue how annoying it is to coexist with a slob, then you might be inclined to get angry. Instead, look at this as an educational process. Just as you taught your kindergartner to tie her shoes, you are now going to teach your teen to be a good roommate.

When your child is a pre-teen, you should begin to emphasize his need to take personal responsibility for himself, his belongings, and his surroundings. Kids who learn cooperation, self-reliance, and thoughtfulness gain confidence, coping skills, and independence. They become better adults all around.

What Has Your Teen Done for You Lately?

As you consider your Svengali task of transformation, keep in mind your goal: You want to create a teen who has the potential to be a good roommate—someone who picks up after herself, takes care of her own dishes, and keeps a room that is tidy enough so that you can identify the color of the carpet and the major pieces of furniture. (And you want to do it soon enough that her current roommates—her family—benefit!)

Reform that lasts is implemented slowly and in small doses, so you should start with something simple, but something that will make a big difference to you. Think of a couple of small chores your teen could do that would help you maintain a better household. For example, how would it feel if your teen was expected to:

➤ Bring snack dishes to the kitchen and put them in the dishwasher?

➤ Leave the kitchen as he found it after fixing a snack?

➤ Put sports equipment in the garage instead of the front hall?

➤ Put shoes away (instead of leaving them all over the house)?

➤ Turn off lights as he leaves a room?

Decide on your new expectations and discuss them with your teen. Explain why it's important that everyone take more responsibility for themselves.

Giving Orders a Teen Can Understand

Your teen is far more concerned about her complexion than she is about the state of your household, and you can save both time and angst by clearly communicating what is bothering you. Be specific. Just as a toddler responds better to "pick up the blocks" than to "clean up your room," the same is true for a teen.

You can make your expectations even more clear by creating a checklist. For example, an index card taped to the mirror in the bathroom might bear this post-shower checklist:

➤ Wring out washcloth and hang on side of tub.

➤ Hang towels on bar.

➤ Use bathmat to dry up puddles on floor and hang over edge of tub.

➤ Put shampoo back in cupboard.

For a while, you may have to remind your child of her new responsibilities—expect to, and don't get angry. You're teaching a new behavior, one that she has been able to avoid doing for a good number of years.

If your child still doesn't comply after a time, though, you'll need to take stronger action. Establish age-appropriate consequences. It's best if the consequence has something to do with the offense: "If you don't have time to help around the house, then that means I have to devote extra time. For that reason, I won't be able to drive you to the game this weekend."

If a new habit has been particularly difficult to develop, you might consider reward system. For example, if he remembers to clean up after himself in the kitchen for a full month (with two days off for bad days), it's worth a new CD. After a month of good behavior, chances are good that the reform will

Tuning In
If your teen still doesn't "get it" (picking up the family room, for example), ask what the problem is. It may turn out that his nine-year-old sister is responsible for some of the mess in the family room, and he's rebelling because he doesn't feel he should have to clean up after *her*. This is good for you to know. If you can instill responsibility in your nine-year-old now (a perfectly acceptable expectation), your son will be happier because you really listened to him, and your family room will be neater.

be complete. (Remember, though, that this is a reward system, not a payment. After earning the first reward, your child should be expected to do the chore on his own.)

As each new behavior becomes habit (when you're no longer tripping over his size 11 sneakers as you come in the door, because he's finally "gotten the message"), add a new one or two without making a big issue of it.

In an ideal world, no one else would have to empty someone else's pockets before throwing jeans in the wash, remove clothing from the floor, or trip over backpacks and shoes left all over the house. Though nirvana is difficult to reach, you should set "improvement" as a goal. Choose the responsibilities you want your teen to handle, and with love and patience keep reminding her of them.

Why Nagging Doesn't Work

Your kids are used to you by now. They recognize your sighs and your shouts, they know your tolerance level, they know that after you blow up, you'll calm down. That's why nagging won't get you very far.

Lead with principles (remind them that all family members need to work together) and gentle reminders. If you need to, you can draw up a list of fines for undone chores, or continue the occasional withdrawal of privileges.

Keep things fair. The list should include obligations for all family members, and fines should be levied against adults, as well as kids, who don't pull their weight. Put the money in a centrally located container and agree to spend it on something fun that the whole family can enjoy, like a volleyball net for the backyard or a dinner out.

Tuning In

As a member of the household, there are certain expectations that need to be met to make the household work. If you've ever had a craving for ice cream and found that when you opened the freezer it was all gone, you understand that cooperation is key to having a pleasant, well-organized household.

Here are a few common-sense household rules to get you started. Build on these to create your own list:

➤ Write down the groceries you need when you are low, not out.

➤ Clear the table after you've eaten, and put the dishes in the dishwasher.

➤ If you've used the last of the toilet paper, get out a new roll.

➤ If the wastebasket is full, empty it.

➤ Everyone in the family (babies and toddlers excepted) is responsible for putting away their own laundry.

➤ If you track mud in the house, clean it up.

➤ Let the dog in (and wipe his feet) when he bangs on the door. (Yes, a teen can sit two feet from the door and ignore a deafening bang.)

While your teen probably already does a good number of these "good citizen" tasks, start adding new ones that are important to you. If you do it slowly, it won't seem like you're on her case.

And always remember to compliment your teen for being helpful: "It was terrific of you to clean up after the little kids—they left the kitchen a mess!" or "Thanks so much for picking up milk on your way home. I didn't realize we were so low." Words of praise are gratifying to everyone, and teens are no exception.

Start with Chore Choice

All family members should have household chores to do that are appropriate to their age—it's part of any type of cooperative living. And if your teen lives in two households as a result of a divorce, she should hold responsibilities in both locations.

Schedule a family meeting to discuss a redistribution of chores. You'll need a list of daily chores (setting and clearing the table, washing dishes, laundry, walking the dog, taking out trash, watering the plants, etc.) and those that must be done weekly (grocery shopping, dusting, vacuuming, errands).

A happy worker is a better worker, so ask if any family member has a particular request. Most teens prefer chores that display an instant benefit ("If I help with dinner, I can eat it"). And a new driver will do almost anything that involves being out in the car. (You may never have to run another errand again!) A chore such as dusting is less rewarding because most teens don't care much about what they consider invisible dirt anyway. They also like chores with flexibility. Having to do the laundry on Monday will probably be less popular than cleaning out the car once a week.

Some families rotate chores; others prefer to make permanent assignments. While rotating chores offers variety and allows all family members to learn to perform various tasks, it becomes more difficult as your children become older. If your daughter goes to school and is on the swim team, chances are she's only home for brief periods during the weekday. Taking on a weekend task may be all that she can do. Another benefit of a constant assignment is that it promotes pride in a job well done. If someone notices how neat everything is in the family room, there's a specific person to thank. (And do remember to notice and thank!)

Chore assignments will go more smoothly with a check-off chart for all family members. If your teen is responsible for breakfast dishes and your ten-year-old helps with dinner, your family chart might look like the following daily chores calendar:

Daily Chores Calendar

	Mon.	Tues.	Wed.	Thurs.	Fri.	Sat.	Sun.
Feed dog							
Wash breakfast dishes							
Make dinner							
Do laundry							
Take out garbage							
General household pickup							

Weekly chores could be done at the convenience of the chore-doer, as long as they are accomplished (and checked off) sometime during the week. Weekly chores can be charted on a weekly chores calendar:

Weekly Chores Calendar

	7/6	7/13	7/20	7/27	8/3	8/10
Vacuum						
Dust						
Bind up newspapers for recycling						
Change bed linens						

This system also allows for swapping. If your son knows he has to leave for school early on Monday, he can ask his sister to cover for him and he'll help out at dinner instead.

Setting Deadlines

Chores need deadlines—relatively tight deadlines for daily chores, and more lenient deadlines for less frequent chores. On evenings when everyone has eaten dinner together (perhaps at 7 p.m.), family members should know that dinner dishes must be done by 8 p.m. (and you can always point out that with a chore such as kitchen clean-up, the sooner they do it the less difficult it is). Laundry should be folded shortly after the dryer stops to reduce wrinkling. If your teen is in the middle of something at that point, ask him when he can do the folding (in 15 minutes? in 30 minutes?) and set the kitchen timer to remind him.

An advantage to setting a loose deadline for weekly chores (such as wiping down the porch furniture before Friday at 6 p.m.) is that your teen can feel more freedom as to when the chore is done and will learn a different type of responsibility. If he does it Thursday, then Friday afternoon he can get the weekend off to an early start with his friends.

If you're at work in the afternoon when your teen arrives home, you've got a perfect opportunity to delegate specific chores with a set deadline. Your child can start dinner or organize the house for you in the afternoon, at her leisure—so long as it's done before you get home. Leave a checklist for each afternoon, detailing what dinner is planned and what must be done ahead of time.

As schedules change, you'll need to conduct a chore review so that family members still have an assignment they can maintain with their new schedule.

Info Flash

A study conducted by Dr. Laurence Steinberg of Temple University revealed that a higher incidence of anxiety, depression, behavioral problems, and alcohol abuse was found in children of overindulgent families than in children from homes in which parents set consistent boundaries and responsibilities.

Taking on household responsibilities really is good for children!

Boiling Water 101: Teaching the "How to" of Chores

Believe it or not, it's perfectly possible to be alive for 15 years and not have any idea how to make a grilled cheese sandwich.

Once you give your teen a new chore, assume that she knows nothing about how it should be done. (Anyone who has ever watched a teenager "wipe the counter" by using a sopping wet sponge to push the crumbs onto the floor will know that is not a bad assumption to make.) An obvious benefit to teaching the chore carefully is that eventually it will be done more or less the way you would like it to be.

Here's how to introduce your teen (and younger children) to a new chore:

➤ Explain the job. Why do you sort laundry by color? What kind of soap do you use? What does loading the washer "evenly" mean? (Nothing is too basic to explain, but don't talk down to your teen—after all, you want to teach, not to lecture.)

➤ Break the job down into steps and demonstrate it. A full vacuuming of the family room, for example, is going to involve removing couch cushions to vacuum for crumbs, putting the cushions back, and then switching vacuum attachments to do the floor. (Make sure you demonstrate how to switch attachments.)

➤ Show her where any supplies are kept. It doesn't ease your burden (or put her in charge) if she has to come and ask where things are.

➤ Keep an eye out for how she's doing, and compliment her regularly and often.

Info Flash

Be sure that your chores transcend gender barriers. If you've taught your son some basic repair skills, your daughter should be taught them as well. And your son should be as capable with a frying pan and an iron as your daughter is.

Most families assign chores that perpetuate gender stereotyping. Studies indicate that girls are more likely to do dishwashing, clothing care, and cleaning chores; boys are more likely to be assigned maintenance, yard, car, and pet-care chores. (Some teens may actually prefer chores that perpetuate the stereotype, but be certain that both genders know how to do all chores.)

And there's a big disparity in the time spent on chores, too. (This should be no surprise to mothers.) Girls log in 6.1 hours weekly, to boys' 4.2 hours.

The True Value of Chores

Maintaining a household is easier when everyone helps get chores done. But there are other reasons why it's important that your teen learn to do chores. Her popularity is going to plummet when she moves into a dorm with her friends and they discover she leaves the bathroom a mess, or when his first question on entering the shared kitchen is, "How do I fix a hamburger?" And for the teen who moves out on his own, you've provided him with the skills he'll need to run his own life.

While no one really considers housework when they talk of raising confident, capable children, housework—like it or not—is part of life. A teen who can make pasta primavera for his vegetarian friends or who thoughtfully tidies up after himself in the bathroom will exhibit a thoughtfulness for others that will take him far in life.

Tuning In

Don't pay for general household responsibilities or regular chores. And don't link allowance and chores either. (See Chapter 21, "Money for Today," for more tips about allowances.) Do pay for extra chores that go above and beyond the scope of normal responsibility.

For example, your teen may have certain regular responsibilities, just like every other member of the family. However, if your teen tackles a major task like cleaning out the garage (which goes above and beyond what any other family member is doing that week), extra pay is certainly in order.

The Least You Need to Know

➤ Begin teaching responsibility by expecting your teen to pick up after himself. Work on these behavior changes a few at a time.

➤ Each family member should take on general responsibilities (adding to the grocery list, putting away laundry) that keep the household running smoothly.

➤ Let your teen choose some of her chores; assign those that are left over, keeping her schedule in mind.

➤ Teach the chore carefully (don't assume he knows how to do it), and set a regular deadline for when chores must be completed.

➤ Chore assignments should transcend traditional gender boundaries.

Chapter 4

Teen Rooms: Livable Solutions

In This Chapter

➤ Why order ranks low in teen priorities

➤ Making the room fit your teen

➤ Room neatness tips

➤ Helping your teen keep track of belongings

"The place is a pig sty."

"I just close the door…"

"I'm afraid there's mold growing in there."

"I wouldn't go in there without a survival kit!"

The subject, of course, is "teenagers' bedrooms." If you have ever uttered one of these comments, it may make you feel better knowing that the state of a teenager's bedroom is one of the top two issues families fight about (telephone use is the other one; see Chapter 13).

However, there is encouraging news. With thought, open discussion, hard work (room reorganization will help a lot), and mutual respect, it is possible to set up a teen room that suits all members of the family.

As you read, keep in mind these three principles concerning your teen's bedroom:

➤ It is her space.

➤ It should be a place that reflects her interests.

➤ It should adhere to your cleanliness standards because it's a room in your house.

Reading this should already make you feel better—most parents just close the door and fume. Remember, you do still have some say over that space.

"This Room's a Mess!"

Most teens don't mean to be messy. It's just that neatness isn't that important to them. (And they do have a cultural stereotype to live up to—aren't teens supposed to have messy rooms?) In most families, the state of the bedroom is not an act of teen rebellion (unless it's become a major family issue); it's an honest response to housework—who thinks it's a fun thing to do?

Look at it from a teenager's standpoint. If you had to try on seven different outfits before leaving for school like your daughter did, the floor in your room would be a mess, too. And remember, she did have her priorities in order: She opted to leave for school on time rather than staying home to hang up those seven different outfits.

Despite the disorder, teens do want their room to be a place where they can stake their independence. You can help them achieve this in ways that don't involve half-eaten sandwiches on the desk and old gym socks under the bed.

Is This a Room Fit for a Teen?

One reason your teen's room is a mess may be because the storage arrangement no longer works. Just try stacking sweaters for a 14-year-old in the same space where sweaters for a 6-year-old were stored, or putting ice hockey equipment where a baseball bat used to go, and you'll begin to understand that your teen's needs are changing.

Answer the following Teen Room Questionnaire to help you form an action plan.

Teen Room Questionnaire

➤ Is it a shared room? If so, is there adequate room for each sibling and his or her belongings?

➤ How does your teen use the room? (For homework? To hang out with friends? Or only for sleeping and "passing through?")

➤ How is it decorated? (If the room still sports a childhood theme, it's time to redecorate.)

➤ What types of things are hanging on the walls?

➤ Is there enough drawer or shelf space for putting away folded clothes?

➤ Is there adequate space in the closet to hang clothes?

➤ Are provisions made for removing out-of-season clothes to make this season's clothing more accessible?

➤ When was the last time you or your teen sorted through the closets, weeding out what is outmoded or outgrown? (For example, clothes that no longer fit, whites that look gray, and anything that hasn't been worn recently.)

Based on this evaluation, make a list of some of the changes that you can make that will create a better room for your teen.

If you decide that redecorating is in order, resist the urge to make the decisions yourself. Talk to your teen. He may offer color or design suggestions, and you can let him make choices from pictures in a catalog or swatches you bring home from the fabric store.

Explain to your teen that while it's his room, it's your house, and though you'll try to let him have what he wants, you both may need to compromise. For example, if he wants an all-black room, you might suggest that black be the accent color, since you would find black walls very difficult to live with. If the two of you enter into it with goodwill, there should be a way to make each of you reasonably happy.

Tuning In

Once parents have a teenager, they often experience a tremendous urge to "help" their kids grow up by getting rid of stuffed animals and tossing out baseball cards.

But what's the hurry? Teenagers are in transition, and by letting them keep one foot in childhood for days when they need it, you help make the passage to adulthood a gradual one. By letting them keep some things, you convey the message that it's okay to take two steps forward and then a step back. They'll get where they are going faster and easier if you let them.

If space is at a premium, there are solutions. Ask your teen to choose the items that are most important to him. Offer to box up the rest and store the box on a shelf or in the basement indefinitely.

Re-Thinking the Space

Consider the function of the various parts of your teen's room. Most bedrooms should accommodate a dressing area with a mirror (near the closet and/or dresser), a quiet area (the bed and perhaps a comfortable chair), and a work area (a desk). Consider traffic flow from the main door to the various parts of the room. (The bed is generally the largest piece of furniture; don't place it so it disrupts flow.)

If siblings share a room, consider whether there's a way to create privacy within the shared space. Some families use bookcases as room dividers. You could also rig up some type of cloth divider. Or think about glass block (large bricks of glass). It's opaque but translucent, so it provides privacy but allows light to filter through to the internal side of the room. If the space is not big enough to divide (or if the siblings don't want a divided space), try to create separate storage areas. Having adequate space for each person's belongings can make shared living much more pleasant.

Does the room make a statement about the family attitude toward studying? A room with no bookshelves or study space may be a self-fulfilling prophecy. Even if your teen prefers to study elsewhere in the house, provide space in his room for additional study materials. There should always be shelves for books—with room for both his old favorites and new discoveries.

Lighting is important. In addition to an overhead fixture, there should be good supplementary lighting by the bed, by the desk, or in any area where your teen may read or work.

Many home supply superstores sell new "closet systems" that are great space savers. They can help make a small closet seem larger by providing double hanging and shelf space in closets that were wasted with a single pole. You can have professional companies install this for you.

If you're having shelves built for additional storage, have a coat of polyurethane added. It makes for better storage and easier cleanup.

Most teens like to express themselves through what they hang on the wall. Tackboard that can be painted the same color as the wall can be cut to fill an entire wall, leaving plenty of space for tacking posters, pictures, photographs, and small mementos on the wall without doing any damage. This system also permits a teen to update her interests regularly.

Tuning In
The more healthy outlets you give teenagers for self-expression, the less need they'll have to find unhealthy ones.

Though teens report that the state of their room is a relatively low priority most of the time, they do look at the space as a haven. If you can instill a sense of control that will bring with it pride, you'll have gone a long way toward creating a neater room.

Organization, Teen-Style

If you think your teen is capable of reorganizing her room on her own, think again. Reorganizing a room is an overwhelming task for an adult, and you're going to need to help out. It's best if the two of you work together. (Even if you're not organized by nature, the following guidelines will give you the basics to straighten out a room. You may like it so well, you'll implement these measures throughout the house!) If your teenage son has no patience for folding and putting away T-shirts, let him handle a more difficult project that is his responsibility anyway, like sorting through memorabilia or deciding which books he wants to keep in his room.

Set aside several blocks of time or a full day to reorganize. You'll need a spray cleaner, dust cloth, vacuum, garbage bag, and laundry basket. Also bring in some boxes and label them "To Store Elsewhere" and "To Give Away." You'll also want boxes (or you can create piles) of the items that will stay in the room: desk items, books, mementos, collections, sports equipment, and so on.

Working clockwise around the room, sift through all items and classify them, dusting or cleaning each area as it's emptied. You'll need your teen's input on which items to toss and which to save.

Consider where the "To Store" items will be kept. Oversized sports equipment might belong in the garage or basement (buy a basket or bin to keep items from rolling around and tripping up the whole family); a plastic box might be perfect for holding a baseball-card collection; and it may finally be time to buy your daughter a makeup organizer.

If you use storage containers, make them accessible. The key to getting a teen to put something away is to make sure that she won't have to lift or open anything extra in order to do it. (Stacked baskets and storage units within a closed cabinet just don't get used.)

Neatness Counts: Creating a Room that Won't Be Condemned

Some parents think they'll wait out the messy room phase and simply close the door. If you're considering this, you've got a long wait, and you've provided no guidelines for how the room is going to be cleaned—a hygienic necessity.

The first step in establishing guidelines for a neater room is to make your teen's job as easy as possible. You can help with this:

➤ Invest in a comforter or quilt rather than putting a bedspread on the bed. A simple toss of this heavier style of bed cover in the morning can cover a multitude of wrinkles.

➤ Put a laundry basket in the closet and stress the necessity of putting all laundry in it.

➤ Make it a family rule that if dishes are permitted in the bedroom they must be brought back to the kitchen the next morning. (The first ant or mouse your teen finds in her room should cure any lapses in a hurry!)

Your next job is setting the "neatness standard" to which your teen must abide. Here, you've got to be respectful and realistic. You do need the room dusted and the carpet vacuumed once a week, but you don't need the place looking like a hotel room. The best way to provide guidelines is to list the tasks that must be performed once a week. These will probably include:

➤ Changing the sheets on the bed

➤ Putting the laundry in the hamper

➤ Putting clothes away

➤ Emptying the wastebasket

➤ Clearing and vacuuming the floor

➤ Dusting the furniture

Set a time when all cleaning chores must be complete. There are a lot of advantages to setting deadlines prior to the weekend. Your teen's school schedule may slow down toward the end of the week, and she's got weekend privileges in view. Without being punitive, you can certainly make it clear that room chores must be complete before the weekend begins.

While positive reinforcement works best with everyone, including teens, you can try other measures if you find that you're not getting through. The best measures are cause-and-effect:

➤ If your teen has not had time to do his room chores, then he does not yet have time to go out on Friday night: He can go out as soon as he's taken care of his room.

➤ If you have to vacuum her room, then you do not have time to drive her to the mall as she wants you to do.

While it's easy to get emotional about how many times your teen has ignored requests to clean his room, humor, goodhearted reminders, and a possible reduction of privileges will take you a lot farther. A teenager needs to learn that you'll give him his space, but it has to live up to the agreed-upon family standards.

Tuning In

"Can't you just throw these out?" How often have you felt like saying that about your son's mineral collection or your daughter's old set of exercise tapes? While the remnants of hobbies that have definitely been outgrown might be candidates for the trash, be supportive of other interests your teen may take on—regardless of how you perceive their value.

Like anyone else, many teens become quite passionate about collecting old record albums or current CDs, creating a great sound system, building a comic book collection, or acquiring an amazing wardrobe of footwear. Your teen is beginning to establish an identity, and this is part of the process.

Know When to Step Back

If your teen has just taken an after-school job, sports season has started, or her play is one week away, ease up. Teens are only human and they deserve to have a week off here and there.

Don't look the other way indefinitely, however, because disorganization creeps in one shirt and one piece of paper at a time. (See it from his vantage point: If there are three old T-shirts balled up in the corner, why should the fourth one be put in the laundry basket?) If you see that a formerly acceptable room is beginning to look like a trash heap, offer your services—free of criticism. A teen who has been doing a pretty good job with his room will continue to do so if you help get it back in shape.

"I Can't Find My _____!"

If your teen is constantly misplacing things and running late because he has to tear apart the household looking for them, there are some things you can do to help out. Consider:

➤ Is there any consistency to what she loses or where she loses it? (Consistently losing or forgetting homework might call for a parent-to-teen talk. Something else may be bothering her.)

➤ Are mornings the worst time?

➤ Does he forget to bring home all the things he needs to do homework after school?

➤ Does she need a better organizational system for the things she keeps losing?

Once you've evaluated what the circumstances are, you can help create a system for solving the problem:

➤ A teen who leaves for school without his homework should be taught to put his homework in his backpack as soon as he finishes it. Remind him of this for as long as it takes to become a habit.

➤ The number of misplaced items should decrease as her room reorganization takes place. As your teen learns to put things away, she'll begin to see that it's easy to find them again.

➤ If there is some item he needs regularly (car keys, student ID), show him how to create a special storage place (a hook, a bowl, a place on a shelf) and always put the item in that one place.

➤ Teach her to make reminder notes for herself. Does she need to take an extra snack today? A permission slip for a field trip? Tell her to write a note and leave it where she'll be sure to see it (by her backpack, perhaps, or at the breakfast table). This is the type of responsibility you should be shifting to her shoulders. You don't need a family fight that begins, "You forgot to remind me to take my permission slip!"

Both adults and kids need reminder systems, and if you can teach your teen a few, you'll both have an easier time!

Teen Space, Teen Privacy?

Can your teen shut you out of her room, claiming privacy? No. While certain elements of your teen's life certainly are private, her room isn't really one of them. It's your house, and it's perfectly appropriate for you go in and out of her room occasionally (daily or weekly). What if she's left candy bars on the floor and now has mice? These are issues you need to know about.

If you've kept the computer, TV, and sophisticated sound system elsewhere in the house (as recommended in other chapters in this book), you may want to consult a professional if your teen is spending enormous amounts of time in her room alone. But put this in context—if your teen is an avid reader, she may simply be shutting out the household noise in order to enjoy her latest book. That's a good reason for checking in on her now and then—if she's reading, you'll know it.

Should you snoop while you're in the room, and she's not there? No. Would you want her snooping in your room? Respect goes both ways. Does this mean you should *never* snoop or ask questions? No, not at all. Here are some guidelines:

➤ If you overhear your teen talking about doing something forbidden (drugs, beer party, "doing it," someone being beaten up, etc.) 'fess up to your teen that you overheard. You may be right to be concerned and will want to get involved.

➤ If your teen leaves something in your path (a letter from a friend, a diary, or personal notebook) more than once, you can assume she wants it read. Sometimes teens purposely want you to "find" something because they know no other way to bring up a sensitive or troubling subject.

➤ While your teen's room needs to be open territory, he ought to have the right to a private drawer or area of the closet. This private area should be investigated by you only if you observe some type of worrisome behavior: He's suddenly hanging out with a very different group of friends whom you don't know, his behavior changes drastically (he's become very secretive, for example), or he's acting in such a way that you fear he might be hiding drugs or alcohol in his room.

Every teen needs privacy, but if your teen walks into the house, strides to her room, and slams the door, check on her in a little while. She may actually want to talk. (Knock before you go in, just as you would want her to knock on your closed door.)

The Least You Need to Know

➤ Consider whether your child's room still meets her space needs.

➤ Do what you can to reorganize the room.

➤ Consult your teen if you redecorate.

➤ Provide storage that is user-friendly.

➤ Establish a "neatness standard," and ask that your teen achieve it once a week.

➤ If your teen occasionally neglects to keep the room clean, offer to help out before it becomes a disaster area.

Part 2
Teens Inside and Out

You may look at your teen and wonder, "Who is this?" Teens grow, they change, and they alter their appearance. Even when you live with them, their transformations can catch you by surprise!

This part of the book tells you what physical and emotional changes to expect. Helping your teen manage his growth and development (and feel good about it in the process) will boost his self-esteem. And a teen with positive self-esteem will weather these years far better than one who isn't sure of himself.

So just before you get totally fed up with his newest hair color or nose ring, do yourself a favor: Get out some photographs of when you were a teen.

Point proven?

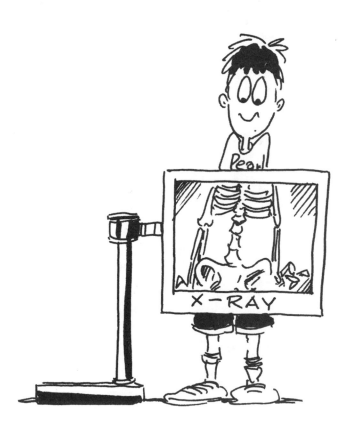

Chapter 5

How They Grow: Physical Development

In This Chapter

➤ Physical development for boys

➤ Physical development for girls

➤ Choosing a good doctor for your teen

You need only walk into a seventh grade classroom to get a view of the variety of growth and development at this age. Most of the boys will still look very young; they may be shorter than some of the girls, and they will show little sign that they're approaching adulthood.

The girls are another matter. While a few will look like they still belong in elementary school, many of them will be growing to their adult height, and most will show some signs of breast development.

They're all gathered together, labeled "seventh graders," but about all they have in common at this moment is their grade level. Everything else is changing, and don't think for a moment that they aren't comparing and wondering whether they're "normal."

Though of course you, too, were once an adolescent (not that your teen will believe it), this chapter will help remind you of the changes that are transforming your adolescent's body as he or she develops from a child to an adult in a very few short years.

This is a "just the facts" chapter. For too long, body parts and sexual development have been discussed with funny words and evasive descriptions. I want to provide you with the straight facts so you will be well prepared to have accurate and informative conversations with your teen on a topic that is important to everyone.

Info Flash

Growing pains are for real. (Teenagers grow so much, small wonder it hurts!) Approximately one in five adolescents experience aches in their shins, calves, or thighs. The attacks most often happen at night and can last up to a half hour at a time. They can occur over a period of months or even years.

Growing pains are not a cause for alarm: massage, heat, or occasional use of a pain reliever can help your teen feel better. If your teen suffers severe or chronic leg pain, consult your doctor.

Growing Up Physically

During puberty your child will grow faster than at any time since the first year of life. At times they will seem to grow overnight. In preparation for this growth, both boys and girls may add a little fat before puberty. This fat gain is normal, and parents should assure a teen who is concerned that the extra weight is simply the body's way to prepare for getting taller.

Info Flash
All parts of the body do not grow at the same time or rate. The hands and feet usually grow before the arms and legs, and the arms and legs before the torso. If your teen seems awkward and gangly, it's because he is! You can assure him that he'll soon "grow into" his size 13 feet.

As a result of all the hormonal changes they are going through, both boys and girls are prone to acne at this time. Teens of both sexes are extremely self-conscious about looking pimply-faced; see Chapter 7 for more information on skin care.

While your teen can't escape the awkwardness and confusion that these rapid growth changes will bring, patience with his body will help make this transition easier. (See Chapter 17 for more information about diet and health.)

Growing Up, Boy-Style

Boys are every bit as aware of their bodies as girls are, and in locker rooms, bathrooms, and gyms, they compare themselves to others constantly. Usually the tallest, strongest boys command the greatest stature among their peers, and the later your teen enters puberty, the more difficult it is for his self-esteem.

During their growth spurt, some boys become tall and reedy, and they may develop an interest in muscle-building (looking like a "weakling" makes them vulnerable to teasing). However, boys should wait until late puberty before they begin any type of weight-lifting program (at least Tanner stage 4). Refer to the section, "What Do You Mean, She's Stage Three?" later in this chapter for more information on the Tanner stages.

In addition to wanting to grow taller and more muscular, your son will be interested in the development of his reproductive organs. Growth of pubic hair is the most obvious indication of male puberty, but penile growth and enlargement of the testes actually begins before that. (Some boys start changing as early as age 10, and almost all boys will see some signs of development by the time they're 13 and a half.)

Teenage boys will also notice that although they've had penile erections for their entire lives, these erections will become much more frequent during early or mid-puberty because of an increase in male sex hormones. All boys begin to experience erections when they don't anticipate them. (Sometimes these erections occur at the most awkward moments, like while standing in the hall talking to a girl or when called upon in class.)

They also occur frequently during sleep and sometimes result in nocturnal emissions. These are described as "wet dreams" because semen is released during sleep. This ejaculation is perfectly normal and is a sign that a boy is maturing sexually. With age, wet dreams will become less frequent because of masturbation and intercourse.

Boys sometimes are concerned about the development of the testes and penis. In most males, one testicle (usually the left) hangs lower than the other. Penis size also brings up feelings of anxiety, because

> **Info Flash**
> To their great embarrassment, almost two-thirds of boys develop some swelling around the nipple during the early stages of puberty. This is normal. The puffiness will disappear within 12 to 18 months. The swelling is caused by a temporary imbalance in hormones.

> **Tuning In**
> Sweat glands change in both boys and girls at this time, and you'll want to encourage your teen to start using deodorant—for peer acceptance as well as your own aromatic pleasure.

boys with small penises are often teased by their peers. Most boys don't realize that the size of another boy's flaccid penis may be a poor indication of how large it is when erect. Also, male sexual function has nothing to do with penis size. Give your son the facts and tell him there's no reason for concern.

As a boy's larynx grows, it causes his voice to "crack"—a source of embarrassment for many boys. Once his larynx has enlarged to its full growth, your son's voice will deepen. Gone will be the days when he's be mistaken for his mother or sister when he answers the telephone!

Tuning In

It's vital that you talk to your teen about what's happening to his or her body. Ideally, parents should initiate basic discussions about growth and bodies, in age-appropriate ways, from the time their children can talk. This helps make the topic easier to talk about later on. (For information on talking about sex, see Chapter 18.)

While most parents realize that they have to talk to their daughter when she's about to start having periods, some neglect to have any discussions about development with their sons. (This discussion is best handled by Dad, or a male substitute if no father is present in the household.) Casual discussion is best, particularly in a situation where your teen can avoid eye contact (such as when a parent drives him somewhere, or as he moves around the kitchen helping to prepare a meal).

Even if he claims to know it all, he may be secretly relieved to know what's happening when he has a wet dream, and that he'll never ejaculate involuntarily while at school.

Growing Up, Girl-Style

In girls, breast development can begin any time between the ages of 8 and 13. (Later development may be considered "delayed" but is not necessarily abnormal.) As the breasts grow, pubic hair will begin to appear, and your daughter will grow very rapidly.

Early breast development can be a source of embarrassment, and if your daughter is among the first in her class to develop breasts, she may be very self-conscious about it. She may favor big shirts, and bras that flatten rather than "point" her breasts during these early days. She will probably be uncomfortable until some of her friends begin to develop, too.

Bra shopping is another milestone. It's actually become much easier, given today's wide fashion selection. While there's a limited selection of bras for the new wearer, your options increase with cup size.

Young girls who are developing often like the look of sports bras; otherwise, pick up one white or skin-colored bra for her to wear under white or light-colored shirts, and then let her select whatever other color and style she likes. Designers are making bras in every style, from zebra-stripe to polka-dot. They've certainly made growing up more fun! Let her enjoy it.

Approximately two years after the first sign of breast development, your daughter's first menstrual period will occur. (Your pediatrician will be able to give you a slightly more accurate timetable based on the progress of your daughter's development.)

Prior to menstruation, glands within the female genital system often secrete a fluid ranging from clear to white in color and from watery to thick in consistency. This is quite normal and can persist for several years.

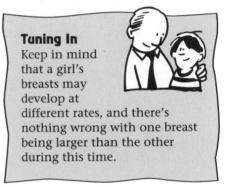

Tuning In
Keep in mind that a girl's breasts may develop at different rates, and there's nothing wrong with one breast being larger than the other during this time.

Early menstrual periods are almost always painless, because cramps don't usually occur until ovulation takes place (which can be 6–20 months after the onset of menarche). Irregular periods are normal and they will become more regular over time.

It's All in the Attitude

How you present menstruation to your daughter may have a big effect on her attitude. Just as some cultures celebrate boys becoming men, you might consider treating menstruation in the same positive light—as a celebration of the wonderful woman she is to become.

Mothers should avoid referring to menstruation as "the curse" or complaining about PMS or terrible cramps. Negative references will convince your daughter that she's entered a bleak phase of her life. (It's hard to persuade a 13-year-old that the "miracle of giving birth" makes it all worthwhile.) A positive attitude about the manageability of mood swings and menstruation will take her far.

Also check with your doctor. Tampons are very liberating, and many physicians will say that as soon as your daughter is willing to try, there's no problem with using them. (Learning to use tampons is an art; give her a box and show her the general directions on the instruction leaflet, then let her experiment. She'll get the hang of it after a few tries.)

Tuning In

If your daughter chooses to use tampons, tell her about toxic shock syndrome, a relatively rare but extremely serious illness that can result from tampon use. To avoid TSS, doctors recommend changing tampons regularly, wearing a pad instead of a tampon at night, and using the lowest-absorbency tampon appropriate. (In other words, stuffing in a "super" and figuring she won't have to change her tampon all day is not a good idea.)

Symptoms of TSS include a high fever, feeling faint, vomiting, diarrhea, chills, headaches, sore throat, rash, and a vaginal discharge. These are also symptoms of many other illnesses, but if your daughter does come down with a high fever or what seems to be a bad virus while using tampons, have her remove the tampon and check in with the doctor.

"What Do You Mean, She's Stage Three?"

When your son or daughter gets an annual physical, the doctor may describe the stage of reproductive development according to an adolescent growth scale established by J.M. Tanner (and known as the Tanner stages of development). The following figures illustrate these stages, so that you'll be aware of what the doctor is telling you.

Male genital and pubic hair development reflecting the Tanner developmental stages.

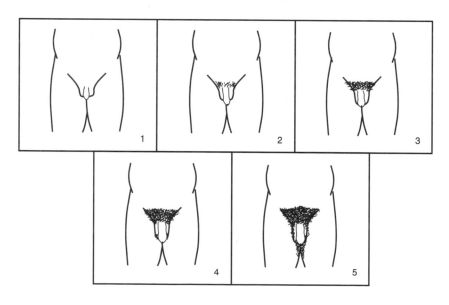

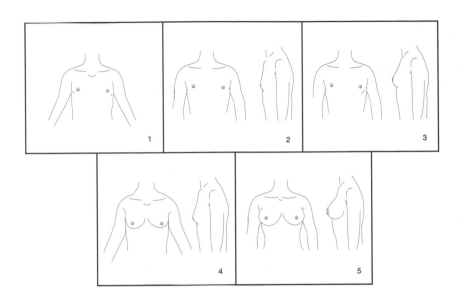

Female breast development reflecting the Tanner developmental stages.

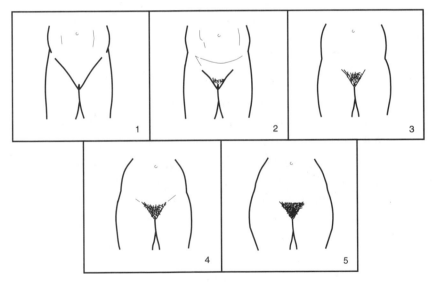

Female pubic hair development reflecting developmental stages.

It's perfectly normal for girls to be at one Tanner stage in breast development and at another stage in pubic hair development. These ratings can be particularly helpful in that the doctor will be able to come up with a fairly accurate estimate of the onset of menstruation.

Tuning In

As your teen develops, he or she will need help with hygiene.

Shaving for boys: Most boys are thrilled when it's time for them to shave. Don't laugh when your son tells you he needs to remove the "duck fuzz" from his lip. Get him a razor and let him get started. Before long he'll be threatening to grow a beard or goatee.

Shaving for girls: As soon as your daughter decides she wants the underarm hair to go, give her a razor. As for leg hair, it's nice to be able to forego shaving (as any adult woman can tell you), so if your daughter has light hair, counsel her to wait. Some daughters like to try hair removal creams, but they may sting. The tried-and-true razor is probably still the best hair-removal method.

Girls may also develop a light "mustache." Commercial cream bleaches usually take care of this, but some teens eventually opt for electrolysis (a more expensive and painful, but permanent, option).

Tuning In

Many parents are still uptight when it comes to sexual matters. For that reason, your teen may have learned from toddlerhood on that touching himself or herself is bad.

If you have the opportunity, you might want to set your teen straight: Touching yourself to feel good is okay. Particularly in this day of sexually transmitted diseases, a teen who finds this natural, harmless way to relieve sexual tension may be grateful to know that it's nothing to worry about—or be ashamed of. Your teen should also know that masturbation doesn't cause warts, acne, physical weakness, blindness, or insanity.

If you don't want to discuss the subject with your teen, try leaving this book open to the appropriate page where your teen will find it.

Your Teen's Doctor

When it comes to your teen's medical care, you have one very specific job: to let your teen gradually take charge of his or her own health and to eventually disappear from the examining room. But first there are a few issues to tend to.

Is your current doctor appropriate for your teen? Whether you remain with the doctor who has been seeing your child (most likely a pediatrician), really depends on personality.

Most pediatricians provide full care for adolescents; however, if they don't have a special interest in teenagers, their advice and suggestions may not be as comprehensive as you might like. There are some doctors who specialize in adolescent medicine, but they aren't always easy to locate in every community. In deciding what to do, consider the following questions:

➤ *Does the doctor respect your teenager?* By this stage, a good doctor will talk about most medical issues directly with your child, and they should be developing a rapport with one another.

➤ *Is your child comfortable with this person?* If the doctor is male, be particularly aware of how your daughter feels discussing sexual issues with him. She may feel more comfortable with a woman doctor during these years.

➤ *Is your doctor concerned about the other issues surrounding your teen's life?* Before an exam, most doctors will talk with an adolescent patient about home life, school, and extracurricular activities. They should probe for signs of trouble, like social disengagement or difficulties at home.

➤ *Is your doctor alert to danger signs?* In addition to general questions, doctors should ask about diet, drugs, sex, and thoughts of suicide—all big issues for adolescents. This is good news for you. If your teen isn't talking to you about any troubles in these areas, there's always the possibility that he or she will open up to someone else who will be a good influence or resource over the years.

Info Flash

One condition your teen's doctor will screen for is *scoliosis,* curvature of the spine. Girls are particularly at risk for this problem, and anyone with a family history of it has an 11 percent greater chance of developing it.

If left untreated, scoliosis can lead to a prominent shoulder blade, an uneven waistline or hip, or even breathing impairment.

Most cases are mild and just need to be monitored. More severe cases may require a brace (newer styles are fairly lightweight and unobtrusive). Though it may be difficult to put your teen in a brace, leaving a severe case untreated is simply unacceptable because the resulting complications are so serious.

Let your teen decide whether you should stay in the examining room or not. Most doctors will generally call in the parents for a final doctor-child-parent discussion where you can find out how your teen is doing.

Part of parenting is setting up a helpful network for your teen, and finding a good doctor is an important part of this connection.

What About a Gynecologist?

A girl's first gynecological visit usually comes between ages 16 and 18, or when she experiences some type of gynecological irregularity. Any teen who is sexually active should also be examined by a gynecologist.

For reasons of privacy (hers), consider taking your daughter to a different gynecologist than the one you use. If you take her to the same gynecologist you see, she may not request birth control or bring up any subjects she's afraid you may end up hearing about. If you prefer to use the same gynecologist, reassure your teen that anything she discusses with her gynecologist will stay between them. (You will not be trying to pry details out of the doctor at other times.)

Spend some time looking for referrals to a doctor who has experience working with teens. Ideally, a good gynecologist will do the following with your teen:

➤ Explain what will happen during the exam.

➤ Show her the instruments that will be used during the exam.

➤ Discuss various forms of sexually transmitted diseases and be prepared to offer information on how to avoid them.

➤ Help your daughter feel comfortable talking about sexual issues or problems.

➤ Give your daughter a pelvic exam and discuss birth control if she is sexually active.

➤ Discuss and examine any problems your daughter experiences, such as menstrual problems, vaginal discharge, secondary amenorrhea (the loss of her period), or any sort of pelvic pain.

The Least You Need to Know

➤ During adolescence your child will grow more quickly than at any other time since the first year of life. Good nutrition, extra sleep, and patience with one's body will come in handy at this time.

➤ Talk to both sons and daughters about the changes they should expect during puberty. Reassure them that they're normal.

➤ Take a positive approach to growing up, and treat adolescent worries about breast development or penis size seriously.

➤ Let your teen establish his own relationship with a doctor.

➤ A girl's first visit to a gynecologist should occur between the ages of 16 and 18. She should be seen prior to that if she is sexually active, or if she is suffering from some type of gynecological irregularity.

SON, CAN WE DISCUSS THIS DEATH THING...

Chapter 6

How They Grow: Emotional Development

In This Chapter

➤ The emotions of the younger teen

➤ The emotions of the older teen

➤ What teenagers worry about

At first glance, it might look like most teens live the "good life." They spend most of their day at school, where they get plenty of time to be with friends and to socialize. After-school time is often devoted to special interests, such as playing softball, singing in the chorus, or acting in a school play. Weekends get booked up quickly: sleeping until noon takes time, and hanging out with friends and going out at night takes care of any possible boredom. The temporary inconvenience of having to do homework and take exams is a small price to pay for what seems like a pretty good life.

Yet anyone who really watches a teenager knows that underneath this seemingly carefree lifestyle there's a world of work going on. Whether they're vegging out on the couch, shooting baskets with friends, or hanging out in the mall, teenagers are researching: they're taking notes, making comparisons, and testing theories in a wonderful "experiment" of trying to find out who they really are (or want to be).

And as you watch, you'll see that the old adage, "one step forward, two steps back" must first have been said about a teenager. (Well, maybe not, but it definitely applies.) One minute your teen sweetly offers to play catch with his little brother, a sure sign of growing up; the next, he's upstairs ranting because he can't find his football cleat, and somehow it's become *your* fault.

Viewing this uneven metamorphosis can get frustrating. Just keep watching for those "steps forward"—they'll come faster and faster with time.

Ultimately, the emotional work of a teen involves transforming from child to adult: becoming comfortable with a changing body, gaining good judgment through decision-making, learning to be friends with peers of both sexes, and making some early choices about school, education, and career. In the process, your teen must learn to accept herself for who she is—complete with likes and dislikes, strengths and weaknesses, all in the process of achieving her identity.

Info Flash

In addition to beginning to look more like adults, teenagers begin to think more like them, too. Adolescents have reached the age of reason, and they're beginning to master the ability to think a problem through and understand the possible consequences.

No matter how you do it, these are turbulent years, filled with feelings of insecurity, confusion, ambivalence, frustration, and anxiety.

So the next time you're thinking your teen has a pretty easy life, remember that anyone who starts the day shrieking about a new pimple or figuring the bio teacher won't really care if she hasn't finished her homework is guaranteed to have a *very* long—and not so simple—day.

Different kids hit different stages and maturity levels at different times, but generally speaking, younger teens and older teens face different emotional challenges. This chapter will show you what those challenges are and how you can help your teen face them.

The World Through the Eyes of a Young Teen

Young adolescence is a confusing time. During these early years of teenhood, kids aren't sure who they are, what they are, or how they (should?) feel about things. The work of these early years is beginning to feel comfortable with how they are changing and what they are to become.

Mirror, Mirror, on the Wall...

As your child enters his teen years, he will become very egocentric, and the mirrors in your house will suddenly become very important to him. In many ways, this constant "mirror check" expresses what he's going through inside. His body is changing and he feels different; if he keeps tabs on his outer appearance, maybe he'll find out who he is and how he's doing!

Girls who develop early and boys who develop late are more likely to be self-conscious about their bodies and may worry whether they are "normal." While many teens will often suffer silently, if your child does bemoan his state of development within earshot, provide reassurance that he is, indeed, normal. You can probably produce a story or two about your own awkward teen years—being the tallest or the shortest in the class or whatever—and how it all turned out all right. (These types of "historical" stories also help because they provide your teen with helpful information—for example, that people in your family are "late bloomers.")

Teen Doublespeak

Your young teen will also be very aware of a new "public"—her friends. More than anything, most teens want to be accepted and well-liked. This is hard because her friends are an erratic group. Many of their emotional responses are immature, and they give off mixed signals, making it difficult to interpret what they mean. The teens are heavy into "group think" at this age, and because most of them are unsettled about their identities, this makes for confusing days.

Here's a multiple choice quiz that will show you the communication difficulties of this age:

Maddie invites Susan to walk home from school with her. Susan responds with a very snippy, "Sorry, I have plans."

Why did Susan reject Maddie's invitation?

A. "I'm walking with Jo, and I'm afraid she'll make fun of me if I invite you along."

B. "I just had a fight with my mother, so even though I'm free this afternoon, I'm taking my bad mood out on you."

C. "I have to walk my little brother to the library, but I don't want anyone to know that I have to."

D. Any of the above. All could apply on any given afternoon.

If you answered D, you win a prize. (Unfortunately for you, it's a tube of anti-acne cream.)

As you can see, this is a confusing time. Susan is so concerned about maintaining her "image" that she's sure Jo will think less of her if she includes Maddie; and she's afraid her image will be totally destroyed if she's ever seen hanging out with her bratty little brother.

As for the fight with her mom, she'd hate to admit that it upset her—but it did, so she lashed out at the nearest possible victim.

Breaking Family Ties

Emotionally and financially, young teens are still very reliant on their parents. Yet, in their own minds, they picture themselves as more mature, more independent, and altogether more cool. A shy young boy may imagine that he's the swaggering lead guitarist from his favorite band; an unpolished girl may fantasize that she's the poised model on this month's cover of *Seventeen*.

Your teen is trying to establish his independence and to differentiate himself from his family; but the resulting behavior may express itself in strange ways.

He may snap at you over the strangest questions, like when you ask, "What time are you leaving for school?"

Sure, you meant, "What time are you leaving for school? I'm going to set the alarm." But your teen may have heard it as, "You're never ready! Why are you always late?" And so he tells you to get off his case. His snap may actually be a very positive sign of a kid who's trying desperately to get it together to get out the door on time!

This is also the age when your teen will walk a dozen feet ahead of you in the mall or on the street (when she condescends to go out in public with you at all). This, too, shall pass—although unfortunately, it may take quite a few years.

Moody Blues

Are you confused? Your teen certainly is, and that helps explain her mood swings. One day she imagines she's in charge of her world, ready to tackle anything; she doesn't hesitate to tell you that you were born in the Dark Ages and you don't have a clue as to what's going on with kids today.

The next day, she feels overwhelmed. A rough time at school, a personal slight, and she's curled up in your favorite chair (claiming your space as her space, the way she used to when she was little), asking you what should she do next.

Just what you have time for, right? You're working, you're harried, you've got two other kids (or a lousy ex-spouse) to worry about, and here's your teen looking like a storm cloud part of the time. (If your teen looks like a storm cloud *all* of the time, talk to your pediatrician for a referral to a counseling group of some type. Excessive bad moods are a call for help. Also see Chapter 20 for information on helping a teen in crisis.)

Otherwise, just try to weather the storms without getting involved, and try to create opportunities for improved interaction between the two of you. No matter how busy you are, inviting him to a quick lunch at the diner may do both of you a world of good.

These are interesting days, and they're destined to get even more interesting. So hold on.

Tuning In

Your teen's growing maturity and capacity for advanced thinking is good news for you. You're in for some good times if you seize the moment and listen when he's ready to talk.

Even the teen who never seems to pry his thumb off the video game controls may amaze you with his opinions on everything from the current U.S. government to the state of our environment.

Your maturing teenager can enrich your life—if you listen to him.

The World Through the Eyes of an Older Teen

The older teen is more secure than he was in early adolescence. He's beginning to understand who he is, what he's good at, and which friends he can depend upon. These are important—and rewarding—developmental steps.

Settling Into Their New Bodies

By the time your child hits her mid-teens, she's probably become somewhat more comfortable with her body. (Though the high interest in dieting for girls and body-building for boys suggests that many teens aren't completely happy with their bodies yet.) Though boys will continue to grow for a few more years, most have overcome the "shrimp" stage of immaturity.

Young Love

When it comes to sexuality, though, most teens are unsure of themselves. They worry about—and measure—the strength of their allure. They may start to develop, and start weighing the possibilities of serious relationships and sex. They will also experience the emotional highs and lows of young love.

While you may be tempted to classify your teen's first relationship as "puppy love," remember that it's serious for your teen. He will begin to learn how to build a relationship and to acquire the skills that will enable him to create long and lasting bonds. (You'll find information on what to expect as your teen navigates these new relationships in Chapters 11 and 18.)

Circle of Friends

Peer interaction is more normal at this point, as all of your teen's friends gain in maturity. They are kinder to each other (there will be fewer episodes of purposeful exclusion of one or another member of a teen group), and your teen's friends will be more dependable than they were when they were younger.

However, this peer stability comes and goes, depending on the security of your teen's friends. The transition to high school, for example, throws many kids off-balance and may cause great social upheaval among the ranks. Your child may get cut off from her usual crowd, as friends link up for lunch without her or stop inviting her to the movies on Friday night. In all likelihood, when the dust settles and the teens feel comfortable again, relationships will return to their rightful orbit.

Rebels with a Cause

Your teen will continue to rebel against you as a way to assert his independence. This is a normal part of growing up. If he accepts all your judgments, how is he going to learn to make his own?

Yet as teens get older, the forms of rebellion get scarier. The battleground for younger teens and their parents generally focuses on after-school or weekend activities, bedtime, telephone usage, household chores, dating, the need for adult supervision, and appropriate attire.

Older teens, on the other hand, may challenge you on driving rules, smoking, drinking, using drugs, becoming sexually active, and whether to go to college. Remember how your teen refused to make his bed when he was 13? That'll look simple compared to his blatant disregard of his midnight curfew on his first night out with the car.

While you want your teen to be independent, he still lacks judgment, experience, and wisdom. Part of the art of parenting is to provide your teen with enough freedom to learn his own lessons (the only lessons anyone truly remembers), but also to keep him close enough so that he seldom tangles with true danger (drugs, drinking and driving, etc.).

(For additional information on handling these issues, refer to chapters later on in the book. Driving is covered in Chapter 16; you'll find information on drinking, smoking, and drugs in Chapter 19, and sex is covered in Chapter 18, for starters.)

Measuring Up

The egocentrism of the early teen years is still present in the older teen, but it begins to fade as your teen learns to see the world from other perspectives.

Older teens still value peer opinion, but they also begin to look to the outside world and wonder how they will measure up. They may begin to ask:

➤ "Will I be good enough to get into the school I want to go to?"

➤ "What am I going to be when I grow up?"

➤ "Will I find someone to love who loves me back?"

The better a teen's self-esteem through this period, the smoother his passage will be.

You can weather all this if you work at your job of promoting yourself to "guide" and "mentor." If you're prepared to cruise on the sidelines, surfacing when needed, you'll have a good chance of keeping your teen safe—and even of having a good relationship eventually.

Tuning In

When your teen rebels, the punishment should fit the "crime." Your family motto could be: With privilege comes responsibility.

If she ignores your curfew on Friday night, tell her she'll be spending the following Friday night at home. If he neglects his household chores, he must take care of them before going out Saturday night. (For information on drinking or drug-related transgressions, see Chapter 19.)

What Teens Worry About

Everyone has their stress points, and teens are no exception. Here's what they report makes them worry:

➤ *What people think of them.* Teens are very concerned that they "select" the right identity. They don't want to be viewed in a negative light (as a "dork," for example). Unfortunately, dorkhood may encompass many qualities you admire—like making good grades or playing the viola in the school orchestra.

They may also seek peer approval by taking up habits like smoking or drinking.

The stronger a teen's self-esteem, the less prone she will be to tailoring her image to what she thinks her peers want her to be. (See Chapter 8 for ideas on building self-esteem.)

➤ *Grades.* Believe it or not, most teens—even the cut-up who rides along with the C-average—worry about grades. Good grades are a sign of well-being and achievement, and even though teacher approval may not be as cool as peer approval, it does count.

At heart, kids know that a good grade or some type of honorable recognition buys them the legitimacy they so very much want to have. However, the longer they are discounted as possible achievers, the harder it becomes to get them back on track.

If you're the parent of someone who seems lost, read Chapter 9 for ways that your teen can be recognized. Your child may not be a math genius or an authority on the complete works of Dickens, but if he can find a subject or hobby at which he excels, chances are good he'll start doing well elsewhere, too.

➤ *Lack of time.* Teens, like you and I, are strapped for time. They represent the first of the "over-programmed" generation. (That's what you get for enrolling your kid in dance at age two and karate at age four.) If you didn't teach your kids time management when they were younger, you might want to start now.

Talk to your teen about learning to set priorities and to balance her time. (Maybe you need to conduct a "reality check" on your own schedule, too.) Life holds so many options, but she (and you) can only concentrate on a few at a time.

➤ *Family difficulties.* Most teens have perfected the art of acting indifferent to their families, but this nonchalant veneer belies how they really feel. If there's trouble at home (whether it's emotional or financial) your teen is keenly aware of it. Take the time to explain and to reassure as much as possible.

➤ *The future.* From getting into college to finding a job, teens are well aware of the need to make a place for themselves in the world and the competition that they'll meet in trying to get there.

Keep reminding your teen of the things she is good at and how her qualities (intelligence, sensitivity, patience, sociability) and skills (being great with kids, well-organized, or a computer wizard) are of value to the world. Assure your teen that there will be a place for her, though what it is and where it is may be a surprise. Encourage your teen to be open to many possibilities; sometimes the path to the future may not be predictable, but it can still be filled with wonderful opportunities.

The Least You Need to Know

➤ The younger teen is getting used to his changing body, and is very concerned with peer interaction.

➤ Teens are not always certain how they feel, and their confusion sometimes causes them to give off mixed signals. Don't take what they say at face value; give them another chance.

➤ Teens desperately want approval. Peer approval rates top on teens' charts, but they also care about what you and their teachers think of them. Let them know when they're doing a good job.

➤ Rebellious behavior should be dealt with by deciding on a punishment that fits the crime.

➤ Through interactions with their peers, teens develop important relationship skills. This is an important part of the life lessons learned at this age.

Chapter 7

How They Look: Accepting a New Reality

> **In This Chapter**
>
> ➤ Helping your teen cope with acne
>
> ➤ Your teen's makeup and clothing style
>
> ➤ What you should know about tattoos and body piercing

"Pick your battles" is good advice for many matters concerning life with your teen, but perhaps nowhere is it more applicable than when talking about appearance.

When you were pushing your toddler in a stroller, chances are you saw a punk rocker with shredded leather and spiky green hair, and maybe you harrumphed something about how *your* child would never look like that. Well, guess what. That former toddler is going to surprise you.

And if *you* happened to sport your own far-out style growing up, you'll have a better understanding of what your teen is trying to accomplish during these years!

Inevitably, there will come a morning when he or she will walk out of the bedroom looking quite amazing. Maybe he shaved his head and sprouted a goatee, or perhaps she's sporting smeared eyeliner and ratty hair à la Courtney Love. Or you may hear (ahead of time, if you're lucky) her plans for a tattoo or a nose ring.

Whatever your challenge, you can spare your family a lot of grief by picking and choosing what you comment on. A few issues may concern health and safety; those *are* worth taking a strong stand on. Otherwise, buckle up, sit on your hands, and close your mouth. When it comes to appearance, your best plan is to do what you can to be helpful, and otherwise to react as infrequently as possible.

Tuning In
While most girls take to personal grooming like ducks to water, some young boys need to be told the merits of using deodorant and bathing and washing hair regularly.

Your "good behavior" just might be rewarded. If you're open-minded, thoughtful, and respectful of your teen, chances are you won't have much to worry about. Teenagers sometimes strut outrageous looks to create a scene, so if your teen realizes that you're not going to "pop a cork" over her latest fashion statement, she may well pass these years without trying anything too wild.

This chapter will try to help you think about when to get involved in how your teen looks (or is about to look)—and when not to get involved.

(See Chapter 17 for information on glasses, braces, and weight issues.)

From Black Leather to Blue Hair: How Much Can You Handle?

Teens use their appearance as a way to *explore* who they are (not *define* who they are). If you give them a few months, they'll move on to something else. Most forms of experimentation are relatively harmless; you just have to determine your own tolerance level.

Maybe you can handle almost any color of fluorescent hair, but you have a lot of difficulty with your daughter wearing miniskirts and go-go boots to school. Or maybe baggy pants that droop around your son's feet make you afraid he's going to fall on his face. As particular issues arise, have frank discussions with your teen.

She may half-agree with your concerns about her belly-button-baring halter top, so she might not be as upset by your comments as you think. (Don't expect her not to stomp around about it, though.) Or at heart your son may not want to go along with his friends, who've decided to wear Metallica T-shirts instead of dress shirts to graduation. You may be doing him a favor by making him able to say, "My parents made me change."

Remember, too, that there will be plenty of other voices commenting on your teen's fashion. Right now she's most concerned with how she appears to her peers. Those peers may be tolerable "adjusters." Just as the kindergarten girls had no problem telling her why she "just *couldn't* wear red socks with a pink skirt," they'll do the job now, too. And if her friends look halfway decent most of the time, you're in for smooth sailing.

Maybe you'll get to drive the carpool one day when one of the kids gets in the car sporting a new fashion. Listen carefully to the conversation as the others view her coming down the walk and then listen to what they say when they greet her. (You may feel pity; most teens are affected by catty comments and may be hurt by what's said.)

Ultimately, you have to acknowledge who is really in charge. In high school, how many of your friends brought along "forbidden" clothes and changed into them as soon as they were out of the house? If your rules are too strict, you'll lose before you've begun on the important stuff.

Danger Zone

CAUTION

If you're dismayed by the appearance of your teen's friends—and don't like the look that she wears to fit in—observe her group long enough to determine who they really are.

It could turn out that your teen is hanging out with a great group of kids whose individualistic clothing reflects their creative and imaginative spirit. If, on the other hand, it turns out that her friends actually are bad influences, refer to Chapters 11 and 19 for more information.

Remember to always start by listening to your teen. She may be doing better than you think.

Standing Up for Your Teen

Changes in appearance often invite comments from relatives, and you may want to act as an advocate for your child by reminding family members of what really matters. A grandmother who harps about dyed hair or a ragged beard is doing needless harm to a relationship with her grandchild. Assure her that you doubt his blue hair will show in pictures so it really isn't necessary to discuss it.

You may find some of your teen's experimentation interesting or even kind of fun, and then you should comment positively. Your compliments will offset the times when you have to say, "You just can't wear cut-off shorts to your cousin's wedding."

Other than a few health and safety hurdles, your main concern when it comes to your teen should be how she's doing on the inside. Does she feel good about who she is? Does she have supportive friends? How's she doing in school? If the important pieces are in place, then sit back, put up your feet, and wait for the next version of your son or daughter to come through the door.

"I Can't Go Anywhere—I Have a Pimple!"

Unless you had perfect skin when you were a teen (in which case, everyone in school hated you—so you had other problems), surely you remember waking up on the morning of a dance and discovering that your face sported the largest zit you'd ever seen. Remember how it felt?

Acne really affects how kids feel about themselves. A recent study by the American Medical Association revealed that adolescents and young adults with acne are likely to have lowered self-confidence, a poor self-image, and are less inclined to participate in social activities.

As adults, most of us begin to realize that physical appearance is less important than other attributes, but teenagers clearly don't feel this way. How they feel about their appearance affects how they feel about themselves—so acne is just one more factor preventing them from fulfilling their potential.

Just the Facts, Please

➤ "Acne comes from chocolate."

➤ "It comes from eating too many greasy french fries."

➤ "She has zits because she never washes."

Info Flash
Eighty-three percent of teens worry at least sometimes about their complexion; approximately one-third or more indicate that they have felt anxious, embarrassed, or frustrated by their acne. Almost one-half of the teens surveyed in a study sponsored by the American Medical Association felt that their complexion affected how other people reacted toward them.

Despite what you hear, there's no proven link between acne and foods (not even soda, chocolate, or french fries). Nor is it caused by dirt; no matter how carefully your teen washes, he can still have acne.

When your teen is moaning about his skin, give him the facts about the causes of acne:

➤ *Heredity.* If other members of the family have had acne, your teen is more likely to.

➤ *Hormones.* At the onset of puberty, hormones trigger oil ducts on the face, back, and upper chest to begin producing oil. Additional oil leads to the third contributing factor about acne:

➤ *Plugged oil ducts.* If your teen is susceptible, the cells that line the oil ducts in the skin tend to get plugged. When the ducts plug up, whiteheads form and eventually bloom into the pimples of acne.

A few other factors may aggravate acne. Some teens find that stress makes their acne worse. Girls may suffer worse skin during menstruation when hormone levels change. Anything that rubs on the skin (a chin strap, a headband, and so on) may cause a break-out in that area. Some types of makeup cause acne to get worse.

"Pizza Face" No More

There is no true cure for acne, but there are ways to keep it under control. According to the American Academy of Pediatrics, the best over-the-counter remedy is benzoyl peroxide lotion or gel in 5 to 10 percent strengths. (Benzoyl peroxide is available under many brand names, so check the labels on skin-care products in your pharmacy.)

Benzoyl peroxide is very drying, so your teen should start slowly, using the milder strength once a day. If your teen's skin isn't red or peeling after using it for a week, she can increase to twice a day.

If there's no improvement after she uses it twice a day for four to six weeks, then visit a dermatologist who can prescribe something more effective.

In addition, tell your teen that *popping pimples just makes acne worse.*

A teen can also improve her skin by keeping her hands away from her face and by keeping her hair clean and pulled back; oily bangs or greasy hair can lead to a forehead dotted with pimples. (If she has bangs, she should clip them away from her forehead at night.)

Acne is worth your attention—there are solutions, and it can cause scarring.

Tuning In

Like your teenager, you may believe acne myths that sometimes stop you from being sensitive to your child. Here's what you should know about a few of the myths:

Myth: This is a stage teenagers just have to go through. Your dermatologist can recommend excellent products to help your teen. It's worth paying attention to acne now because it can be a problem for years to come and can even lead to permanent scarring if it isn't treated in time.

Myth: Sunlight will dry up the skin. (Remember sitting under sunlamps to cure acne?) With skin cancer on the rise, the sun and sunlamps are no solution.

Myth: The doctor won't recommend anything better than what you can buy at the store. Your dermatologist can give your teen a better understanding of how to use acne-fighting products properly. Teens who start "self-medicating" may soon end up with skin reactions to the products they use in addition to acne.

Beauty and the Makeup Box

Most parents have strong feelings about their daughters and makeup. It's a particularly difficult issue, because makeup represents more than putting some stuff on a face. When your daughter begins to apply makeup, it's a sure sign that she's growing up and that she's becoming aware of her own sexuality. These are difficult issues for a parent to face. However, rather than restrict her to no makeup, you might have better luck with the concept of light makeup. You may decide on an age when you'll agree to let her wear light makeup; however, she may already be experimenting.

What to do? Try to tolerate normal experimentation. If she's wearing a look that's objectionable to you and different from her peers—such as heavy eye makeup and red lipstick at 12—you may want to look deeper at what's going on in her life. Otherwise, if makeup is forbidden at home, she may well put it on at school or somewhere else.

While you can certainly request that makeup be used minimally (no thick eyeliner or scarlet lips to Grandma's), your best approach is to try to compliment your daughter when it looks nice and guide her so that, if she's going to wear makeup, she wears it tastefully.

That said, you don't have to pay for it. (And believe me, you don't want to—you can drop a small fortune on cosmetics.) Expect her to use her baby-sitting money or allowance, and sit tight. It's going to be awhile before she discovers that no amount of high-priced potions and lotions will transform her into Cindy Crawford.

Clothes Make the Teen

It's important to be seen in the right clothes at this age, and chances are your teen and his friends all sport the same look—whether it's hip-hop, preppy, grunge…the list goes on. Should you say anything? Only if the attire is indecent, or if you're headed to a family occasion where wearing an appropriate outfit is important.

Shouting at her when she appears in a belly-button-revealing T-shirt on her way to school is not the way to build a great relationship. You could instead say something like, "I hate to make you change, but I really don't think that shirt is appropriate for school. I can live with you wearing it on the weekend, but I just can't imagine what your teachers would think about it—it's quite revealing. I really have to ask you to change."

If you have a good relationship with your daughter, she might change (although she may put the shirt back on once she gets to school). If you don't, you risk having her storm out of the house in the forbidden shirt. If that's the likely outcome, you may want to avoid such confrontations until you've had an opportunity to work on your relationship (possibly with the help of a therapist).

Info Flash

Many educators and politicians back a movement for school uniforms or dress codes. Supporters suggest that the "one look" solution will reduce gang violence, improve attendance, keep students focused on books—not looks, reduce clothing costs for families, and reduce school theft.

How do kids feel about these measures? While many agree that it would be nice not to be judged by their clothing, many also feel that uniforms and dress codes would interfere with their right to self-expression.

The Supreme Court has ruled that students have rights of free expression, and fashion—in most cases—can be regulated only if it disrupts education or poses a safety or health issue. Under this ruling, distractingly short skirts, bare midriffs, and gang colors could be prohibited. Otherwise, kids are free to "express themselves."

Another problem with dress codes or school uniforms is the time that would be spend on enforcement. What would you rather have your school principal worrying more about: the curriculum or what your son wears to school?

If your school district is considering uniforms or dress codes, you might speak up in favor of practicality. Uncomfortable ties or impractical skirts should not be the only options. School clothes should feel comfortable and look up-to-date.

For some kids, having the right look and the right brand becomes very important. As a result, major family battles are fought over designer jeans, sneakers, and jackets. Turn to Chapter 21 to learn about clothing budgets. Forcing your teen to buy within a budget will bring reality home to roost, and your teen will soon learn to choose between having a larger, less expensive wardrobe or a smaller "name brand" one.

Primal Teen: Tattoos and Body Piercing

You may have taken your daughter to get her ears pierced when she was still in elementary school—so now you're shocked that she wants extra holes? Or that your son wants some, too? Go figure. (You ought to be smarter than that.)

Tattoos and body piercing (nose rings, nipple jewelry, and belly button rings) are some of the latest forms of self-expression among teens. Because they can be dangerous, you may want to get involved.

Like any other serious discussion you'd like to have with your teen, it's important to know all you can about the issue.

Body piercing, if done safely, is not harmful. Unfortunately, the profession is unregulated in most areas, and many consumers are getting pierced under unsafe conditions (at a sloppy tent at a music festival, or in some rickety tattoo shack on the outskirts of town).

People who get tattoos and body piercings run the same kind of health risks as anyone sharing needles. While the Centers for Disease Control and Prevention has never traced an AIDS case to a tattoo parlor, a very real danger is the risk of contracting hepatitis B or C. That's primarily because the HIV virus dies on a surface in 12 minutes, but the hepatitis virus can live for up to 10 days.

Currently, it's up to the consumer to select a piercer or tattoo artist who practices in a safe, hygienic manner.

Danger Zone

A few facts about tattooing and piercing:

➤ Piercing guns are safe only on earlobes. They cannot be properly sterilized and when piercing other parts of the body there is a greater likelihood that the gun will become contaminated with blood.

➤ Holes in noses and near the top ridge of the ears are vulnerable to problems if the cartilage is pierced instead of the soft tissues.

➤ Body jewelry is a different size than ear jewelry, and smaller jewelry can become embedded in other areas of the body.

➤ Remind your teen that tattoos are permanent and can only be removed with expensive (and not always successful) laser surgery.

The Association of Professional Piercers is clamoring for state regulations that would outline proper sterilization. In the meantime, the organization recommends the following guidelines

➤ Get pierced or tattooed at a sanitary studio (rather than a booth at Lollapalooza).

➤ Piercers should not accept clients who are not sober. Many kids get tattoos when they are drunk, and alcohol in the system can lead to heavy bleeding.

➤ Piercers should use disposable or autoclaved instruments; sterile, disposable needles; and jewelry that has been disinfected and stored in sterile bags.

➤ New and sterilized needles should be used for each tattoo or piercing.

➤ Practitioners should wear clean latex gloves, dispose of the needles in puncture-proof containers after each use, and throw away tissues in plastic-lined containers.

➤ Tattoo artists should not dip into contaminated bottles of ink; they should use small, disposable containers of ink, and any ointments should be removed from containers with sterile spreaders.

➤ Belly-button piercing takes up to a year to heal and should be done only after great consideration. Teenage girls should be especially careful because the belly button is just a few inches from the fallopian tubes—it isn't a good place for infections.

➤ After-care is extremely important in any type of tattooing or piercing, so a true professional will offer very specific instructions. (Tattoos should be treated with an antibacterial cream and kept out of water and sunlight. Pierced areas should be washed at least twice a day with a surgical scrub/water solution.)

What's a Parent to Do?

If you notice that your teen's friends are sporting tattooed biceps or bejeweled belly buttons, or if you think your teen is interested in piercing or in getting a tattoo, you might want to step in.

Begin by opening a conversation. You might comment: "How do you think John will feel about a scar by his eyebrow when he decides to quit wearing the ring?"

You may immediately learn that your teen thinks body piercing is "gross" or "dumb," in which case you can breathe a sigh of relief.

If you sense that your teen thinks it's an interesting idea, you might say that though you're not crazy about it, if he's going to do it you would like him to go to a trained professional. (Offer to cover the cost difference—it's *that* important.) Point out that a "scratcher" (inexperienced tattoo artist) can leave him with a blotchy mess as well as an infection; and a bad piercing can lead to infection or scarring.

Because tattoos and body piercing are often ways of rebelling, you may find that your offer dampens your teen's enthusiasm. If you offer to help pick out a tattoo, it makes getting one a lot less interesting. If you're lucky, you can relax knowing that the next "autoclaved instruments" your teen will see will be at the dentist's!

Because ideally you want to discourage tattoos and body-piercing totally, continue to express your negative feelings about the process under consideration. You should only offer to help if it seems inevitable that your teen is going to take action with or without you. Then you'd like to see that it's done safely.

Professionals also note that multiple tattoos or body piercings are often a sign of some type of emotional problem or immaturity. If your teen has already become tattooed or pierced several times, you might want to take a deeper look at what's going on.

The Least You Need to Know

➤ Try to make appearance an issue as infrequently as possible.

➤ Take acne concerns seriously. Purchase benzoyl peroxide for your teen, and if the condition doesn't improve in six weeks or so after regular use, visit a dermatologist.

➤ Let your teen spend her own money on cosmetics.

➤ If your teen wants a tattoo or body piercing, be as discouraging as possible. If that fails, offer to get him to a professional.

Chapter 8

How They Feel: Keeping Tabs on Self-Esteem

In This Chapter

➤ The importance of self-esteem

➤ Self-esteem in girls

➤ Self-esteem in boys

"Self-esteem" has become such a buzz word today that, like other over-used words or terms, its meaning has become fuzzy. But I'm going to spend a chapter clarifying it here, because it could be the single most important factor in getting your teen (and your family) through these years with everyone's sanity intact.

Sometimes self-esteem sounds like a "feel good" remedy: make someone feel special (even if they aren't particularly), and they'll go far in life. But that isn't the true meaning of self-esteem. Self-esteem is the perception you have about yourself that defines who you are. No matter what your environment, the beliefs you hold about yourself remain constant and determine your behavior.

Danger Zone
At some point, you may feel yourself getting upset at your teen when her friends are around. If at all possible, hold your anger until the two of you can speak privately. Don't damage her self-esteem (or trust in you) with a "public flogging." Bite your tongue if you have to, but try to hold off.

If your teenager feels secure about who he is and what his strengths and weaknesses are, he's got the world by the tail. He may falter or stumble here and there as he encounters new challenges, but he'll always be able to find his way because *he knows who he is.*

So this chapter isn't about saying "good job" to your teen when he does marginal work on a science project, and it's not about telling her she's great at soccer when she isn't; this chapter is about helping your teen become confident of who she is and what she values.

What Do You Value?

Strong people tend to grow from strong families, who can identify what they value and express it to others. Some experts recommend that families create Mission Statements that clarify what is important. You can do that if you like, or you can simply live your values.

Specific beliefs will vary from family to family; what mustn't vary is establishing those beliefs so your teen has a railing to help him find his way along. Here are some examples of what a teenager might know about his family's beliefs:

➤ "I have to be home by 11 p.m. If I'm not my parents will kill me."

➤ "My parents won't be upset I got a B-; they know I really worked hard in chemistry."

➤ "Once a year my dad and I go away for a weekend, just the two of us."

➤ "My sisters and I are best friends."

➤ "My mother is so honest. If she gets the wrong change, she'll run back to the store to give them back their 50 cents."

➤ "My parents agree that the teacher was wrong, but they say I have to go along with it, because she's the teacher."

➤ "My parents don't smoke. My grandfather died of lung cancer, and I know that really affected them."

➤ "Family is important; we visit my grandparents every week."

Whether this teenager decides to rebel against some of these beliefs and values at various times doesn't matter. What's important is that when he needs to find his base, he'll be able to find it easily because it's been well-defined for him.

Defining Who They Are

Part of being a teenager is defining oneself in relation to one's peers. This is a process that your teen will go through on her own, but there are some things you can do to make it easier.

You're not going to have much to do with whether she eats lunch with Mary or Susie, but what you can do is try to build her a platform from which to operate.

The best platforms encourage adolescents in their special interests. You may have a talented teenager who excels at the piano and loves it. His love of music and ability to play well can get him through rough times with other things.

But the teen years are ones of transition, and many times the young piano player enters middle school and promptly quits; or the boy who loved shooting baskets decides he's never going to grow and refuses to try out for the basketball team.

If up until now your teen has derived great pleasure from an interest, take time to open a discussion on the topic. It's a shame when an adolescent drops something he's terrific at, and perhaps there are ways you can make this break a short vacation rather than a permanent rupture. Or perhaps you can change things to make it better.

For example, the young basketball player who is suffering because he's so much shorter than his peers might be encouraged to stick it out one more year because he'll surely grow. And the piano-playing teen who wants to quit because she doesn't like her music teacher might be encouraged to continue if you include her in the search for a new teacher.

Otherwise, encourage him in other interests. Whether it's baseball-card collecting, tinkering around with the computer, or collecting jazz CDs, encourage it.

This also offers you an avenue where you can enhance his experience. You can bring home special music magazines, or offer to drive him to a baseball-card convention (if he doesn't yet drive). By showing support and interest, you do a lot to increase his self-esteem.

Danger Zone CAUTION
Some parents start collecting show tunes if their teen collects show tunes, or start gardening if that's what their teen is into. That's usually the wrong thing to do. It's important that your teen "own" the experience independent of you. She's creating her own existence.

Gotcha! Caught Doing Something Good

One great self-esteem builder is catching your teen doing something good:

➤ "Boy, did I appreciate your doing the dishes last night. I was so tired."

➤ "Helping your little sister with her painting was really sweet of you. She's been feeling left out, and you made her feel like a million dollars."

➤ "Bringing your friend Max's homework home for him now that he's been out three days was really nice of you."

As a whole, teens are probably the least-complimented group. Stereotypically, they are viewed negatively and because there is frequently tension in the household ("You want to go out again tonight?" "You still haven't cleaned your room?"), paying compliments often falls by the wayside. Think back to the early days when all of her accomplishments garnered praise: "Look at how well you tie your shoes!" or "Wow! Look how neatly you printed your name!"

Any opportunity you have to reward the positive will help reinforce your values and what your teen is particularly good at.

Remember how terrific you feel when your boss, your spouse, or a good friend praises you for something you do well. This is your opportunity to provide this gift to your teen.

Heard it Through the Grapevine

Also remember to pass on any compliments to your teen:

➤ "Mr. Reilly from next door said you did a great job shoveling the snow on his walk."

➤ "I ran into Mrs. Smith downtown today. She mentioned that all of you were so polite the other night at her house. It made me feel great to know you're always welcome there."

When your teen knows that he gets a good rap, he suddenly has something to lose through negative behavior.

Tuning In

The other evening a local cable station aired the graduation ceremonies of a local high school. The camera was focused on the graduates, one boy in particular, during a portion of the principal's speech:

"Every class has a reputation, a word or a phrase that describes the class," explained the speaker. "This class has always been known for being 'nice.' From the time you entered as freshmen you were described as being a really nice group of kids, and you've always lived up to that very positive reputation."

The boy on whom the camera was focused had been sitting slouched down in his chair when the principal began his remarks. At the description of the class, and the mention of the word "nice," he sat up and started listening.

"Nice" words are always heard. Use them frequently.

Accepting What They Look Like

During early adolescence your teen is getting to know a whole new body, and feeling good about her changing body reflects a healthy dose of self-esteem.

If kids are concerned about something (such as their appearance or size or some way in which they fear they don't measure up), treat their worries with respect.

Encourage them to focus on their strengths, talents, and positive attributes. They may have to accept being short, but they don't have to feel penalized by it. "I may be short, but I am a great tennis player."

"That's Not Fair!"

If your kids frequently cry that you're unfair, you ought to examine how you're handling things. Equal treatment among siblings is an important goal to strive for.

Research reported in a 1994 issue of *Adolescence* confirms what many parents suspect: we're more protective of our daughters and more permissive with our sons. While a 6'2" teenage boy is, indeed, more likely to be safe walking at night than a 5'3" teenage girl, every time we treat women differently we communicate that they need to be dependent on someone's protection for their well-being.

Though there are very real safety issues that will dictate some decisions, try as often as possible to make the same decisions for both your sons and your daughters. Thus far, note what researchers say:

➤ Sons are permitted to work outside the home at an earlier age than daughters, thus providing them with earlier independence.

➤ Girls do more housework than boys, sending the message that the home is a woman's domain, and teaching boys a "learned helplessness."

➤ Fathers are more encouraging to their sons about participation in competitive sports than they are to their daughters.

➤ Teens perceive that boys get to use the family car more often than girls, thus granting them greater independence.

The Not Tough-Enough Boy

How gender sensitive are you as a parent? Try the following exercise:

"My teenage daughter got terribly homesick while she was away visiting her cousin, so my spouse and I decided to _____."

"My teenage son got terribly homesick while he was away at camp, so my spouse and I decided to _____."

"Pick her up early" is a logical fill-in for the first sentence concerning the daughter, but would you pick up a teen son who was feeling homesick? In most families, the answer to that would be "not likely." The son would be expected to tough it out.

Perhaps you would handle both son or daughter in the same way, but often, fathers have difficulty with what they consider "babying" their son.

Boys are raised to be self-reliant, achievement-oriented, tough and aggressive, sexually assertive, and emotionally controlled. (And by all means, they must avoid all things feminine!) What a burden.

In her book, *The Courage to Raise Good Men*, psychologist Dr. Olga Silverstein puts forth a theory that more and more experts are espousing: boys are pushed away from the family too soon, and the greatest gift parents can give their boys is the ability to acknowledge their feelings. In her book, Dr. Silverstein relates a touching story about a teenage boy who wanted to live at home for an extra year after high school; he didn't feel he was ready to move away yet. As a therapist, her chore was to help the father understand that his son's choice didn't mean the boy was a failure.

The Not Good-Enough Girl

Our daughters carry another burden. While parents tell them that they should be strong and independent and men's equals in every way, society also says, "Yes, be strong and independent, but be feminine, passive, and above all, polite (which often translates into being unassertive and compliant) at the same time."

The damaging effects of this mixed message have been well-documented in "Shortchanging Girls, Shortchanging America," a study conducted by the American Association of University Women (AAUW). The study showed that many of the girls studied felt good about themselves at age nine. But by the end of adolescence, external influences had chipped away at the self-images of the majority of the girls.

Encourage your daughter to be academically competitive in everything from English to science and math. There is no reason for girls to do less well in what have been considered "male" subjects; make sure she knows you believe that. (Some schools report that girls do better in math classes divided by gender. If your school system offers that option, you might want to look into it.)

Info Flash

In the AAUW study, boys who reported doing poorly in math and science usually ascribed their performance to the topics' lack of usefulness, while girls who reported a lack of success in these areas often attributed the problem to personal failure.

Perhaps the greatest favor we can do for our boys' and girls' self-esteem is to break stereotypes and simply work to raise good people.

A Sense of Place

In *A Good Enough Parent*, psychologist Dr. Bruno Bettelheim talks of a feeling of place:

> According to the dictionary, "to belong" means to have a rightful place. A rightful place is not one that is granted by the powers that be, not even by parents; this is too shaky a source for a true feeling of belonging. A rightful place is the place we gain for ourselves, first through loving and being loved in the right way, later through one's own efforts. This alone makes the place secure, one's very own.

A parent's job is to try to set our teens on the pathway of finding their rightful "place."

The Least You Need to Know

➤ Communicate your values clearly to your teen. He may reject or deny some of what you teach, but having values will help him know who he is.

➤ Encourage your teenager to develop her interests. Having something she loves and can control will give her strength when other things in her life that are outside her control are going wrong.

➤ Compliment your teen for positive behaviors, and always remember to pass on the compliments of others.

➤ Treat siblings of both sexes as equally as possible.

➤ Resist gender stereotyping and look for gender discrimination in your own attitudes and behavior.

Part 3
School Life

Your teen's job is school, and how she approaches it will have a major effect on the choices she makes in later life.

It may have been easy for you to help your child when she was in elementary school. But many parents aren't sure how involved they should become in their teen's middle-school or high-school academic experience.

This part of the book shows you how you can help your teen juggle responsibilities and perform well in school. It also tells you when and how (and whether) you should get in touch with the school. And since no discussion of school would be complete without a peek at after-school life, this part also touches on extracurricular activities, including dating.

If your teen wants to go to college, you've got a lot of thinking to do—so don't wait until your teen is a junior or senior to take a look at Chapter 12.

Chapter 9

Academics: Making the Grade

In This Chapter

➤ Helping your teen get organized

➤ Homework: To monitor or not to monitor

➤ Motivating your teen

➤ Initiating and maintaining parent-school contact

Because of his excellent upbringing, your teenager comes straight home from school, doesn't turn on the radio or the television, hardly glances at the phone, proceeds directly to his room, and settles right down to do his homework. (He doesn't even pause to empty out the refrigerator for what he loosely refers to as a "snack.") The efforts pay off in spades, and at his high school graduation, you have the privilege of hearing him give the valedictory...

Wake up, wake up! You're dreaming, right? Whether they're 12 or 16, most kids need a little homework guidance from you; not necessarily to help solve equations or to understand *The Odyssey* (what a relief!), but help with organization and time management.

Providing your teenager with the guidance and skills for getting homework done is well worth the time because in the process, she'll learn positive, lifelong work habits.

"But I never did my homework before the last minute…" you may be saying. Don't worry. If you roll up your shirtsleeves and follow the guidelines in this chapter, you'll probably learn something, too!

Setting the Stage for Homework

At this point, your teen has probably established his favorite place to do homework, so your main role at this point is to stop nagging. If you were to visit households of some "grade A" high school students, chances are you'd catch one doing homework with MTV blaring in the background; another talking on the phone while completing a history paper; another working in the kitchen with his feet on the table; and yet another sprawled across the family room floor keeping up her A average. If you looked really hard, you might find one actually working at a desk in a quiet bedroom, but boy, is she the exception.

Despite that, get a desk for your teen's room—be it a hand-me-down from Grandma's house or something from the unfinished furniture store. Why? Because whether or not he uses it for study, it represents a concrete family commitment to schoolwork—and provides an excellent place for storage, too.

If the desk doesn't have a file drawer, visit a stationery or office supply store and buy a file box (they cost under $20) so your teen will have a place to store the current year's papers. A simple, accessible filing system will let your teen find previous notes, tests, and reports quickly and easily.

Items you want to save for "posterity" are best stored in accordion file folders with elastic wraps. Place the best-written papers or projects in them, label them with your teen's name and the year, and store them somewhere out of the way.

Tools of the (Homework) Trade

Just as cooking is a drag when you find you don't have the right ingredients, homework is tough without the necessary tools. At the beginning of the year, ask your teen what school supplies she needs. Don't be surprised if she mentions paints, nails, or textiles; with the new emphasis on experiential learning, many middle and high school students have to create, cook, or fashion something for class.

Be flexible. If the plastic protractors he uses for math keep getting broken in his backpack, do the smart thing: buy two and tell him to keep one at home and leave one at school.

Stock your home library with a dictionary, thesaurus, and possibly an atlas. A good dictionary is worth the $30 price tag for hard cover; and thesauruses are available in paperback.

Consider whether you can afford a computer (see Chapter 14). If you can't add one to your household, investigate other ways your teen can work on one. Some communities give access to school computers during specified evening hours; some schools are investing in laptops that can be checked out like a library book; and many public libraries feature computers that anyone can use.

Homework Made Easy

By the time your teen enters middle or high school, your teen has almost certainly established some type of pattern for the way she does her homework, so you may feel your job is done.

Not so fast. Even a bright, well-organized student may have trouble pacing herself for long-range assignments and juggling the work of six or seven classes every night.

As a parent, you want your teen to get homework done without having to impose rules; you want your teen to assume responsibility so you don't have to stand over him menacingly with a ruler (just kidding!).

To help, you might begin each year with a discussion of your teen's upcoming schedule. If she plays soccer or has a role in the fall play, then talk about when it makes the most sense to do homework. When she gets home? After rehearsal? Or maybe after dinner is the best time for her to buckle down to work. To help establish this pattern, you might pick an amount of time—say, 30 to 45 minutes a day—and state that even if she has no homework she's expected to read or do mentally challenging work during this "homework period."

Homework Time Management: Teen-Style

Perhaps the greatest gift you can give your child is the gift of time management. (Okay, okay, so *you're* disorganized. Don't worry; what you need to teach your teen is right here. And wouldn't this be a perfect time to get better organized yourself?)

➤ Some schools provide students with school planners. If yours doesn't, then you should. Take her to a stationery store and let her choose a daily calendar that she's comfortable carrying. One that devotes a page per day and leaves plenty of room for keeping track of assignments. (Some students prefer a small flip-top notepad for assignments.)

➤ Teach her to note the following information for each assignment in each subject: date, subject, assignment, due date, and date handed in.

➤ Purchase homework folders for each subject, and teach your child the merits of categorization. That way, when it's time to pull out the social studies handout, your teen knows just where it will be.

➤ If your child needs help with time management, hold his telephone calls until after his homework is done.

Doing Homework in Bites

Help your teen to break a long-term assignment into parts. Sit down with her and help her break down the steps that might be involved in writing her year-end term report on China, for example. Those steps might include the following:

1. Choose a specific topic by doing some general reading.

2. Get the topic approved by the teacher.

3. Visit the library and check out books, periodicals, and computer reference materials on the topic.

4. Read and take notes. (Most students could benefit from some guidance here. Slogging through an entire 600-page book on China's Long March is overkill for an eight-page report. Show her how to use resources selectively.)

5. Write a rough draft and edit it.

6. Produce a finished copy.

Starting with the project's due date, show your teen how to calculate how much time she can devote to each stage. Mark a due date by each step.

Foiling Procrastination

A lifelong bad habit like procrastination starts with simple things, like chores and homework. If you sometimes procrastinate (and don't we all?), you know the feeling. You wait and wait, hoping the task will go away…then when it doesn't, you're stuck sweating it out at the last minute, doing a halfway job. You never feel good about it—not before, or during, or after the project.

Here are the five major reasons people procrastinate, and what you can do to help your teen get past each of them:

➤ *They don't know how to do something.*

If your teen is stuck, encourage her to go in early to get some help. Middle school kids are usually quite open about problems, so if you start this "academic coaching" early, you're more likely to have some influence later on. If you're a math whiz, for example, you may find that you and she develop an extra bond because she can turn to you with her algebra questions.

➤ *They have poor work habits.*

Much of the advice in this chapter will help here. A good time management trick that can take your teen a long way is teaching her to do the hardest assignment first. After she's finished with that, it makes the rest of the night look easy.

➤ *They're afraid of not doing well, so they don't try.*

This has to do with your teen's mind-set. Don't pressure her when it comes to scholastics. What you want to instill is curiosity and a pleasure in learning that will help her tackle things she's never tried before.

➤ *They'd rather be doing something else.*

This is where plain old self-discipline comes in. You can help by setting guidelines; for example, homework should come before television or telephone time.

➤ *They feel it has to be perfect.*

Perfectionism is equally insidious. Writing and re-writing an assignment before it is finished is not good use of homework time. Teach her quick-fix methods (like using correcting fluid, erasable pens, and computer word processing programs) and don't push for "perfect." If you already have a perfectionist, give her a limit on the number of times she should allow herself to re-do something (two times?).

Raising an Enthusiastic Reader

Your child learned to read in first grade—that's all there is to it, right? Nope. Reading is a skill that's acquired over many years, and although by the teen years the basic ability should be there, your teen still needs to develop a more sophisticated vocabulary, and she needs to learn to understand complex thought.

So does this mean you ought to sit her down with the writings of Thackeray, Shakespeare, and Dostoyevsky? Not at all. But you do need to create an environment where reading is practiced frequently (just as you would practice horseback riding, speaking French, or playing the piano). Constant practice and exposure should help her increase her reading speed and ability to understand. Here's what to do:

➤ Keep reading material—everything from current books to *People* magazine—in every room in the house. If your teen finds himself eating breakfast with the morning paper spread out on the table, chances are he'll check the sports scores or even read the front page.

➤ Don't impose your own will. Maybe you loved *Huckleberry Finn*; you can recommend that he read it, too, but don't dictate. (And take another look at the complexity of the dialect used in *Huckleberry Finn* while you're at it.)

Tuning In

Teachers say a lot of students get turned off to reading because their parents won't let them read sci-fi, series books, or "trash" like Stephen King. Let your son read every Stephen King book he can put his hands on, if that's what he likes. He's building a skill, and if you leave him alone, the next thing you know he may move on to other horror writers—like Edgar Allen Poe.

➤ Make reading a priority for all family members. Spend quiet time reading on your own. It doesn't matter whether you're reading a novel, the newspaper, a home-remodeling magazine, or a cookbook, the point is that you are demonstrating the importance of the written word. Suggest that all children in the family spend at least 20 minutes per day reading, too.

➤ Share reading when you can. This may be as simple as reading part of a funny Ann Landers column out loud, or it could be a more involved situation where you and your teen recommend books to each other. This will give you some perspective on what interests your teen, and sharing something in common creates a meaningful bond for both of you.

➤ If your teen has a special interest (blues music? ESP?), help him pursue it through reading about it. A visit to the library, a bookstore, or a newsstand may help you find material that your teen will find irresistible to read.

➤ Extend the reading experience. If your teen loves reading about baseball, try to get her to a professional game. And if he loved the last Michael Crichton movie, buy the next Michael Crichton novel before the movie is out.

Tackling Tough Reading Assignments

Beowulf and *The Canterbury Tales* have not gotten easier to read with time (or were you one of those students who enjoyed studying them in school?). If your teen comes home with a daunting summer reading list or a tough assignment, here are a few things that might help:

➤ Help your student map out a plan of attack. How long is the book? When must it be finished? Plot out how many pages must be covered per night. (Be flexible. Some kids do better with longer, less frequent reading sessions because they like to "get into" the book, rather than reading small pieces nightly.)

➤ Check the library for audio recordings of a difficult book (she can listen and read along in her text). Movies or video versions of a book or play will also heighten understanding of the material. A good example is Shakespeare. Reading it and seeing it (even on video) are two totally different experiences, and the teen who sees it enacted has a far better chance of appreciating and remembering both the story and the characters than the teen who doesn't.

➤ Some books really are exceptionally difficult; no 15-year-old should be expected to trudge through them alone. Look for study guides. Teachers don't want them used in place of the real text, but they most certainly don't mind a good guide being used to help explain what's going on.

➤ If you're really motivated to help (and your teen doesn't mind), read the book at the same time your teen is. That way you can discuss it with her as she goes along.

If your child frequently has trouble with reading assignments, talk to the teacher. You both may want to look deeper into the cause of the problem, or discuss new teaching strategies that will help.

Tuning In

Should you pay for good grades? In general, you want your teen to learn that good work is its own reward.

That said, you might find other ways to reward improvement (not just achievement). Promise nothing in advance, but if your teen makes significant gains in a certain area (say, pulls his Biology grade from a C- to a B), consider staging some type of celebration that your teen would enjoy. He might like to be taken out to dinner or you might spring for coveted tickets to a hockey game, and the two of

continues

you can go to celebrate his improvement. If he showed noticeable improvement in a subject that was difficult for him, that's something worth setting off some fireworks about!

Families who do pay for grades sometimes stipulate that the money earned goes into a college fund. This type of enforced savings certainly doesn't do any harm.

Underachiever (and Not So Proud of It)

Most parents find it difficult to tolerate a teen whom they feel isn't trying. His or her refusal to do homework is often an indirect way of expressing anger and confusion. Under-achievement in kids can be caused by many things:

➤ Emotional upset. The teen who has experienced a death in the family or whose parents are going through a divorce is very likely to go through a period of under-achievement.

➤ Mild learning disabilities (see Chapter 10) or an unrecognized physical problem such as a vision or hearing difficulty.

➤ Overly high parental expectations. Dad may be a neurosurgeon, but Johnny may want to play in a rock band right now, and if the academic pressure is too strong, Johnny may rebel.

➤ Peer pressure, especially among teens: "If I do too well, my friends won't like me."

Before trying any "remedies," get a second opinion. If your teen's teachers feel he's doing pretty well (and if they have the test scores to prove it), it's worth listening.

Next, you might consider whether your underachiever has hit a downward spiral because she's disorganized or just doesn't know how to cope with a busy schedule with several subjects to work on every night. (Refer to the earlier part of the chapter on helping your teen get organized.)

Sometimes, one of the best ways to help an underachiever is to not get directly involved in homework. Find out how much time he should be spending on homework every night and then require that that amount of time be invested. Make sure he touches base with you, your spouse, or an older sibling to show that he made an effort to do his work. Then check to see that the work makes it into the backpack. (Doing the work but not taking it to school is another form of self-sabotage for the underachiever.)

After the elapsed time, encourage your teen to do something he likes—whether it's painting or biking or tinkering under the hood of his car. Having him do something in which he excels will help bolster the confidence he needs to try school challenges.

Offering emotional support (underachievers generally have low self-esteem) helps immensely, but ultimately, the under-achiever has to decide to do it for himself. Show acceptance and affection for your child and make certain that he knows you love him no matter what his academic standing.

Progress may be exceedingly slow, but express pleasure in anything. An improvement from a C to a C+ is a good start. A few forays into grades of B- and above will prove to the under-achiever that he is capable of better work and nothing terrible will happen if he does it.

If you feel you're making no progress, consult a professional. (See Chapter 20 for information on finding counseling help.) Underachievement often has deep psychological roots, and if you're not making headway with your teen, you'd be wise to contact someone who can help discover what's bothering him.

Tuning In

Though it may be hard for parents to accept, not all children are academically inclined. But even if your teen isn't a scholar, he can be great at many other things. He may be a wonderful jazz pianist, or have excellent painting skills. Or maybe he's just a really nice kid. Your job as a parent is helping your teen find what he's good at, and what he really loves—whether it's helping the poor, working with tools, or starting a business. Many things are possible for people of all abilities, and if you believe in your teen—no matter what—you make his road that much easier.

Not Making the Grade

What should you do when your teen brings home a grade of D-? It depends on the circumstances:

➤ *An isolated bad grade.* Chances are it's a temporary misstep. Perhaps your teen just didn't understand the subject matter, or maybe it's a case of a hate-hate relationship between your teen and the teacher. If this is the case, talk to your teen as well as the school counselor. With mediation there may be a way to patch up differences.

➤ *The bad report card.* If a bad report card appears suddenly and unexpectedly, you first owe your teen a hearing: "It looks like you had a rough marking period. What happened?" Your teen may be having a tough time socially or in a single subject, and the problems have pulled him down in all areas. Or perhaps there's a physical problem, such as an illness or even a drug problem that needs to be handled (see Chapter 19). Even if your teen seems to be capable of explaining what happens, touch base with the school. They should be on the look-out for your child, too.

➤ *What to do.* You need to tell your teen how you feel about what has happened. If she just doesn't "get" math, look into after-school tutoring, either by a teacher, a friend or family member, or a local college-age kid.

Depending on the circumstances, you may want to tighten up on homework requirements—not by punishing and making her hate you and the work, but by reducing interruptions during homework time or by offering incentives for a job well done. Three math test grades of 80 or above earns her lunch at the local diner. Take her yourself, or better yet, offer to let her go with a friend—and tell her you'll pick up the tab for both.

Cheating: Passing Phase or Doomed Destiny?

"My child a cheater?" No parent wants to think that way. While occasionally trading homework and notes seems to be part of the fabric of teen school life, a consistent pattern of copying or cheating on tests may be a cry for help. Cheating may not always signify dishonesty or laziness; it may have to do with insecurity, peer pressure, a quest for perfection, and the desire to please.

If your teen is accused of cheating, you need to get her back on track. If a teacher has notified you of the problem, set up an appointment and see if you can learn anything more about the situation. Is this the first time this has happened? (Maybe she just fell asleep while she was supposed to be studying for the quiz.) How will the school handle the situation? (If they're doling out punishment, that should affect how you handle the situation at home.) Is your child in a class or program that's too difficult for her? Is there pressure among her peers in the class? What does the teacher think might have led to the cheating?

Talk to your teen about what led her to this point. If you can find out why it happened, you may be able to correct the situation without ever raising your voice.

➤ Try to reduce grade pressure ("You'd better bring home an A") or any need she must feel to "measure up"; stress that you value her for who she is, not for her chemistry grade.

94

➤ Check out her homework organization and her time management system. She wouldn't cheat if she knew the answers, so any help you can provide (possibly including getting a tutor) can make a big difference.

➤ All throughout childhood and into the teen years, do what you can to model honesty and integrity. If Uncle Joe brags about cheating on his tax return, discuss that with your children. When a cashier gives you too much change, make a point of giving it back. If your kids see you as someone who's consistently honest, they're not going to go down the wrong path.

Info Flash
Remind your teen that eating right and getting enough sleep before a big test will boost her performance, but that "cram- ming" until the last minute will create an information overload that will sabotage her.

Tuning In

What if a friend is cheating off your teen? Here's what you might recom- mend. Before the next test, suggest that your teen offer to help his friend study. If the offer is denied, then the next morning, encourage your teen to say: "I'm sorry. I worked really hard on this, and I'm worried we'll get caught if we keep coming up with the same answers." Your teen may feel this solution is nerdy, but by suggesting it, you're conveying that he has the right to protect his work.

While saying negative things about your teen's friends is always risky, you may want to point out that in this particular case, his friend is using him: "He's really put you in a tough position, saying you're not a true friend if you don't let him copy off you...That doesn't sound right to me." Your teen may come to view his friend in a different light.

Getting Involved

Your child's education is a cooperative effort between the family and the school—all the way up through senior year of high school. If you speak positively of the school and take time to be involved, you're saying to your teen, "I value your world, and it's important to me."

There are two ways your child needs you at school.

Pitching In

Studies have shown that teens whose parents are involved in the school do better academically and have better attitudes. You don't necessarily have to give up a lot of time; if you can't be there to help with the school car wash, tell your child you'll donate the buckets they need.

Get into the school to help out occasionally—you'll find it very rewarding. You'll get an inside view of your teen's world and you'll get to see the kids firsthand.

Stay in Touch

Attend back-to-school night; watch for interesting meetings; and try to stay in touch with the parent grapevine.

If you don't act as an advocate for your child, chances are no one else will. When your teen is assigned a counselor, set up an appointment to meet him or her, then stay in touch periodically by phone. It's nice to know who is looking out for your teen.

At the initial meeting, ask what to do if you need to talk to a teacher about something specific. Maybe it's easier for the counselor to initiate contact, or maybe you should get in touch with the teacher directly. Any good teacher or counselor will welcome your concern or interest. You all have the same goal—to give your child the best education possible.

Info Flash

The Freedom of Information Act gives you the right to see your student's complete school records. You might have reason to invoke this right if you're worried that something negative may end up in your teen's official records. Schedule a meeting with the school administration and have a rational conversation about your concerns. With luck and goodwill, you may be able to work everything out.

The Least You Need to Know

➤ Provide your teen with space and equipment for doing homework, and avoid criticizing his homework "environment."

➤ Help your teen with time management by teaching her to keep track of assignments, and to break big assignments into small parts.

➤ To encourage reading, keep printed material all over the house, and bring home books or magazines that will spark her interest. Don't comment if she settles into a Stephen King phase and you think it's junk. She'll move on, and the important thing is that she's reading.

➤ If your teen brings home bad grades or is accused of cheating, talk to her or her teacher about what's going on.

➤ Participate in activities at your teen's school to demonstrate that his world is important to you. Being around will also clue you in on what's going on!

Chapter 10

Catching Previously Undetected Learning Difficulties

In This Chapter

➤ What you should know about learning difficulties

➤ Signs to watch for

➤ A parent's role as advocate

If your middle school or early high school teen is struggling with his scholastics after faring well (or well enough) in elementary school, don't call him lazy. He may have a mild learning problem that has gone undetected until now. Don't worry: there are specific ways you can help him, ranging from medication to new study strategies. If you detect his problem now, he may emerge as the good student you want him to be.

"But why hasn't it caused a problem before now?" you may ask.

Experts say it has to do with changing teaching styles and expectation levels. In elementary school, teachers break down concepts into easy-to-understand segments, and material is repeated frequently until it sinks in. Kids also tend to get more help with their homework during their early school years.

By middle school, academic expectations are changing. School work demands more abstract thinking and the use of applied knowledge (meaning that a student must be able to remember material she learned last week and apply it to her work today). And as students begin to rotate classes, they need stronger organizational skills. A child with learning difficulties may struggle with these new challenges, even though she's done well in previous years.

So if your teen now seems lazy and unmotivated in her studies, or if a teacher is suddenly describing her as "slow," "sloppy," or "incapable," don't write it off to the "teen years." In this chapter, you'll learn whether there is more going on than you might expect.

What Is a Learning Disability?

Generally speaking, a learning disability is a life-long neurological disorder that affects the way people (with average or even above-average intelligence) select, retain, and express information.

A learning disability can affect several methods of learning and thus cause a child problems in several areas (say, both reading and arithmetic), or it may be present in a single subject (such as having trouble only with mathematical calculations or getting thoughts down on paper). That's one of the reasons spotting some difficulties is so tricky.

Another tricky aspect is terminology. Even experts disagree on the terms used to describe learning problems. Just remember that it doesn't matter whether it's called a "disorder," a "disability," or any other condition that causes difficulty with learning. If experts can identify the problem, there's usually something that can be done to make it better.

Just the Facts

Here are some facts about learning disabilities:

➤ An estimated 15 percent of the U.S. population has some form of learning disability.

➤ Learning disabilities can affect one's ability to read, write, speak, and compute math, and can impede socialization skills.

➤ Learning disabilities often run in families.

➤ Because they are often "hidden handicaps," learning disabilities are not easily recognized, accepted, or (in some cases) considered serious.

➤ Learning disabilities never go away, but they can be compensated for.

➤ Learning disabilities are *not* the same as mental retardation, autism, deafness, blindness, or behavioral disorders.

Watching for Warning Signs

The National Center for Learning Disabilities has developed a checklist of common warning signs. The organization stresses that this is merely a "guidepost" for parents. Because all children exhibit some of these behaviors throughout childhood, what you're looking for is a *consistent* pattern of a group of these behaviors that indicate your teen is not progressing at an appropriate rate.

If you recognize some of your teen's traits as you read this list, *don't panic*. Teenagers are infamous for many of these qualities! For example, disorganization, distractibility, and difficulty with planning are a few of the "symptoms" listed here. Now really. How long do you wait in the morning while your teen locates everything she needs for school? What teen isn't easily distracted? And if you've ever watched your teen try to hatch a plan with friends, you know that it simply cannot be done without 42 phone calls—and even then it may not work out.

Remember, too, that a teen who isn't interested in English literature may not pay attention in class, may show poor recall of material, and may not do well on the tests. That doesn't mean he's learning disabled; it simply means he doesn't like Jane Austen or Thomas Hardy or he has something else on his mind.

So you've got to read this list carefully. Do you notice that your child seems to be progressing in a certain subject or with a specific skill at a much slower rate than his friends? Kids vary greatly in their rate of progress, so what you're looking for is consistency: Do all the other 13-year-olds seem to "get" something, and your young teen just doesn't ever pick up on a particular type of skill or concept when everyone else does? Is he suddenly bothered by his inability to master certain tasks? And is there a dip in performance in some aspect of his life—be it social or academic? If this is the case, then there is reason to look for further advice, observation, and assessment.

The National Center for Learning Disabilities (NCLD) has created a checklist of some common warning signs of learning disabilities. The NCLD notes that all children exhibit some of these behaviors at various times; what you are looking for is a *consistent* showing of a *group* of these behaviors. If, after reviewing the list, you have any concerns, contact the school counseling department or a psychologist for further information and possible assessment.

Learning Difficulties Checklist

Does your teen have difficulty with:

Organization

Knowing time, date, year

Managing time

Completing assignments

Organizing thoughts

Locating belongings

Carrying out a plan

Making decisions

Setting priorities

Sequencing (placing things in order)

Physical Coordination

Manipulating small objects

Learning self-help skills

Cutting

Drawing

Handwriting

Climbing and running

Mastering sports

Spoken or Written Language

Pronouncing words

Learning new vocabulary

Following directions

Understanding requests

Relating stories

Discriminating among sounds

Responding to questions

Understanding concepts

Reading comprehension

Spelling

Writing stories and essays

Attention and Concentration

Completing a task

Acting before thinking

Poor organization

Waiting

Restlessness

Daydreaming

Distractibility

Memory

Remembering directions

Learning math facts

Learning new procedures

Identifying letters

Remembering names

Remembering events

Studying for tests

Social Behavior

Making and keeping friends

Social judgment

Impulsive behavior

Frustration tolerance

Sportsmanship

Accepting change in routine

Interpreting nonverbal cues

Working cooperatively

Reprinted with the permission of the National Center for Learning Disabilities—381 Park Avenue South, New York, N.Y. 10016.

The following chart, provided by the National Center for Learning Disabilities, offers some guidelines as to what warning signs are particularly relevant to specific ages. For example, poor reading ability in a child in the early elementary years is not a problem; but if that child is not comprehending what he reads by the middle grades, then this would merit investigation.

Learning Disabilities

What to Look For: Some First Signs of Trouble

Keeping Up with the Flow of Expectations

	Language	Memory	Attention	Fine Motor Skill	Other Functions
Pre-school	Pronunciation problems. Slow vocabulary growth. Lack of interest in storytelling.	Trouble learning numbers, alphabet, days of week, etc. Poor memory for routines.	Trouble sitting still. Extreme restlessness. Impersistence at tasks.	Trouble learning self-help skills (e.g., tying shoelaces). Clumsiness. Reluctance to draw or trace.	Trouble learning left from right (possible visual spatial confusion). Trouble interacting (weak social skills).
Lower Grades	Delayed decoding abilities for reading. Trouble following directions. Poor spelling.	Slow recall of facts. Organizational problems. Slow acquisition of new skills. Poor spelling.	Impulsivity, lack of planning. Careless errors. Insatiability. Distractibility.	Unstable pencil grip. Trouble with letter formation.	Trouble learning about time (temporal-sequential disorganization). Poor grasp of math concepts.
Middle Grades	Poor reading comprehension. Lack of verbal participation in class. Trouble with word problems.	Poor, illegible writing. Slow or poor recall of math facts. Failure of automatic recall.	Inconsistency. Poor self-monitoring. Great knowledge of trivia Distaste for fine detail.	Fist-like or tight pencil. Illegible, slow, or inconsistent writing. Reluctance to write.	Poor learning strategies. Disorganization in time or space. Peer rejection.

	Language	Memory	Attention	Fine Motor Skill	Other Functions
Upper Grades	Weak grasp of explanations. Foreign language problems. Poor written expression. Trouble summarizing.	Trouble studying for tests. Weak cumulative memory. Slow work pace.	Memory problems due to weak attention. Mental fatigue.	Lessening relevance of fine motor skills.	Poor grasp of abstract concepts. Failure to elaborate. Trouble taking tests, multiple choice (e.g., SATs).

Melvin D. Levine, M.D., F.A.A.P., THEIR WORLD, 1990

These lists are guideposts for parents, teachers, and others involved. They should not be used in isolation, but may lead you to seek further assessment. Many children will, from time to time, have difficulty with one or more of these items. They should always be reviewed in a broader context of understanding about a child.

Reprinted with the permission of the National Center for Learning Disabilities—381 Park Avenue South, New York, N.Y. 10016.

Types of Learning Disabilities

The following sections will give you a little more information about the types of learning disabilities that can present themselves in the teen years.

Dyslexia

Approximately 10 percent of the population suffers from some level of dyslexia, a disorder that makes the learning of reading, writing, and spelling exceptionally difficult—to the point that it interferes with progress in personal growth, in school, and in work. Many dyslexics are quite bright, which is one of the reasons why it isn't always detected early.

Dyslexics may reverse letters, such as *b* and *d*; write *p* for *b*; see the word *was* for *saw* or *left* for *felt*; or *nuclear* may appear as *unclear*. They sometimes have trouble finding the right words when they speak. Math can also be difficult because of the challenge of sequential ordering (placing things in order). Dyslexics also often need help with time management and organization.

Dyslexics can usually be taught to manage the situation. They do need more help than others in sorting, recognizing, and ordering letters, words, and numbers. After dyslexia is diagnosed, there is special training available that will help.

Other Possible Problems

Other learning problems include:

➤ *Apraxia (Dyspraxia).* The inability to make an appropriate body response.

➤ *Dysgraphia.* Difficulty in producing legible handwriting at an age-appropriate speed, both in the technical as well as the expressive sense. These students also demonstrate difficulty with spelling.

➤ *Auditory discrimination.* Difficulty perceiving the differences between sounds and sequences of sounds (such as being tone-deaf).

➤ *Visual perception.* Difficulty understanding and interpreting what one sees. Color-blindness is a good example of a neuro-physiological problem that affects someone's ability to perceive information visually.

Attention Deficit (Hyperactivity) Disorder

Teenagers with Attention Deficit (Hyperactivity) Disorder (ADD or ADHD) have difficulty paying attention. Because these teens are not "screening" for what is important in the classroom, they become distracted and their attention wanders. They may be attentive and participate positively in class one moment; the next moment, they're focusing on something else.

Tuning In
What causes learning disabilities? Experts don't know precisely. A variety of factors may contribute to their occurrence: heredity; problems during pregnancy and birth (such as illness, injury, drug or alcohol use, birth difficulties); or incidents after birth (such as head injuries or nutritional deprivation). In addition, high levels of lead in the blood can cause disabilities. Experts stress that parents should not feel guilty or feel that a child's disability could be prevented.

Sometimes hyperactivity is part of this disorder; it often is not. Teenagers who exhibit hyperactivity are impulsive and have a heightened inability to sit still or concentrate for long periods of time.

Some children with ADD or ADHD aren't diagnosed early on because teachers (and parents) think that maturation will solve the problem. Other children perform well academically, so the difficulty goes undetected. (Some ADD/ADHD children have above-average intelligence and can actually get by pretty well even though they listen only 20 to 30 percent of the time.)

ADD and ADHD are conditions that require medical diagnosis. They can be managed. Some sufferers will find relief with medication; others will benefit from teaching strategies that provide them with additional study skills.

What Now?

If you suspect a problem, your child's school is your first resource. Contact your child's counselor or school psychologist. Evaluations can often be arranged through the public school system (at no cost), private clinics, private evaluators, hospital clinics, and university clinics. (Some school districts do not honor test results from sources other than the school system, so check this out before paying for an outside evaluation.)

According to Public Law 94-142, the public school system must evaluate students who are referred by parents or professionals to determine if special education is warranted.

Observation by professionals is an important part of verifying the existence of a disability. In addition, assessment should be conducted by a team of professionals using a variety of standardized instruments and informal tasks. Depending on the nature of the problem, the assessment team might consist of (but not be limited to) any of the following professionals: a pediatrician, a pediatric neurologist, a psychologist, an occupational therapist, and a classroom and learning disabilities teacher.

When parents or the school detect a diagnosable problem at this stage, teens are often relieved. They knew they were different or that they weren't learning the same way their friends were, and they are relieved to know they aren't "stupid"—they just learn differently than others.

Looking for Help in All the Right Places

If your teen has a learning disorder or disability, here are the levels of help you might expect at your child's school:

➤ Students with more serious disabilities may spend all or part of the day in a resource room for specialized teaching.

➤ Other students stay in the regular classroom but are taught differently than other students. Adjustments may be made in the teacher's methods and the learning environment. (This may involve simplification or modification of assignments or tests.)

➤ Other students are candidates for medication that is intended to help improve behavior and learning.

Parents should know that Ritalin and some similar medications are overprescribed. Sometimes teachers who are burdened with large classes will urge parents to get a prescription for their child (because a medicated child may be easier to deal with in the classroom). However, keep in mind that these medications should not be taken without cause, and if your teen is placed on a particular medication, its use and effects should be carefully monitored.

At this point, identifying someone who can act as liaison between you and the school is important. Your child's counselor is a logical person to fulfill this role, or he or she can suggest someone else. You need someone who will regularly update you on your teen's progress in school.

What You Can Do

Most teens with any form of learning disability will benefit from being shown better organizational systems. The following tips will help you help your teen:

➤ Emphasize the importance of keeping track of homework assignments, test dates, and other deadlines in a daily planner. (In the beginning, you may want to go over your teen's planner with her daily.)

➤ Note-taking can be a great help at stimulating recall. Work with your child—or talk to a supportive teacher—about what you can do to help her get lessons down on paper and in her own words.

➤ See if your teen can be allowed to get assignments early. If it takes your teen longer to get through a book for a book report, then he should have the benefit of extra time to read it. (Another idea: visit next year's teacher and get the reading list ahead of time so your child can get a head start.)

➤ Use the summer to improve skills in a fun, pressure-free way. If your child has a problem reading, for example, you can pick up her favorite magazines (*Wired*, *Spin*, *Seventeen*, and so on). It doesn't matter what the content is, it's just important that your child keep building her reading skills.

➤ Familiarize yourself with the many books, seminars, and workshops that address your teen's condition. (See the Resource Directory for a list of organizations devoted to learning disabilities; they're a good place to start.)

Coping with a Learning Disability

More than anything else, teens want to be "normal." Why else would they wear the same style of clothes, use the same slang, go to the same movies, and listen to the same music? In all likelihood, your teen doesn't want to be classified as "learning disabled." She just wants to fit in and be accepted.

When you discuss a diagnosis with your teen, you may find that her first response is actually relief—now she knows why a particular skill or subject was giving her trouble!

That said, it's still difficult to be told that you're different—especially for teens. Here are some ways you can help your teen cope with her diagnosis:

➤ Some families put their teens in individual therapy for a brief time once they are diagnosed, partly to provide emotional support for this "different-ness." A good therapist will help a teen focus on her strengths and weaknesses in a way that lets her accept what she'll be coping with in the coming years. Your child's school psychologist may be willing to meet with your student for a few sessions, or she may refer you to an outside source that is affordable.

➤ In addition, some schools run support groups for kids coping with learning disabilities, and this type of support can be very beneficial for teens. If your school does not provide this type of ongoing support, ask for a referral to a place that does.

You, too, may be feeling overwhelmed by this news. When you find a support group for your teen, ask if there are resources for parents. Or you may find a special PTA committee dedicated to working for additional services for learning disabled students in your school district. Any group you find will link you with parents who may provide a helpful grapevine for information.

In addition, refer to the Resource Directory for national organizations specializing in learning disabilities. Through these organizations, you will be able to get some literature on the topic; you may also get a referral to local resources in your area. There are also seminars for parents on a wide variety of disabilities, so once you're on the right mailing lists, you'll find yourself surrounded by helpful people and comforting information.

Your Role as a Parent

If your teenager has just been diagnosed with some level of learning disability (or you've found that while there is no disability, your child needs additional academic support), you need to identify and think through your role.

Always, you must serve as your teen's advocate, staying in touch with the school and monitoring what goes on. (This doesn't mean being on-site full-time; an occasional visit and regular phone calls will do.)

You will want to get more involved with your child and her studies. (If you don't have a good relationship with her, maybe someone else can help out. Your spouse? An older sibling? A favorite grandparent? A private tutor?) Because organization must be emphasized, you and anyone working with your teen should emphasize an orderly approach to all aspects of life.

As the process evolves, remember your ultimate goals:

➤ Your teen should be acquiring and strengthening skills that will prepare her to take full responsibility for her own learning.

➤ Throughout your teen's adolescence, your role should be constantly diminishing.

Yes, he will forget his math text one day, and yes, she will be inadequately prepared for her biology test because she never buckled down to study over the weekend, but that's part of being a teenager. If you get your child to the point that her problems are within normal teen range, then you've done a good job.

The Least You Need to Know

➤ If you're concerned that your child may have a learning disability, watch for a consistent pattern that indicates your child isn't progressing at a normal rate.

➤ If you suspect a problem, contact your child's school. Your child is eligible for a free diagnostic assessment.

➤ If your child is diagnosed with a problem, don't feel guilty. Just pitch in and figure out what you can do to help.

➤ Learn as much as you can about the particular disability and be prepared to act as an advocate for your child.

➤ Your long-term goal is to provide your teen with support and strategies that ultimately make him as independent as possible.

HEY MOM, I FIGURED OUT ANOTHER CHORD!

Chapter 11

Extracurricular Activities and Social Life

In This Chapter

➤ The importance of friends

➤ After-school activities

➤ Weekend activities

➤ Dating and your teen

As your teen moves into the wider world, part of her job is becoming more independent—well, independent from you. She won't be truly independent because she's going to replace you with her friends.

If she's excited because the boy at locker 31 smiled at her, or if she has a problem with her best friend, or if she wants to talk on and on about the new kid at school, her friends will be delighted to listen. They will be turning to her for the same things as well.

Info Flash

Kids are more likely to turn to their friends when they believe that parents have little experience about something, for example drugs, or when parents seem unable or unwilling to advise them about something, such as sex.

Info Flash
Studies of adolescent friendship show that while peer influence may reveal itself in clothing, hairstyles, language, and substance abuse, parental influence is most important in the long run in choices of career and religious values.

So her friends are useful to her—and useful to you. (What can *you* say after she describes the boy at locker 31 and how he looked at her? Kind of a conversation-stopper if you're over 18.)

Her friends are useful to you in other ways, too. Study after study has shown that peer influence is one of the major factors in whether or not a teenager abuses drugs and/or alcohol. If this is so, then it follows that if your child is hanging out with Honor Society kids, their positive influence might rub off on your teen.

Simply put, if your teen associates with a nice bunch of kids whom you like, your parenting days (and nights) are going to be a lot more carefree. (You still have to stay on duty, but you can probably sit down part of the time.)

"So What Are You Doing After School?"

After-school activities are the first and most important step in guiding your teen toward a positive peer group. Although kids are beginning to have strong feelings about their outside interests by middle school, parental prodding can still accomplish a lot.

Tuning In
Don't judge a book by its cover, and don't judge your teen's friends by their clothes. Future valedictorians (and corporate presidents) have sported long locks, spiked locks, and nose rings. Get to know your teen's friends before making any sort of assessment.

First, you can suggest that your child do something with his after-school time—whether it's playing softball or joining the Spanish club or practicing the trombone. Idle time is dangerous time, and by linking him with a special interest (school band, soccer team, art club, and so on), he has the potential to make friends with kids who have other things to do besides just "hang out."

If your teen maintains his interest into high school, you'll find that his core group of friends probably share the activity. Having a bunch of kids lay out the school newspaper over your kitchen table is a far different experience from entertaining kids who've had no outside interests for the last few years.

Tuning In

Particularly during the early teen years when your child is still forming new friendships, it's in your best interests to subtly convey your feelings about your teen's friends. You can express approval of certain kids by including them in family activities: next time you're having a barbecue, suggest that your daughter invite her friend Lucy. By doing so, you're expressing your approval of Lucy.

If you dislike a particular friend, your options are more limited, because expressing your feelings may cause a needless rift between you and your teen. If the situation is not dangerous, try to go along with your teen, and hope that he'll soon get bored with his friend. You might also try to learn the attraction to this person. Maybe he knows everything there is to know about comic-book collecting, and that's why he's interesting to your teen.

However, if the friend is not a positive force, you may want to comment—tactfully. You might say: "I've noticed that when you spend time with Ben you aren't very cheerful." This may help him identify what has been bothering him.

Or if it's the child's household you don't like (for example, it's rumored that his brother is into drugs), you might say: "I'm delighted that you spend time with Doug, but I'd like the two of you to hang out here rather than at his house," and say why.

(If the friend is cutting classes or into substance abuse, you'll need to make your opinion of those activities known and try to involve your teen in activities that do not include that particular friend. Also refer to Chapter 19 for additional strategies on helping your teen remain drug-free.)

Being "In" and Being "Out"

From the vantage point of a teen, cliques are great if you're among the "chosen," and really difficult if you're not.

Cliques change with age. Popularity and social pull lie at the core of early cliques, making them more difficult to penetrate for teens who are on the outside. The peak of conformity comes at around age 13 when teens want desperately to "belong."

Danger Zone

If you're truly concerned about the group your teen is running with, call your school counselor or talk to other parents who may know the crowd. Someone who knows the kids well may be able to allay your fears or verify that it's a bad group. A good counselor may also have some suggestions on how to help your teen gravitate toward a different group.

Later on, cliques become more interest-specific and less exclusive. For example, even if your teen has never fit into a particular group before, he may "bond" with other yearbook staffers and gain acceptance that way.

During a bad time when your teen is on the "outs" with his clique or his best friend, the most helpful thing you can do is not comment on it. ("You're making it into such a big DEAL, mom!") If the unringing phone or the free Friday nights pass unnoticed, your teen will feel like he's saving face. In the meantime, re-read Chapter 8, "How They Feel: Keeping Tabs on Self-Esteem." This is when hobbies and special interests can fill a void that you can't reach.

During the early teen years, "dissing" (putting down) other kids is part of many teen cultures. Unfortunately, many kids go through a stage where they find that the easiest way to define themselves is by proving how much better they are than the next person. Young teens and teens in transition are particularly prone to berating others. Try to discourage your own teen from "dissing" others by pointing out that inevitably, "what goes around comes around."

If your teen is the subject of particularly painful ridicule over a prolonged period of time, it can be very difficult for him. Providing support at home and encouraging other activities that involve him with a different (less cruel) crowd is a partial solution; but there is little that can soften the negative impact of being the butt of a class joke day in and day out.

If time doesn't correct the situation, contact the school counselor and/or a teacher to see if they have any suggestions. Perhaps your son could switch classes; distancing your son from the bully or bullies may make them lose interest in teasing him.

What shouldn't you do? Call the parents of the other kid(s). It will mortify your teen, and any parent who has raised a child capable of truly cruel harassment isn't likely to be very helpful to you.

Rolling Out the Red Carpet: Entertaining

You can already guess the drawbacks of entertaining teenagers in your own home (fingerprints all over the walls, no food left in the refrigerator, and so on), but there are some definite advantages. To begin, if they're at your house, you know where they are. In addition, if they're at your house, you'll get to know them (a little, anyway). It's also nice to let your teenager know that you welcome his friends just as you welcome your own.

Another thought to keep in mind: in most communities (especially in rural or suburban areas) the kids don't have a lot of options; movies are expensive, and ice cream parlors or local restaurants often close early. If they're looking for a safe place to simply hang out, they need a home.

And actually "hanging out" at your place is preferable to an official party that carries with it higher expectations than simply letting kids sit around and watch a movie or listen to music.

"There's a Party Tonight!"

If you do step into the role of official "party-thrower" for a birthday celebration or post-prom bash, keep the following in mind:

➤ Ask your teen to draw up a guest list of a limited number of kids. In general, 20–30 kids is a manageable group. (Large parties are almost impossible to control.)

➤ Specify "no crashers." Once teens can drive, party-crashing can and does occur; indicate that you'll be around throughout the party, and if too many kids appear, you'll have to close down.

➤ Agree ahead of time to the hours of the party. An end time gives you added control.

➤ If your teen needs a reminder, say that alcohol and drugs will not be tolerated. If kids bring in beer or any other substance, you can certainly ask them to leave.

➤ Specify that those who come to the party are to stay at the party; kids arriving, leaving, and returning are more likely to be bringing in illegal substances or are partaking elsewhere and then coming back—and you don't need that either.

➤ While you certainly don't want to monitor the party moment-to-moment, try to walk by once or twice during the evening (if only to bring in more food). If the party is in a basement rec room, keep some of the food upstairs. If the kids come up and realize parents are around, their behavior will probably remain more civilized.

➤ Invite another parent to keep you company. This also provides you with someone who knows some of the kids whom you don't know.

➤ If you have agreed to a large party, notify the neighbors, and tell the police. The police may be able to make suggestions regarding parking, and if they're keeping their eye out for you that night, it's all for the good.

➤ See Chapter 19, "Living Dangerously: Alcohol, Smoking, and Drugs," for information about your legal responsibilities regarding teens and alcohol.

Partying Elsewhere

Parents tell horror stories that sound like something straight out of *Risky Business*: they were out for the evening, and their teenagers entertained without permission. The results were disastrous: the neighbors called the police, many of the kids got drunk, and the living room furniture will never look the same.

You don't want to be those parents, but you also don't want your teen to be at that party. That's why I'm going to give you some additional guidelines.

Every book you read says, "Call the parents to find out if anyone is going to be home." I recommend that, too, but with full acknowledgment that it's difficult to call people you don't know to quiz them about their plans and still maintain a relationship with your teen. As alternatives, you might try the following: (Don't tell your teen that you plan to call. It will only make him mad.)

➤ Call, but call with an offer: "How nice of you to have the kids over Friday night. Could I drop off some soda ahead of time, or is there anything else I can do to help you out?" If the party was a "surprise" party for the parents, you've just blown the whistle in the nicest of ways. If the call goes well, you've also made a new contact.

➤ Network. Call people you know who may be able to tell you what the scene will be like, or who can call and find out the arrangements for the party.

➤ Discuss times and transportation with your teen. What are the hours of the party, and how is your teen getting there? Remind her that if she goes elsewhere—for any reason—she's to call you.

➤ Tell your teen that she can call you (or another adult whom you both trust) at any time—no questions asked—if she wants to leave the party.

➤ Remind your teen never to ride with someone who has been drinking. (Refer to Chapter 19 for additional guidelines.)

➤ Stay awake, or have your teen wake you, when he gets home. This is your opportunity to check on what condition he's in following a party.

➤ Be suspicious if your teen frequently sleeps elsewhere after a party. He may not want to run into you for some reason. (Get the hint?)

Tuning In

Throughout elementary school you've probably been in close touch with the families of your children's friends. As your kids enter middle school and high school, it's more important than ever that you keep building those connections. You can stay in touch by meeting them at school functions, or simply chatting if you run into them around town.

If your parent-chain is strong enough, you ought to be able to find out what's really happening on any given weekend with only a phone call or two.

While the Cat's Away...

If you're going to be gone for a few days and are planning to leave your 17- or 18-year-old at home alone, you need to carefully evaluate the situation. Here are a few pointers:

➤ You may want to re-think your plans. If your teen can't hold off a crowd who learns you're not at home, both you and your teen may be very sorry you ever left town.

➤ If you have to be away and your teen can't or won't come along, consider asking a relative or hiring someone to come stay during the night.

➤ Ask if your teen can stay with a friend.

➤ Tell neighbors you trust to keep an eye out while you are gone. Ask that they call the police (or a person you designate) if a large gathering shows up at your place.

One mother of a basically good teen who ran into problems when she went on a weekend trip tells the following story: "This winter my son, who is a senior in high school, said to me, 'Mom, why don't you go skiing on the weekends anymore?' and I replied: 'Because when I went away for a weekend last year, you proved to me why I can't.' And he's a basically *good* kid."

Like it or not, our child care responsibilities don't necessarily get easier as our kids get older. (You may remember fondly the days when relief was a phone-call-to-the-sitter away!)

Setting Curfews: Pumpkin Time

Just as Cinderella's fairy godmother did not hesitate to give her a curfew, neither should you pause before telling your teen a time by which he is to be home.

And just as adjustable mortgages have their advantages, so do adjustable curfews. Most families have success by establishing a set time for nights when the kids are "just hanging out" and another time for special occasions. If you're in sync with the rest of your teen's friends, enforcement will be a snap.

The consequences for missing a curfew and not calling should involve coming in earlier the next night, or not going out at all—depending on how serious you consider the infraction.

Pajama Party

As if parenting isn't tough enough...your 16-year-old daughter skips through the living room and announces, "Bye, Mom. We're all sleeping over at John's tonight."

You really *needed* to deal with coed sleepovers, didn't you? Yeah, right, as the teen set would say.

With this issue, like everything else, you have to decide what makes you comfortable. If the thought of your son or daughter participating in a coed pajama party drives you crazy, then forget it. Lay down the law: he or she just can't, because you say so. (You do have the right to say that occasionally; just not too often, or you'll lose your ability to communicate effectively.)

However, if you're at all open to learning more about today's social scene, consider the following reasons given by parents who permitted coed group sleepovers:

> ➤ "My son went to a coed sleepover the night of the junior prom," explains one mother. "He attended the prom with the group of kids he hangs out with. There are both boys and girls in the crowd, but none of them are romantically linked. When they asked if they could come back to one of the girl's houses for the night, we agreed. We know the family well, and we found it far preferable to them going to clubs or looking for a 'party' in some other way. They're good kids, and all things considered, this seemed like an acceptable alternative."

> ➤ "Kids today aren't dating the way we did," says another mother. "My daughter socializes with a big group of kids, none of whom would be said to be dating. They've had one or two social all-nighters, and because we knew the family—and knew the parents would be home—we permitted her to go. Even though I doubt that the parents stayed awake all night, we felt she would be okay."

Note that in both situations there were no serious couples in the mix, and the exact location where the kids would be was known to the parent giving the "okay."

And what about a sleepover with a "significant other?" Liberal parents have been known to permit it: "I know they're 'doing it,' so I'd rather have them at home," goes the thinking. You have to make up your own mind on this issue. Be sure to read Chapter 18 on sex and sexuality. And if you just don't like the idea, you can always simply say, "I'm not comfortable with that in my home."

So the next time your teenager comes home with a sleepover request, you might double-check the guest list (now you'll know to be heads up on this one!), and if it turns out it's coed, you can consider it with these comments in mind. (In the meantime, you might want to cut these pages out of the book. No sense in giving your teen any ideas!)

What to Do About Other Household Rules

Like boys in your daughter's bedroom!

Life was certainly simpler when you and I were growing up: No members of the opposite sex in bedrooms, right? Well, it's a new day. You need to be reasonable and flexible about some of the issues that come your way.

Because coed groups of friends are a part of many teens' social lives, it's awfully hard to say, "no boys (or girls) in your room" (especially if that's where the CD player is). Try this:

If the member of the opposite sex is a friend, then the bedroom is on-limits, even with an occasional closed door. If the member of the opposite sex is your teen's "significant other," then being in the bedroom is permissible only if the door is open.

Info Flash
When young adolescents say they're "going out" with members of the opposite sex, it doesn't mean going anyplace; it just means being romantically linked.

"I'm in Love!"

While some of the emotional aspects of young love are discussed in Chapter 6 and the sexual ones are covered in Chapter 18, you should also consider some of the practical aspects of your teen having a "steady" or (in today's terminology) "going out" with somebody.

Take her relationships seriously, but not too seriously. In other words, acknowledge that she really is "in love," but don't start measuring her for a wedding dress. These are the years when she should be dating different people and learning all she can about relationships. A serious but light attitude on your part will leave her free to move around as she sees fit.

If you think she's head-over-heels with the wrong guy and the relationship seems to be lasting, you might try uncritical comments:

"I notice it makes you angry that Bill doesn't call you until the last minute for the weekend. It makes it difficult to plan, doesn't it?"

Your remark shows that you're sympathetic, but you're planting the seed that perhaps Bill is bad news. Give her time. If her self-esteem is intact, she'll get the picture that she doesn't have to settle for Bill. (But if you say that explicity, you could end up with him as an in-law!)

Even if you're crazy about the boy (or girl) your child is seeing, limit the amount of time the two of them spend together. For example, in the summer, you might say they can see each other in the afternoon or evening, but not both. Continuous physical contact may lead them both farther than they intended, and it also closes off other options. (If she's at the beach without HIM, another love interest may catch her eye.)

Prom Night News

One thing hasn't changed from your day: the prom is still a big social deal. But proms have changed to become more expensive, less safe, and yet, in many communities, more open. Here's the news:

No date for the prom? No problem. In today's world, going with friends can be just as fun (and may be less stressful for everyone). If your teen doesn't have a date and isn't sure whether or not to go, be encouraging. (Saying, "In my day, no one went unless they had a date," is what *not* to do.)

You also need to accept that prom night should not be like any other night. A later curfew is in order and special privileges—within reason—are probably part of the deal. However, vigilance on your part will help make it work out safely.

Once your teen decides to go to the prom, your ears should be permanently perked. Prom plans will change at least five hundred times, but it's important that you stay on top of what your teen has in mind. (Some of the less positive prom developments include parents who rent hotel rooms for teen couples; the practice of over-drinking and club-hopping; and the pressure to 'do it' on prom night.) If your teen's got your voice in his ear as the kids make decisions about what to do that night, he'll be better off for it.

Your teen will want to link up with others, and safety will be less of an issue if she links up with a safe crowd (a basically good group of kids who generally have pretty good judgment). If she's booked to go to the prom with a group who walks on the wild side, you may need to impose an earlier curfew than you normally might. Getting her home at a certain time is about your only protection that she won't do anything reckless—other than trusting in her good judgment.

Though it may be expensive, ordering a limo to shuttle your teen and his friends to and from the prom might be a good idea. It offers great safety benefits: a responsible adult will be driving the kids, meaning there's no chance a 17-year-old who is drinking will be at the wheel that night. To reduce per-person expenses, suggest that three couples share the limo instead of just two.

Talk to other parents about safe after-prom options. Some ideas include:

➤ Is someone willing to open their home to an after-prom party? If you're game, you can suggest that a group come to your house for Chinese take-out—or that the boys (in a nice role reversal) put together an elegant dinner for the girls.

➤ Is there an all-night restaurant where teens could go for a late dinner or early breakfast?

➤ Someone with older teens may have some great suggestions of things that have worked in the past. (As mentioned earlier in the chapter, one parent had great success with a post-prom coed group sleepover.)

Remember that you cannot make these plans for your teen and her friends, but you can seed your conversation with suggestions of what you've heard others have done.

All Dressed Up and No Place to Go

The *Gannett Newspapers* recently assembled a teen panel in Westchester, New York to discuss the problem of "boredom in the 'burbs" because too much quiet turns kids to trouble. Among the suggestions the panelists made:

➤ Communities should have more teen-friendly businesses. Teens liked pizzerias, diners, and ice cream shops where they were allowed to hang out.

➤ Schools or community centers should offer more activities, including "open gym" during the summers so the kids have a place to go.

➤ Sports facilities should offer teen hours.

The Least You Need to Know

➤ Try to guide your teen toward positive extracurricular activities. They provide a solid base for friendships.

➤ Try to avoid passing negative judgment on your teen's friends. Your teen may become defensive on behalf of a particular friend whom you dislike, which just exacerbates the problem.

➤ Letting your teen entertain his friends at home should be encouraged. Teens need a safe place to hang out, and if it's your place you'll find it easier to get acquainted with your teen's set, too.

➤ Build a network of parents so you have a quick way to find out what's going on or to take a mutual stand on a dangerous issue.

➤ Set a curfew and enforce it.

Chapter 12

Looking Ahead to College: The View from High School

In This Chapter

➤ Preparing for college: the high school years

➤ What colleges look for in students

➤ What students should look for in colleges

Helping your teen select the right college takes time: time spent learning about various schools; time spent finding and visiting schools that are right for your teen; and time spent in the actual application process.

Applying for financial aid is also an important part of the process for most families (see Chapter 23). The good news is that there's money available at many schools (in the form of scholarships, grants, and loans).

Here's a brief guide to what you need to know about the serious (perhaps too serious) process of applying to and selecting a college.

Getting Guidance

Your teen has many wonderful treats in store for him as he enters his high school years. In addition to academic challenges, he'll be making new friends, pursuing new interests, and learning a lot about himself as he navigates these years.

While doing "high school things" is truly his most important job over the next few years, you don't want you or him to be blindsided by not being knowledgeable about college. If you start learning the college application process little by little, your teen won't be caught unprepared in his senior year. (For example, some kids report that they had no idea their school offered a "college prep" track of courses that they needed to take; no one ever told them. Learning about these courses in junior or senior year is regrettable for the child who wants to go on.)

Info Flash
College grads will, over their lifetime, earn 67 percent more than high school grads.

Starting your information-gathering now will assure you that your teen won't regret the way he spent his high school years—he'll be able to look back at the good times, and also know that he handled those years knowledgeably.

As soon as your teen enters high school, set up an appointment with her guidance counselor. When you meet, ask about the following:

➤ What courses will my teen need to take in the coming years?

➤ How will we know about standardized testing and the sign-up dates?

➤ Are there other tests she should take at times we might not expect? (For example, some high school freshmen take biology, and the logical time to take the bio achievement test is shortly after the course. Don't wait for junior year when "brushing up" on the material will be difficult at best.)

As your teen selects courses for the upcoming years, keep in mind that high grades on easy courses are less meaningful than lower grades on challenging courses. Colleges look for students who take on extra challenges.

Communication 101

As your teen finishes his sophomore year of high school, it's time to start considering what he wants to get out of his college experience. This gives both of you extra thinking time before the pressure is on.

Here are some questions you might encourage your teen to think about:

➤ What kind of courses would he like to take?

➤ What activities are important to him (Team sports? At what level of play? Student government? School newspaper? College radio station? and so on)

➤ Is he attracted to a large or small school?

➤ Are there any particular schools that he'd like to consider?

➤ Would he like to come home regularly? (A "yes" to this question will limit him geographically.)

Your first conversation may be vague, but simply by asking the questions, you'll get him thinking and making some decisions.

This is also the time for you to air your concerns. Perhaps you're worried about financing a $25,000-a-year school. Your teen should know that he may need to apply for scholarships or consider financial aid packages.

By junior year, your teen should intensify his research. His high school library or counseling office will have a good collection of brochures, course catalogs, and even video guides for many colleges. He should also ask about college fairs, which offer good opportunities to hear about schools he might otherwise not have thought of.

Danger Zone

CAUTION

Remember that your teen may be under intense pressure. She faces an extra load of tests and applications, and also has to worry about getting into the "right" school. She's also coming to terms with who she is and where her future lies. She can alleviate some stress by locating a few "safe" schools where she could be happy. You might also lower the pressure by agreeing not to discuss anything about college until a certain date; or seeing if she wants to open up to a guidance counselor or a relative who can help her think about the future.

Testing, Testing, 1-2-3

By junior year, your teen will start taking entrance exams, and the scores she chooses (if she takes the SAT more than once, for example, she can choose her best score) will be reported on her college applications. Many colleges require the American College Test

(ACT); others require the Scholastic Achievement Test (SAT); many accept both; and most consider only the better of the two scores. Many schools require various other tests as well; college reference guides will tell you what individual schools require. Have your teen pick up test application forms from the guidance office, and then watch deadlines.

Info Flash
If your teen is suddenly deluged by college brochures he hasn't even sent for, it's probably because he took the Practice SAT (PSAT). Many colleges buy mailing lists from the testing service and then send materials to those students who meet their requirements.

Your teen will do best on college entrance tests if he prepares for the test in advance. Many communities offer test preparation courses; test prep books and computer programs are also available at your local bookstore or library.

Most kids take the entrance tests more than once; this is a good option if your teen's scores aren't stellar the first time. Repeat testing—with or without additional prep— will probably show better results.

Nailing Down the Application

Competition to get into many schools is tough, and for that reason, you should insist that your teen apply to an intelligent range of schools.

A good guidance counselor can do you and your teen a favor by helping your teen select one school where he is *guaranteed* to get in. You don't want your teen to find out in May that he has nowhere to go.

Try to keep your teen from setting her heart on one school. Remind her that there are many schools where she could be happy—then help her find them. College is one of those experiences where a positive person can create a great opportunity almost anywhere. Let her know that you believe that it will all work out so that she'll get a great education wherever she goes.

Once your teen has decided which colleges he'd like to apply to, he should write to each one and request an application. The application is actually a package of documents. There will be a basic form asking for personal information and possibly some short-answer questions. The application will also ask for your teen's academic record, test scores, and letters of recommendation. An essay is required by most schools as well.

Many schools now accept a standard "Common Application"—lucky for today's teen. It can even be filled out electronically. Some schools request an additional essay along with the Common Application, but anything is better than filling out several separate applications.

Acing the Essay

Of all the sections of the application, the essay section causes the most angst for students. In general, essay topics are some form of one of the following:

➤ Tell us about yourself.

➤ Discuss an idea or special interest.

➤ Why do you want to come here or what do you hope to accomplish?

➤ A "what if" question where the student is expected to use some imagination.

Your teen should use the essay to explore some aspect of herself that has not been revealed in the rest of the application. (You should not write it!)

Have your teen read the essay question shortly after the application arrives so she has time to mull over her answer. Then she should write it (leaving plenty of time to polish it). Once she has a draft, she should ask you, another family member, or a favorite English teacher to read it through to make certain the essay is the best it can be.

Who Says She's Good? Letters of Recommendation

Recommendation letters are an important part of many applications. The application will specify, but generally the required letters must be from at least one teacher and your child's counselor. (If your teen had a piano teacher or employer who is dying to extol his virtues, that letter can go along as an added element of the application package.) It's vital that your teen ask for a letter early in the year; popular teachers are usually swamped by requests once application season hits its peak.

Your teen should pick someone who knows him well; just because he got an A in history doesn't mean the teacher really knows what makes him tick. If he can, he should hold out for someone who does. Your teen should tell the letter-writer what he hopes to study, what schools he's applying to, and when the letter has to be mailed.

The Interview: Schmoozing or Grilling?

At some point, your teen will probably have to be interviewed by representatives from the schools to which she is applying. Not all schools require interviews. Those that do may conduct them on campus, or have alumni conduct interviews in their local communities.

Though it will be difficult to keep your teen from stressing out at the thought of an interview, try to emphasize that it will be a conversation—not a grilling. If possible, try to schedule it so her first interview isn't for her number one choice school.

The Admission Decision

Many schools offer several admission options. Here are some of the admission terms you need to know:

➤ *Regular admission.* This generally refers to schools that mail out their decisions in early April.

➤ *Rolling admission.* Applications are evaluated, accepted, or rejected as they're received. Students should apply early to schools that use rolling admission, because they do fill up quickly.

➤ *Early decision.* For students who apply to one school only and who promise to attend if admitted. (If you're concerned the school won't offer adequate financial aid, ask for an early estimate; if it isn't enough, your teen can drop "early decision" status and apply to other schools.)

➤ *Early action.* Students can be admitted early, but don't have to attend.

Tuning In
If your teen opts to go to a two-year college with the thought of transferring, he should learn the transfer requirements of the college he wants to eventually attend. He should make sure the courses he takes at the two-year college will transfer intact.

What Are Colleges Looking For?

There are superb institutions for all students; don't get hung up on an elite few. Approach the process with an open mind, and you won't be disappointed.

Danger Zone
Don't add to the pressure by making your teen feel that he must attend your alma mater or break into the Ivy League. Tell him you want him to attend a college that's right for him. Many a fool has an Ivy League diploma, and many successes have degrees from Smalltown U.

The problem today is that the pool of applicants is well-filled with qualified applicants. More kids than ever before are college-bound. Your teen can increase her chances of admission by knowing that most college admission officers rank application materials in the following order of importance:

1. The overall quality of the transcript, including the difficulty of the courses taken and how well the student handled them.

2. Test scores. (Some schools don't look very seriously at test scores because they realize that a three-hour test may not demonstrate all of a student's abilities.)

3. What makes this applicant special? Does he or she have something unique to give to the school or the community? Letters of recommendation, the essay, and an interview may all help answer these questions.

4. Lastly, they look at the overall impression of the application. How well has the student presented herself?

Info Flash

What really gets a student noticed? It used to be a kid with a variety of activities. Now experts say that a defining characteristic—evidence that the student is 100 percent devoted to something that makes her special—is more valued. (If it's something that will make a contribution to the college, that's even better.) All the more reason to support her passion for song writing or student politics or lacrosse.

Fear of Applying

Applying to college can set off a lot of emotional alarms for your teen. The reality of growing up and probably going away to school is daunting to some; others worry about measuring up. Here are some specific concerns kids air over and over:

➤ *"I won't get in anywhere."* There's a school for everyone, but you have to be realistic. Encourage your child to apply to the reach schools (schools that may be tough for your teen to get into), but to have some safeties as well.

➤ *"I have to know what I'm going to be before I apply to college."* Nothing could be further from the truth. While having a general field of interest doesn't hurt, it isn't necessary. (For example, only 30 percent of kids who start out in engineering stay with it all the way through.)

➤ *"I won't be able to handle the work."* Tell your teen that if she gets in, she'll be able to handle it—that's what the application process screens for.

What you worry about:

➤ *"If only his test scores were higher…"* No matter what his academic ability, there is a school that's right for your teen.

➤ *"Connections will help."* Applying as a "legacy" (to be a second- or third-generation family member to attend a school) definitely helps for admissions; ask for statistics on how many legacies are admitted each year.

Worrying can lead to procrastination, which can just make things worse (applications may be filed late, or, in rolling admission schools, the classes may fill up). Talk to your teen about what is bothering him, and see if the two of you can come up with a solution.

Extra Help = Extra Money: The Role of the College Consultant

A reputable college consultant can assess a teen's potential and serve as a guide through the process—suggesting schools you might never have thought of, advising on courses, explaining what tests must be taken, and helping the family through the application and financial aid maze.

Help comes at a price. Some consultants will work with you on an hourly basis, meaning that you may invest under $100 for an initial consultation; others charge a flat fee of several thousand dollars. Ask around about costs.

Before signing on for any extended service with a consultant, check references. Consultants promise to take a lot of the responsibility; if you're going to delegate this, you'll want to be certain he or she will deliver.

When to call? You may want to consult with someone before your teen's junior year when there's still time to switch courses, if necessary. Or make an appointment for the time when you expect to have your teen's PSAT scores. This and your child's academic records will give the consultant a good working knowledge of the situation.

Road Tripping

When your teen starts her junior year is a good time to visit colleges. It takes the pressure off trying to schedule visits in the senior year, when kids are focused on the application process. Here are a few touring tips:

➤ Try to tour schools during the academic year; you'll get a better feel for the school if you see it in session.

➤ Call ahead to see if your teen can be interviewed by someone in admissions when you visit; many schools grant interviews even before they have received an application.

➤ Before your trip, buy a folder with pockets for each school you plan to visit. Use the pockets to stash brochures and school literature, and make it a habit to record impressions of the school while the experience is still fresh. Your notes might contain comments about financial aid and other details; your teen can record the "I loved it because..." or "I hated it because..." information.

Looking for the "Real" School

A meeting with administrators and a walk around the campus doesn't give you a full picture of what's going on at school. Here are some additional things you can do:

➤ If you know someone who's currently attending the school, see if your teen wants to attend classes or bunk in the dorm with that person. Lots of schools have "little sisters" or "little brothers" weekends that are designed to let siblings (or friends) see the school.

➤ Pick up a campus newspaper and a town newspaper for insight into community life.

➤ A walk around the campus will be more enlightening if you stop and read the flyers posted on the bulletin boards. What's happening on campus? Is your college-student-to-be interested in the events posted?

➤ Encourage your teen to talk to random students. If she wants to major in art, she could hang out near the art building and see what she can learn about the department. (She may be mortified to have you around, so go get a cup of coffee while she scopes out the scene.)

What to Look For

You might want to make several photocopies of the following College Questionnaire and use it to record impressions and information about each college you visit.

College Questionnaire

Name of College: _____

Questions to Consider	Answers (or Your Impressions)

Academics

Are the courses taught at small
seminars or large lecture halls?

_____
_____

What is an average course load?

_____
_____

Is tuition based on how many courses you
take? (Depending on the institution, a
full load is 12-18 credits per semester.)

_____
_____

How broad is the variety of courses
offered? Are there course requirements?

_____
_____

Facilities and Support

How up-to-date are the facilities?

_____
_____

Visit the library and check the collection.
How up-to-date are the resources?

_____
_____

How plentiful are computers? Are there
computers in the dorms?

_____
_____

Financial Aid

Are there special scholarships your teen
can apply for?

_____
_____

What kinds of work-study programs does
the school offer?

_____
_____

What kinds of part-time jobs are available
on campus and in the community?

_____
_____

Questions to Consider	Answers (or Your Impressions)

Faculty

Who teaches introductory courses—
faculty members or grad students?

_____

_____

Walk past faculty offices and notice the
posted office hours. How available do
the instructors seem to be?

_____

_____

Student Body

How diverse is the student body?

_____

_____

Will your teen be exposed to a broad
variety of people?

_____

_____

What percentage of each year's entering
class actually graduates from the school?

_____

_____

Campus

Must students live on campus? Do they?

_____

_____

Are dorms coed or single sex?

_____

_____

Is Greek life important?

_____

_____

How are roommates assigned?

_____

_____

Where do students eat?

_____

_____

_____

What type of recreational, cultural, and
social opportunities are available?

_____

_____

Is campus crime a problem? How effective
is campus security?

_____

_____

133

And the Envelope Please...

After tense months of waiting, in April your teen and her friends will begin getting the long-awaited letters. Her mood will rise and fall depending on the news in your mailbox as well as the news in everyone else's: "Why did *she* get in, and I didn't?"

There are many different schools and all offer wonderful opportunities—tell your teen that.

If your teen selected schools wisely (discussed earlier in the chapter), she has at least one acceptance coming in, and if that's her only option, you're going to lead the parade making the best of it. Call the college for additional information and get names of graduates who have gone on to successful careers in your teen's area of interest. A teen with the right attitude can be what she wants to be regardless of where her degree comes from.

If she's miserable about her college options, tell her that after a semester or a year, if she keeps her grades up, she'll be able to transfer to a school she thinks she might like better. Competition for transfer students is far less intense.

If, on the other hand, your mailbox overflows with acceptances, it's time to shift into high gear and become a picky consumer. Visit all the colleges in which your teen shows serious interest (if you haven't already) and evaluate the school based on the advice in the "Road Tripping" section earlier in the chapter. Does she like the campus? Does she feel comfortable? Can she imagine going here, and do the kids there look like kids with whom she would want to be friends?

"I'm Not Ready"

What if college isn't in your teen's immediate future?

Sometimes kids need to take a year off between high school and college. If you're getting a message like this, you can say, "Fine, but let's come up with a plan." Plans could range from applying for college now but deferring entry for a year, or planning other fruitful ways your teen might spend a year before applying to college.

Keep Your Role in Mind

As the adult in this process, you have a serious responsibility. It's your job to open the search and guide your teen on her way. She will start the process as an adolescent and will come out of it very close to being an adult. At all times, remember that it is not your experience—your personal aspirations should be left behind. Have confidence in her instincts. She'll do what's right for her.

The Least You Need to Know

> ➤ Meet with your teen's high school guidance counselor early on to discuss an appropriate course load.

> ➤ Discover a range of colleges that are of interest to your teen.

> ➤ Start visiting colleges any time during the high school years. On campus, talk to students as well as administrators.

> ➤ Find out which tests your teen will need to take; have her get application forms, and watch deadlines carefully.

> ➤ Don't let your teen procrastinate on filing the application.

> ➤ Guide your child, but let him or her make the final college choice.

Part 4
Special Interests, Special Privileges

Your teen will beg you to read this part first if he ever sits down with this book. To most 15-year-olds, cars, phones, games, and sports are some of the best things that life has to offer.

Once you read these chapters, you'll learn some positive strategies on how to let your teen enjoy certain privileges while still upholding his responsibilities (for example, logging in hours on the phone while still getting his homework done).

This part of the book offers advice on setting guidelines for use of the TV and the phone, the car and the computer, as well as some guidelines on that all-important American pastime: sports.

Chapter 13

The Big Ts: Television and the Telephone

In This Chapter

➤ Cooperative living and the telephone

➤ The telephone as a "parent-teen" connection

➤ Taking a new look at television

Now that your child is a teenager, your frustration over the hours he once spent in front of the television has probably been replaced by your irritation over not being able to use your own phone. Teens do love that telephone, and as a result, time on the telephone is one of the two major issues families battle about (the other being messy rooms; see Chapter 4).

As for that former foe, the television, its allure diminishes as teens get busier and more involved with their friends. However, it's still a powerful force in family life.

This chapter looks at what works and what doesn't when it comes to the double Ts—the telephone and television.

"So, What's There to Talk About?"

Has this ever happened to you? You pick up your teen and her best friend, Trisha, at the mall. As you drop Trisha off, she yells out to your daughter, "I'll call you later." Then shortly after you walk in the house, the phone rings, and it's Trisha again! Yes, they were just together, and yes, they still have plenty to talk about!

Peers are becoming much more important in your teen's life, and the telephone time helps her build relationships. The telephone (particularly for young teens whose social life may not be very active) is a "lifeline" to the rest of your teen's world: It offers her a connection and validation that she's accepted and liked by the kids whose opinions she values. Talking all night on the phone helps accomplish this.

Phone management may become a problem during these years, particularly if you have more than one teen. If you like to make and receive calls at night, you may find that teen phone time creates family stress. There are several solutions:

➤ Set limits on phone time, which helps teach a teen about family responsibility and consideration. Give your teen some say in the matter; the new system will work out better if he has input. Logical options include teen "phone hours": between 7:30 and 9:00 p.m., for example, the phone is his. Or you can limit the minutes per call and the number of calls your teen makes per evening.

➤ Many families get call-waiting service at this time. You'll find it more relaxing to know that if someone is trying to reach you while your teen is on the line, that person will be able to get through. (And of course, your incoming call should take priority.)

➤ Some families find it necessary to add a second line. (If you're adding the second line solely because of your teen, consider asking her to pay for part or all of it through her allowance or paycheck.) An added advantage is that for her next birthday you can buy an inexpensive answering machine for the "teen" line—then you don't have to answer it when your teen isn't home.

Occasional abuse of telephone time (on a night when there's a major issue being debated among teens, like whether or not to go to the big concert this weekend) might earn your teen a warning. Repeated abuse could be addressed by tighter restrictions on phone time, or by withdrawing phone privileges for a night or two (no more than a week, though).

The Telephone as Message Center

The telephone is there so that family members can communicate with the outside world. To do that, you need equipment for both incoming and outgoing calls.

Incoming Calls

How many times have you spoken to a friend, only to learn that she already called, but you never got the message? The importance of message-taking must be emphasized, and it should be stressed as an obligation for all members of the family. To encourage this, keep a pad and pen near each phone.

When a call comes in for you, your teen should:

➤ Handle the call politely.

➤ Take down the person's name (asking them to spell it if necessary) and telephone number.

➤ Leave the message in a predesignated spot so that you will see it.

In return, promise that you will do the same for your teen. If a call comes in while he is asleep or out, leave a message as to who called.

Outgoing Calls

When your kids were little, classroom teachers and Scout troop leaders probably distributed class and troop lists with phone numbers. Having this type of list for your teen can be invaluable. Use a small binder and ask him to write in the names and phone numbers of his closest friends. You can also include addresses and the names of parents (if you know them). That way, you always have a way of getting in touch with your teen.

If your teen thinks this is an invasion of his privacy, you should put the list together yourself. The next time you drop him off at Bill's, for example, you'll probably be able to gain enough information (like last name and address) to get the telephone number from the phone book.

Minding Your (Phone) Manners

Establish telephone guidelines that are appropriate for your family. Some common ones you might consider:

➤ Telephone calls that come in during dinner time (including calls for adult family members) will be returned later.

➤ Who answers the telephone in the evening? If the calls are primarily for your kids, ask that they answer the phone throughout the evening.

➤ How late can telephone calls be accepted?

➤ Do you want to set a time limit on calls? (Unnecessary rules are always a bad idea, so set a limit only if your teen regularly abuses the telephone.)

➤ Some families stipulate that homework must be completed before phoning starts. If your teen handles homework responsibly, this is probably a waste of your breath. Many weekday phone calls begin as questions concerning homework, so you'll likely be asked to bend the rules frequently. Why get into it if you don't have to?

➤ When your teen is on the phone and you need to make a call, don't order or demand that she get off. Ask respectfully. You're setting a tone of family cooperation, and it's important that the cooperation go both ways.

Danger Zone

CAUTION

So what happens on the day that you open your telephone bill and find several 900-number charges?

You have a talk with your teen. The ads for 900-numbers aren't clear about how quickly the charges add up, so your teen may not have had a clue that the call would clock in at $20.

You may also want to explore why your teen made the call. A call to a sex line made in response to a dare from his friends is one thing; if he's making persistent calls to a sex line after he's been asked to stop, you might want to consult a professional as to why he feels compelled to make these kinds of calls.

Asking that your teen cover the expense of the 900-call is reasonable (and will certainly teach him that these calls can be pricey!).

Tuning In

You want to keep family members from running up expensive long-distance calls, but your teen has made some wonderful friends at camp whom she'd like to call. What do you do?

Buy a telephone card for your teen. A phone card is prepaid for a certain number of "calling" minutes, and calls are cut off once those minutes are used up. (This is not the same as a telephone credit card, on which unlimited calls can be charged.)

Phone cards are sold at convenience stores and newsstands, and can be purchased in time increments ranging from 10–120 minutes. They let your teen make long-distance calls as she sees fit, charging them against the card for which you have already paid. (Unused time on one call can be used on subsequent calls.)

Your teen will love having the card, and you'll love not having to worry about your long-distance bill.

Dial 1-800-PARENTS

Toll-free telephone numbers (800 numbers) are among the latest services being promoted by the various telephone companies. Get one. Introductory fees are extremely reasonable, or you can comparison shop among long-distance services. Monthly fees are low—sometimes as low as $5—and calls are billed at the normal rate, which is certainly cheaper than having a teen at camp call you collect.

Why get an 800 number? Because then your teen can—and will—stay in touch with you without ever having to worry about having a quarter. Sometimes the local calls will be most helpful:

➤ "Practice has been changed. Don't pick me up until 5:30 p.m."

➤ "We left Mary's house, and we're in town now for pizza."

➤ "Our ride isn't here yet, so we'll be late."

Or it may help them:

➤ "They put up the cast list, and I didn't make it." (He'll spend two seconds with you on this call, but one supportive or understanding word from you will keep him going.)

➤ A younger teen might even call for strategy: "The kids are being so mean. What should I do?"

During these years, communication is vital to a good relationship. The more accessible you are to your kids, the easier it will be for you both.

The Tube: Its Drawbacks and Benefits

The good news is that if your teen is typical, his peak television viewing years are over. Studies show that childhood viewing peaks at age 12 and declines during adolescence. However, your teen probably still has the television on a good deal—he probably watches a couple of favorite shows each week, and he may keep MTV or a ball game on while he eats, talks on the phone, or does homework.

While television has been blamed for societal ills too numerous to mention, most families hit a point at which television is no longer a major battleground. If this describes your family, yet you'd welcome a little more advice, consider these guidelines for viewing:

➤ Don't put a TV in your teen's room. If your teen has her own TV, her viewing hours are unlimited, and TV-watching becomes an isolating rather than communal experience.

➤ Establish viewing rules. Some teens can do homework with the television on in the background; others can't. If your teen needs quiet, stipulate that the television should stay off until homework is finished. (If you have a VCR, let her record shows she misses while she does homework.)

Under normal circumstances, prohibition of television watching generally doesn't work. One mother explains: "I used to tell my children they couldn't watch television Monday through Thursday because of school obligations. What I found was that they were totally addicted once Friday came." Like other things, television viewing is best done in moderation. By giving your child a choice—with limitations—you also teach her about self-control.

Info Flash

A 1992 study conducted by the American Psychological Association's Task Force on Television and Society revealed that the relationship between TV viewing and academic performance is not always as clear-cut as expected. Children who spend a great deal of time viewing television do poorly in school; however, children who watch a moderate amount of television perform better in school than non-viewers (presumably because they have more sources of information than non-viewers).

Television's Possible Danger

Television exposes your family to people and experiences they would never meet without it. Viewing a ballet on an educational channel, learning about a world event on the news, or watching ski jumping on a sports program can be very exciting. But what about the values and practices your teen views that you don't agree with? You might like to stay in touch on that.

Danger Zone

CAUTION

Monitoring your teen's viewing of sexually explicit material during these years is tough, as he may keep much later hours than you do. One simple way to keep his viewing "clean" is to consider what services you bring into the house.

If you don't have cable service, you have no problem, because local and network stations don't air explicit programs.

If you bring in basic service, you are less likely to be bringing in "hot" shows.

If you opt for movie channels, which offer a variety of, shall we say, *interesting* late-night programming, there are lock-out boxes that permit you to block certain channels. Check with your cable company to find out what devices are compatible with your service.

If your teen orders up a racy flick from the pay channel, talk to him about it. Curiosity may have gotten the better of him, and if he knows you're on to him, chances are it won't happen again. (You can also tell him to pay for the movie.)

Though you don't want to turn this experience into a didactic one, or present your views as criticisms, you can use TV-watching as a time to discuss values. The next time you watch TV with your teen, consider using the following conversation-starters:

➤ "Would any of your friends try something like that because it's supposed to be cool?"

➤ "How come there aren't any black or ethnic people on this show?"

➤ "Do you think he should have been treated that way just because he's gay?"

➤ "It seems like only the beautiful, thin girls have boyfriends on this show."

Commercials also offer excellent fodder for conversation:

➤ "Do they expect us to believe that chewing that gum will improve our social life?"

➤ "It seems like women in commercials always have to be beautiful, even if it has nothing to do with what they are selling. Why is that?"

You might even be able to get into some of the programs your teen loves. Then watching television together can be a pleasant activity that the two of you can share (at an age when she is probably too embarrassed to go to a movie with you), and it can offer a unique opportunity for conversation. By talking about your teen's TV passions and heroes, you'll have a better understanding of her culture—and a better understanding of your teen.

The Least You Need to Know

➤ Stress phone message-taking for the entire family.

➤ To preserve family sanity, consider getting a second line or call waiting.

➤ Set appropriate phone rules for your family (such as no calls during meals and no calls after 10 p.m.).

➤ Watch television with your teen when you can. It offers many opportunities for conversation.

Plugged In: Video Games and Computers

Imagine if computers and video games had been around when you were a teenager. Don't you ever envy your teen, who has time to conquer new worlds in a surreal fantasy land on a computer game or navigate through an intricate maze of puzzles on a video game? And if your teen goes online, she can exchange e-mail with a friend in another state, or write a fan letter to her favorite TV star—and get a response! It's a fast, fun, exciting new world, and most teens want to be a part of it.

As we approach the millennium, electronic media are expanding and will dominate our future. It's becoming harder and harder to find a child over the age of five who doesn't know the basics of operating a computer or how to beat level seven in Super Mario Brothers.

Computer technology is so compelling and intriguing to young people that parents sometimes wonder when time spent in front of a screen intensifies from interactive fun to addiction. This chapter offers some guidance for dealing with the brave new world of technology—both its benefits and its dangers.

From Space Invaders to Mario Brothers: Playing Video Games

Teens are attracted to video games for different reasons. Many games feature dreamy alternative landscapes, mind-bending puzzles, realistic graphics, and, of course, blood and guts. Glance at a game like Mortal Kombat—where winning a fight allows you to do away with your opponent in several inventive and gruesome ways, including ripping his head off—and it's easy to see why parents are concerned.

Info Flash

In response to a Congressional hearing on violent content in video and computer games, the industry has implemented a ratings system. There are five categories:

➤ *EC* (early childhood; three and older)

➤ *K–A* (kids six and older to adults)

➤ *T* (teenagers, 13 and older)

➤ *M* (mature, 17 and older)

➤ *AO* (adults only)

These ratings are accompanied by descriptions such as "realistic blood and gore" and "use of drugs."

Video games do have their benefits, though. Not all games involve graphically killing an opponent. A slew of puzzle games that make you think (such as Tetris and Zoop) are still popular with teens. Also, many video games, from Super Mario Brothers to Street Fighter, help develop eye-hand coordination, and because the games come without instructions or blueprints, teens have a great time sharing gaming secrets and strategies.

However, when the love of video games become too compelling, it's time to pull the plug, or at least set some limits. If your teen is placing video or computer games above chores, homework, or even social gatherings, it's time to lay down some clear rules: No video games until homework is finished, or only one hour of video gaming a night.

Video games are not something that should be banned, but they shouldn't dominate everything else in your teen's life.

Logging On: Using a Home Computer

If you bring a computer into your home, you'll find that it is one of the best educational tools around.

Remember when you were assigned a report back in high school? You went to the library, took diligent notes out of various encyclopedias, books, and periodicals, and then went home and wrote it up.

Today's teens have the opportunity to get research done faster, as well as in greater depth. CD-ROM encyclopedias such as Encarta or Compton's have as much information, if not more, than the heavy tomes of *Brittanica* or *World Book*, because they also often have links to pictures, sounds, videos, and timelines of certain subjects. And because they are so easy to use, kids are more inclined to spend time doing the research.

Online services such as the World Wide Web and the Internet are also tremendously powerful and comprehensive resources for teenagers. With a little online probing, they might be able to find someone who knows something about their topic first-hand. Teens have sent e-mail to F. Lee Bailey about the Simpson trial (and gotten a response), talked to astronauts in space, and conversed with popular authors about their work. Incredible and amazing!

Besides being used for research, computers are often mandatory for school assignments. Many high schools require that all student work be typed; it's much neater. It also helps teens get better acquainted with using computers, a skill they'll need in the 21st-century workplace.

Computer games also have some merit. While a few are just violent video games transferred to the computer screen, there are many that promote thinking skills. Almost any game made by the Sierra company (for example, the *King's Quest* and *Space Quest* series) integrates an interesting and humorous plot with adventure and puzzle-solving. If you want to get more educational, your teen can even learn to type and get tutored for the SAT using certain computer programs.

If your teen develops a great interest in computers, she might want to learn about programming, graphics design, or computer animation.

Tuning In
If you don't have or can't afford a home computer, many high schools and public libraries offer computers and CD-ROMs for public use. You can also rent computer time at many copy centers. And in some places, cutting-edge cafes are installing computers as well, so customers can sip coffee and surf the Internet at the same time.

Setting Up a Home Computer System

Taking the leap into the computer age is exciting, but also scary to many parents. Computer systems are expensive and easily outgrown if you don't select the right kind. Here are a few things to keep in mind:

➤ Select the most recent model of computer and ask the salesperson about how easy it will be to upgrade (technology is changing so rapidly that you want your computer to be as current as possible).

➤ Opt for a computer with a large memory. You want your computer drive to be big enough to handle the programs that interest you.

➤ Check out CD-ROMs. Once you've seen an encyclopedia on CD-ROM, it's difficult to go back to thumbing through a hardbound book edition. The same goes for many of the games, programs, and books that have been put on CD—they're amazing!

Cruising the Information Superhighway: Going Online

The latest computer trend is using online services. People all over the country, and even the world, use modems to link up to a service where they can chat with other members, write electronic mail, browse bulletin boards that cover topics ranging from pet care to favorite movies, and download files of all kinds. Teens love these online services— especially the chat rooms, where they can meet other teens who share their interests.

These online services provide access to a wealth of information. Most have a search function where you can locate information on everything from aerobics to Zurich, and possibly talk to people who are experts on your needed topic. One of the services even has a special classroom section where students can interact with teachers online and get help from them.

Tuning In

A hidden bonus of online services is that your teen will become a much faster typist. You've got to have quick fingers if you want to get your point across in a fast-moving chat room!

Danger Zone

If your teen is going online, establish the following guidelines:

➤ Never give out your full name, address, or home phone number to people you meet online.

➤ Never give out your user password or credit card number to anyone.

➤ Be wary of people you meet online; some online users try to steer every conversation into a sexual pick-up. Don't continue a conversation with someone whose first question is, "What are you wearing?"

➤ If you are concerned about your teen accessing cyberporn sites, most services have a way to control which areas your teen can visit and which are off-limits.

If you subscribe to an online service, expect your teen to be consumed with it for the first month. Let her explore the Information Superhighway for a few weeks; although you don't want to discourage her from using a tool she will need to be fluent with by the time she gets a job, you do need to talk seriously with her about monthly costs, and how much time you think should be allowed per month. If she wants to spend more time online, tell her it should come out of her own pocket. Going online can be very expensive and your teen needs to know this.

If you decide to get an online service, you might want to think about putting it on a separate telephone line. Using your modem (the tool that connects you to the online service) ties up the phone line, so calls can't come through when someone is online. If you have call waiting, a call that comes through while your teen is online will cause him to be bumped off the service, which can be frustrating. If you're worried about missing calls, you should definitely get a second line. It will be worth it in the long run.

The Autobahn of the Information Superhighway: The Internet

At school, your teen will definitely be dealing with the mother of all online services, the Internet. The Internet is a vast area with more information than anyone thought existed. On the World Wide Web, you can look at Web pages (conglomerations of text and pictures, sounds, and even movie files) that are made by everyone from major corporations such as Disney Studios to random individuals.

Tuning In

Although the difference is less among very young children, it doesn't take long before boys begin to outstrip girls in their use and knowledge of the computer. If you have an adolescent daughter, do everything you can to keep her interested in this tool that will be a key part of her generation's future. Watch for some of the new games that are intended to be of greater interest to girls.

Make sure your daughter never feels like she shouldn't be as good as your son on the computer simply because of her sex. They should have equal time to learn and grow.

You might also tell her that more and more females are beginning to excel in this field. Two of the head programmers at Sierra, Roberta Williams and Jane Jensen, are women who got started just playing around with their computers as teenagers.

A computer will be a great boon to your teen. If she isn't computer-literate already, get her started today. Who knows, it may be the first suggestion you've made lately that she'll actually like!

The Least You Need to Know

➤ Check out the ratings on the video games your teen chooses.

➤ If your teen can't control the amount of time she spends playing video or computer games, set time limits.

➤ Computers are the way of the future. If you can, invest in one now.

➤ An online service offers access to incredible resources.

➤ Talk to your teen about online costs. Encourage working "offline" and make him liable for expenses over a certain limit.

➤ Stress online safety: Never give out your full name, address, or home phone number to people online.

For Love of Sports

Sports are great for the body and great for the mind, so encouraging your teen to get moving on the field or in the gym has many benefits. In addition to producing a more physically fit body, sports participation will help your teen learn team cooperation, develop mental strategies, and master the art of winning and losing.

For many youngsters, the sports arena is a place where they can carve out a special identity for themselves and where they develop skills that will last a lifetime. Sports also expose teens to friendships they might not develop otherwise.

Yet, like everything in life, sports ability doesn't come instantly. While there are a few "natural born stars," most teens need to develop their skills, which means that the road to being a solid team player can be a bumpy one. And even the "naturals" will benefit if you're on top of the issues surrounding safety and nutrition. In this chapter you'll learn how to raise a healthy, happy athlete!

Info Flash

According to a Lou Harris survey of high school students,

➤ The majority of student athletes said sports helped them avoid drugs.

➤ A large proportion of student athletes also reported that sports helped keep them from dropping out of school.

Safety First

Schools require a physical before your teen can participate in a sport. While general medical problems should be picked up through this type of check-up, school doctors also rely on your child's health history. Take responsibility for filling this out yourself, and do it carefully and accurately. Also be sure your teen is scheduled for a more thorough annual physical.

After your teen passes the physical and becomes involved in school sports, you should check out the following safety tips:

Info Flash
The Academy of Sports Dentistry recommends mouth guards for anyone playing a contact sport. They're mandatory for high school athletes in football, ice hockey, field hockey, and lacrosse. There are three basic types of mouth guards; your teen's coach or dentist can recommend the best kind for your teen.

➤ Be certain that the sports program is safe. At the beginning of the season, come a little early to pick up your teen and watch the practice, and listen to the kids when they talk about the team, the coach, and the sport. They'll speak up when they—or their teammates—are being pushed too hard.

➤ Careful training and safety rules should be emphasized. Practice sessions and workouts should not be excessive. Players should be encouraged to stop playing when something hurts. Also, observe whether the kids feel a lot of pressure to win.

➤ Make note of safety gear. Does it seem adequate for the sport? Is it in good condition, or is it old and frayed? Are athletes shown how to wear it correctly? Is it required for every practice?

Info Flash

Girls' athletic teams sometimes wear less protective gear than boy's teams do. If you sense that your girl's team is not adequately protected, you can ask a school sports administrator why. Sometimes, parents are told that boys' sports have a greater contact element than girls' sports, and so protective gear is not necessary. However, you won't agree if you see the girls sustaining injuries during play (which proper equipment might have prevented).

➤ Emphasize year-round conditioning. You might even find an activity to do as a family. Though training for a specific sport is part of the seasonal regimen of school, year-round, regular exercise such as swimming, cycling, in-line skating, or walking (all of which build muscle tone, flexibility, speed, and endurance) will get your young athlete in good shape. Then the specific sport training can emphasize skill-building rather than body-building.

➤ Keep your teen out of practice when she's sick— her reaction time will be slower, and thus her chances of injury are greater. Sports specialists also worry about any activity that increases the heart and respiratory rate while the body is fighting an illness. Viral illnesses may put the heart at risk and can lead to cardiac arrhythmia or heart palpitations during the time of the illness.

Info Flash
The American Academy of Pediatrics recommends that weight lifting and body building be delayed until after puberty (see Chapter 5). Until then, damage to the musculoskeletal system is possible.

Pain: Your Teen's Personal "Body Guard"

Though the benefits of playing sports far outweigh the drawbacks, sports injuries can lead to lifelong problems, so they should be taken seriously. Many teens who play interscholastic sports are injured each year, and one-quarter to one-third of these injuries are significant.

Teach your teen to listen to pain. While an over-the-counter pain reliever may be okay to alleviate occasional soreness, get medical attention if he suffers from recurring pain.

If he gets injured during a game or at practice, your teen should remember "RICE":

REST the injury.

Put **I**CE on the injury.

Use **C**OMPRESSION to help reduce swelling.

ELEVATE the injured body part as much as possible.

Consult the coach for details of the injury, and check in with your doctor, who may want to take a look at the injury or get it X-rayed.

Feeding (and Feeding and Feeding) a Teen Athlete

Feeding the adolescent athlete is a sport in itself. Strenuous exercise will increase your teen's caloric requirements (which are already enormous) by as much as 25 percent! Chapter 17 will show you how to provide enough food for your ravenous teen. This information covers what you might do differently to see that your teen is well-fed during sports season.

(If you were an athlete, you should know that the thinking on sports nutrition has changed quite a bit in recent years, so don't rely on what you did "in your day." Get up-to-date information.)

Watch for nutritional "red flags." If your teen becomes obsessed with some type of special diet (particularly if it involves calorie-cutting) check it out with her doctor.

You should also discover the coach's attitude toward food. A coach who becomes overly involved in keeping your teen wrestler at a certain weight may inadvertently ignore his other nutritional needs.

Watch, too, for signs of eating disorders. Female athletes—particularly those who are judged on appearance, like gymnasts, skaters, or dancers—sometimes become obsessed with weight, and this can lead to serious problems. (See Chapter 17 for more information about the warning signs and treatment of eating disorders.)

Pre-Game Eats

You probably can't control your teen's pre-game diet—partly because she wants to be in charge of her own body, and partly because she may often leave for games or practice directly after school, which gives her (and you) little or no time to think about food. (You can suggest that she tuck a high-energy food, like a granola bar or some unsquashable fruit, into her backpack for an after-school snack.)

Despite this, you might still be able to slip in a nutrition lesson or two. By stressing that food is fuel and that good food makes for strong athletic performance (you wouldn't put cheap gas in a race car, would you?) you might be able to spark her interest in a topic that generally draws a deaf ear. Keep in mind:

➤ The pre-game meal is not as important as eating balanced meals daily.

➤ The healthy eater should need no vitamin or mineral supplements or protein powders.

➤ The purpose of any pre-game meal is to provide ready energy without causing an upset stomach. To meet these goals experts recommend a diet high in carbohydrates and low in protein and fat. (Protein is a poor source of quick energy, and high-fat foods can cause an upset stomach.)

  A nutritious and teen-approved pre-game meal could include pasta (with little or no meat) or a thick-crust pizza.

➤ Ideally, food should be fully digested before game time. Large meals should be eaten three to four hours ahead of time; smaller meals require only two to three hours to digest. A light snack, such as fruit or cereal, could be eaten up to a half hour before play.

➤ Encourage young teens to drink a lot of fluids (water, juice, sports drinks) before, during, and after a game—even if they don't feel thirsty. The dangers of dehydration (muscle cramping, nausea, and vomiting, as well as less than ideal performance) often go unacknowledged. Unfortunately, the body fails to register thirst until it approaches a danger point. It isn't unusual to lose 1.5 to 2.5 liters of fluid during strenuous exercise on a warm day, and it's impossible to replace this fluid while still exercising.

Whose Game Is It, Anyway?

When teens are asked what parents should know about teens and sports, they frequently reply: "Tell them to let the kid choose whether or not to play."

Hopefully, you've exposed your teen to various types of athletic activities during his childhood, and by the time he reaches high school he knows which sports he likes and what his abilities are.

Yet some parents have difficulty drawing a line between what's best for their child and what they want for themselves. Parents who dream of recapturing athletic glory from their own youth, or of producing a teen athletic superstar, often can't step back and let their teen choose his own activities.

Because high school sports can be so competitive and require so much time (often a couple of hours per day, five or six days a week), it's important that the dream be his now, not yours.

Competition is tough, and if your teen wants to quit—or switch sports or shift over to intramural play—suggest that he sleep on his decision for a while. You may also want to suggest intramural sports as a good alternative. They are still athletic but less competitive.

In the end let him decide on his own. His body may be giving him messages you can't hear, or he may sense bad team "vibes" that you can't feel. This is one of the many times when it's important to let your teen learn to trust his own judgment.

Your teen may just need time off from a sport, and he may come back to it if you're off his case. Or maybe he'll find something new. If you're overly involved, you rob him of the ability to play for the right reasons—because it's fun.

Tuning In

What if your kid doesn't like competitive sports? This is perfectly understandable, but it doesn't mean that she should be permanently benched or relegated to the life of a couch potato.

American kids are more overweight than ever, and the reason is primarily because they're getting less exercise. (See Chapter 17 for more information on fitness.)

Talk to her about other physical activities. She may be dying for a pair of in-line skates, or maybe she'd like to play tennis recreationally—without the pressure of being on a team.

Look into community programs, or call your local YMCA to see what classes it offers. Regular exercise is a great way to develop a stronger, healthier body, to develop a new skill, and to meet some new friends along the way.

"I Didn't Make the Team!"

Skip the "lessons of life" lecture with this one. Not making the team—when many of your schoolmates did—hurts! The best you can do is offer a shoulder to cry on and give some understanding advice.

After the initial disappointment fades, talk to your teen about his commitment to the game. Does he genuinely love the sport? Or is he more hurt by being cut out of the opportunity to be with his friends? Does he want to continue practicing so he's good enough to play next year? Or maybe the sport isn't really that important—he's just angry because being cut was extraordinarily humiliating to him?

After you know where your teen stands, you'll be better prepared to suggest a possible solution.

Could he serve as a team manager for the season? Some kids choose this option. It will give him an opportunity to be with his friends, and he may get to work out with the team, which will improve his skills and increase his odds of making the team next year. Sticking with the team also demonstrates his dedication and commitment—qualities you hope the coach will remember later on.

If this option isn't right for your teen, you could investigate whether there are town, recreation, or club leagues for the sport where the game is played on a less competitive basis. For many teens, playing at this more relaxed level of commitment allows them to maintain other interests.

Otherwise, encourage him to find other ways to be physically active, and begin focusing on his other talents. Perhaps he can devote more time to playing the trombone, learning how to design a Web site, or writing a column for the school newspaper.

Tuning In
"I'm the worst one on the team!" your teen cries. I think we can all sympathize with this feeling. Remind him of good plays he's made, or comment on his attitude, effort, or cooperation—these elements are vital to team success, too.

It's Not Whether You Win or Lose...

One danger of playing competitive sports is that kids begin to think that if they don't win, they're failures. (Some coaches reinforce this philosophy.) This is obviously a recipe for major disappointment.

From the time your child first sets foot on a field or court, it's important to convey a love of the game, not a love of winning. If you feel your teen is overly wrapped up with winning, it's not too late to try to change her attitude. (Talking about what Tonya Harding was willing to do to win is a good start.)

Point out that success is embodied in lots of athletes who don't win or come in first place. Why is the team that loses the Super Bowl viewed as the Big Loser, when it was a good enough team to make it to the Super Bowl?

You might also make note of sports events where people compete even though they know in advance they'll never win. (Tune in to any marathon.)

Danger Zone
Here are some comments *not* to tell your teen:

"You've got to play your best; it's the championship, and the team's counting on you."

"If you play well, we'll be so proud of you."

"I've got ten bucks riding on you getting a home run."

Try to help your teen focus on improving her own performance and skills, not on the number of games her team wins. That's the point of it anyway.

Modeling good sportsmanship is also important—and hopefully something you've been doing since your kid's first days at peewee football. Kids sometimes tell stories of teams that curse their opponents, or hold out spit-filled hands during the final handshake of the game. Chances are they were taught by parents or coaches who cared way too much about winning the game. (When Little League dads duke it out on the field, as they have in some communities, what are the kids supposed to think?)

Model positive attitudes before, during, and after a game:

➤ Emphasize that the point of the competition is for fun, not for winning. Encouraging and cooperating with teammates is just as important as making the best play.

➤ Don't applaud when the other team makes a bad play, and do applaud when they make a good play!

➤ Don't belittle the umpire or second-guess the coach.

➤ Don't coach from the sidelines. It will only confuse the players (and mortify your teen).

➤ If she loses a game, you may want to acknowledge the toughness of the other team. Then note something your teen or another team member did that made for a really good play. (Few games are a total disaster!)

Danger Zone
Teen boys (and an occasional teen girl) who are heavily involved in sports—particularly wrestlers and football players—may think about using anabolic steroids (hormones that stimulate muscular development). Their use has been banned by sports organizations, and you should stress that they shouldn't be used. Steroids can be very damaging, particularly during periods of growth.

If Your Teen's the Next Sports Superstar

Your teen is the best player on the team, so your problems are over? Not so fast, say the experts. While it's great to have a child who's terrific at anything, your super athlete needs guidance, too.

First, compliment your teen on her successes so it's clear she's always "number one" in your book.

But even if your teen saved the day for the team, don't cast her as the game hero. Repeated often enough, this kind of praise may turn her into an insufferable teammate. Instead, focus on a specific moment that was particularly terrific. Teach your teen that she has something wonderful to share, and that only through cooperation can a dynamite player end up on a dynamite team.

You may consider yourself a sports "expert" and be inclined to make suggestions about how she can improve her game. Tread cautiously here. If you talk about ways to improve right after a well-played game, she may think, "I was good, but I'm still not good enough to please my parents." That can put tremendous pressure on her at an age when her self-esteem is particularly vulnerable.

Sometimes parents of a child who is particularly successful at something—whether it's playing baseball or writing poetry or solving equations —fall into the trap of over-emphasizing that single gift. No matter where his special talent lies, appreciate all aspects of your teen. In addition to enjoying the way your teen pitcher controls the ball, let him know that you also think he's a great storyteller or amazing at math. No one should be valued for their strike-out record alone.

Worshipping False Icons

Boxer Mike Tyson goes to jail for rape. Baseball player Pete Rose tarnishes his sports reputation through illicit gambling. Star baseball player Darryl Strawberry is treated for a drug problem. Former football star Lawrence Taylor gets picked up for buying cocaine.

A noticeable number of professional athletes are picked up with some regularity for drinking and behavior problems. Because of their status as respected professional athletes, their misdeeds bring celebrity-style attention, and it's hard for kids to be unaffected. The actions of professional athletes serve to blur and confuse morals and values, making it that much harder for parents to manage.

The best approach is an open one. You might start a conversation about it: "So what do you think about what happened to Lawrence Taylor?" (Don't lecture; open a discussion—your teen's comments may be enlightening.)

Your teen probably has an opinion, and if he doesn't know what happened, send him off to the newspaper or sports magazine to catch up. You may find that he realizes that gifted athletes are capable of throwing their lives away through stupidity. Or he may wonder why someone who "has everything" would get in so much trouble.

Like many aspects of parenting, the best you can do is register your opinion: that playing on any team is a privilege, not a right, and that those who participate should uphold good values. Your opinion holds far more weight than you'll ever know.

A League of Their Own

According to the Women's Sports Foundation, women who participate in sports have high self-esteem, are in better physical condition, suffer less depression, and are more satisfied with their lives than women who do not participate. In other words, if your daughter is physically active, she can reap great rewards—both on and off the court.

However, despite Title IX (a federal law that guarantees women athletes the right to equal opportunity in sports programs in all schools), it is still taking time to correct gender inequities in school athletics. The Women's Sports Foundation reports:

➤ Only 38 percent of all high school athletes are girls and only 36 percent of all college athletes are women, despite the fact that male:female enrollments in high school and college are about 50:50.

➤ Less than 33 percent of collegiate athletic scholarship dollars are awarded to women athletes.

➤ Women athletes are often trivialized in media coverage. Commentators refer to women athletes as "girls" and/or use their first names, while male athletes are referred to as "men" and are called by their full or last names.

Info Flash
There are two million girls in high school sports today, compared with 300,000 in 1972, says the Women Sports Foundation.

There are steps you can take if you're concerned about your daughter's treatment as an athlete:

➤ Look in your community to make sure the same sports opportunities are offered for both boys and girls. Girls should have equal opportunity to play, and equal provision of equipment, supplies, coaches, practice facilities, and so on. If this isn't the case, talk to the school athletic director or principal.

➤ If you aren't pleased with the response, write to your school board or to the Board of Trustees to express your concern.

➤ Remember that, ultimately, your daughter is protected by Title IX.

The Least You Need to Know

➤ Put safety first. Pay attention to safety gear and teach your teen to listen to her body.

➤ Teen athletes have high caloric requirements, so stock your kitchen with healthy, filling foods.

➤ Let your teen call the shots on what sports he wants to play and what level of commitment he wants to devote to athletics.

➤ If your teen doesn't make the team, be sympathetic and help him cope.

➤ Help the teen couch potato find some sort of physical activity she enjoys.

➤ Teach that sports are for fun, not for winning.

Chapter 16

Teen Wheels: Creating a Responsible Driver

In This Chapter
➤ Rules for the road
➤ The license and the new driver
➤ In case of emergency...
➤ What you need to know about insurance

From the moment your child starts talking about driving and getting a license, there are seven important words you can say: "You're going to be a great driver."

By starting with the premise that this very important rite of passage will be a smooth one, you create a teen who feels he is viewed as responsible and trustworthy, and who will want to live up to your prophecy.

That said, you should also know that your teen is embarking on a dangerous journey. According to the Insurance Institute for Highway Safety, traffic accidents are the number one cause of death for youth, with 5,000 teens killed in car crashes every year.

In this chapter, you will learn some specific measures that will increase the likelihood of safe passage for your teen.

Rules for the Road

You are your child's role model, so regardless of her age, start practicing the following rules (which will become your first rules for your new driver).

1. Drive safely and obey all traffic laws. This means no running yellow lights and no speeding. You don't want your teen to do these things—so you can't, either.

2. Wear a seat belt at all times, and don't move the car until all passengers are belted in. Studies show that teens are less likely to use seat belts when they're out with their friends. However, by making the behavior routine, you increase the chance that your teen will feel guilty when her seat belt isn't on.

3. No drinking and driving. If your children are out with you and you have a couple of drinks, let your spouse drive. If both of you have too much to drink and you're at a group gathering, ask to ride home with someone else. If you're at a restaurant as a family with no non-drinking drivers, make a point of waiting until you are completely able to drive.

4. Lock the doors every time you get into the car. In case of a breakdown or collision, this provides you with an added element of control, and it's a good safety precaution.

Riding with Others

Set guidelines on riding with others. In 1993, two out of every three teens who died as passengers in crashes were traveling in vehicles driven by other teens. And fatal crashes involving 16-year-olds were much more likely to occur with three or more occupants in the vehicle. Set some guidelines for your teen:

➤ If the person with whom she is to ride is "under the influence," let her know you'll come and get her, or pay for a cab, anywhere and anytime. She should also feel free to call you any time she senses trouble.

➤ She is to wear a seat belt, regardless of what others are doing.

➤ High school parking lots frequently feature some questionable "specimens," and you don't want your teen riding in a car in which the brakes are likely to fail, or that may stall on the highway. If your teen hangs out with a friend whose car is frequently experiencing mechanical problems, you'll want to discuss it with her. While it would be ideal to keep your teen out of her best friend's wreck altogether, it may not be possible. Your best bet is to limit the range your teen can travel in a poorly maintained car (local driving only is a place to start).

So how will you know that your son doesn't use his seat belt, or that he went cruising down the road in his friend Andy's coughing, sputtering jalopy against your wishes? You might hear, but you probably won't. What you're offering your teen are guidelines for his own safety; all you can do is hope that he takes appropriate care more often than not. And if you do see him hopping out of Andy's pile of junk? Talk to him about why you suggested the rule you did. Maybe he'll hear your words before he and Andy go for their next spin down the highway.

Getting Licensed

Though the legal driving age varies from state to state (ranging from 14 in South Dakota to 17 in New Jersey), the initial application process for a license is much the same.

First-time applicants must generally provide some form of identification that includes full name and date of birth (such as an original birth certificate, a certified copy of school records, or a valid passport). Photocopies are usually not accepted. Many states also want to see a Social Security card. Applicants under 18 must usually be accompanied by a parent or legal guardian who also has proper identification. (The booklet your teen will use to study for the written test will outline your state's requirements.)

In 30 states, first-time drivers must get a learner's permit before they can apply for a full license. To obtain a learner's permit, applicants must usually pay a fee and then pass a written exam and an eye exam. A road test is required for a full license. Some states also require first-time drivers to take a short course of some type (such as road safety, alcohol awareness, and so on).

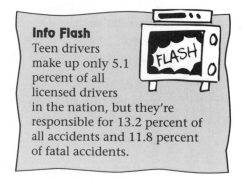

Info Flash
Teen drivers make up only 5.1 percent of all licensed drivers in the nation, but they're responsible for 13.2 percent of all accidents and 11.8 percent of fatal accidents.

Behind the Wheel in Driver's Ed

When humor columnist Dave Barry's son was learning to drive, Barry took issue with the driving law, which required only that his son must have a licensed driver over age 18 in the car. Barry proposed a revision to the law: "If he's going to drive, he must be accompanied by a licensed paramedic and at least two Supreme Court Justices."

As your teenager takes to the wheel, you, too, may feel somewhat inadequate at protecting him, but there are some specific measures you can take.

Have your teen take a driver's education course. Having a trained instructor (who has no emotional involvement in the process—not to mention nerves of steel) in a car with dual controls is a safe, effective way to teach the rules of the road and provide driving experience. (In addition, your teen's successful completion of the course may reduce your insurance premium.)

Unfortunately, school-sponsored driver's education courses have been cut back drastically in recent years, so if your teen won't be able to take it at school, start asking around for reputable driving schools in your community.

Yikes! Licensed to Drive?!

Every parent wonders, "So what can I do to make my teen a better driver?"

The biggest problem with teen drivers, say the experts, is lack of experience. Driving errors were the overwhelming cause of 82 percent of 16-year-old drivers' fatal crashes nationally in 1993, according to the Insurance Institute for Highway Safety. As drivers become more experienced, alcohol becomes a much greater cause of accidents (see Chapter 19 for information on drinking and driving).

According to a spokesperson for the Insurance Institute for Highway Safety, most teens find it relatively easy to steer and maneuver the car; what's difficult for them is scanning the scene, learning to predict danger, and developing the maturity to make responsible decisions. Here are some safe driving guidelines:

➤ Convertibles, "hot cars," and Jeeps with roll bars are accidents waiting to happen in the hands of a teen. Select a good-sized, safe vehicle for your teen to drive—nothing smaller than a mid-size car.

➤ Give your teen lots of supervised practice, before and after she gets her license.

➤ In the beginning, restrict your teen to daytime driving. Roughly half the fatal motor vehicle accidents involving teenagers happen at night. That's partly because visibility is more difficult, and also because night driving is generally for recreational purposes and kids are likely to be less responsible drivers at night.

Info Flash
In areas which have teen curfews, auto crashes have been reduced by as much as 69 percent during restricted hours.

➤ Don't allow your teen to drive on highways (without supervision) for a time. Handling a car at higher speeds requires additional practice.

➤ Friends can be distracting, so your teen's first "solo" runs should be truly solo. Permit her to add passengers gradually. If one of her friends is a "cut-up" who worries you, ask that she wait a little longer before driving that particular kid around.

➤ Reward violation-free, accident-free driving by lifting these restrictions one by one. If you learn that your teen has violated one of your safety guidelines, talk to her. While any violation of your guidelines is a violation of your trust, you may want to treat the offense according to its seriousness. If she's had one extra friend in the car, you might give her a warning. (You may decide that she's responsible enough to handle a passenger or two soon anyway.) If she took off for the open road with a ton of kids packed into the car, you might suspend her privileges for a week. If she drove on the highway without permission (which is illegal in some states for teens who have only a junior license), you might take away her privileges for a longer period of time.

➤ Temporarily suspend your teen's driving privileges for speeding, driving without wearing a seat belt, or driving under the influence of alcohol. Driving without a seat belt is illegal in many states, and you should warn your teen that he doesn't want any tickets at this stage of his driving career. Speeding or driving under the influence should be treated firmly and strictly. You might consider requiring that he attend an extra driver's lesson (that he pays for himself) in addition to suspending his driving privileges for a while. Then let him regain his privileges gradually; for example, you might let him use the car only to get to school or his job before he can start using it again for social occasions.

➤ Driving in bad weather requires extra practice. You may want to drive your teen yourself, or at least specify that he cannot drive friends in bad weather.

Info Flash

Some safety experts advocate staged licensing programs that permit young drivers to gain driving experience gradually.

The recommended program generally consists of three stages: a learner's permit stage, during which all driving must be supervised; a restricted license stage, which allows unsupervised driving in limited circumstances; and a full, unrestricted license for eligible drivers who have remained free of violations or crashes.

Experts stress that staged licensing programs are the safest way to learn to drive, because it isn't acquiring the skills that's the problem, it's getting the experience.

Whose Car Is It, Anyway?

Once your teen is driving regularly, you may find that all the drivers in your family are jockeying for use of the car. Here are some of the questions and rules you'll want to review as a family so that these issues are settled fairly:

➤ When will the car be available for teen use? Are there hours (such as when you're at work) when it will *never* be available?

➤ Who pays for gas?

➤ Who takes responsibility for car maintenance?

➤ Traffic tickets should be paid for by the person who gets them. (The punishment for parking tickets should be the fine itself. You may want to suspend driving privileges if your teen is ticketed for driving violations.)

➤ The car is not to be lent to anyone.

➤ Your teen must report where he's going before he takes the car out.

What if your teen decides she wants her own car? To buy or not to buy a car is an individual decision, but remember: Too many students work 20 plus hours per week for the sole purpose of paying for their wheels. These are some of the same students who fall asleep in class and who have no time to do assignments.

While there's nothing wrong with expecting your teen to cover some automobile expenses, consider whether she really needs a 2,500-pound monster that's her sole responsibility to keep "fed." You may want to suggest that she hold out and share the family car (or cars) for as long as possible.

If sharing the family car becomes difficult for logistical reasons, the two of you may decide that getting him a car is necessary. It's highly unlikely that your teen will be able to afford a car himself, so the two of you will probably have to collaborate on the financial terms. And as long as you are contributing financially, you still have some say over the car he'd like to buy. If you're purchasing a used car, have it checked out by a mechanic so you're sure it isn't a clunker.

Danger Zone

Most adults take safety precautions that teens never think of. Here are a few specifics to point out to your teen:

➤ The number of passengers in the car should be dictated by the number of seat belts. The greater the number of kids in the car, the greater the chance of an accident.

➤ Stay on well-traveled, well-lit roads. Avoid high-crime areas, even if it means going out of the way.

➤ Don't drive late at night or when overly tired. If your teen is going to a concert or to an out-of-town game and will have to drive back very late, she should consider staying overnight and driving back in the morning. Drowsiness reduces awareness, impedes judgment, and slows reaction time.

➤ Both daughters and sons should be cautious of empty parking lots and isolated areas (both in the daytime and at night). Teach your teen to locate her keys ahead of time so that when she arrives at the car she can get right in.

Tuning In

At this stage, some parents consider the expense of a cellular phone a worthy investment in peace of mind.

"A cell phone?!!" your teen will shriek. Yes, but not for carrying around school or for calling friends from the car. For emergencies.

A cellular phone provides you or your teen with the capability to call for help from the road; if your teen is stuck in traffic and won't make his curfew, for example, it's reassuring to know that he can call from the road to let you know what's going on.

Because calls from cellular phones are extremely expensive, you may want to restrict calling to emergency use only. You should also make the rule that any calling must be done by a passenger, or when the car is at a standstill. No driver should attempt to dial a number—or carry on a distracting conversation—while behind the wheel.

When Accidents Happen...

If your teen is in an accident, he'll be flustered. To prepare him, write down the following information on an index card and keep it in the glove compartment in case of emergency.

If there is an accident, your teen should:

➤ Call for medical help if anyone has been injured.

➤ Notify the police and do not leave the scene of the accident before they arrive.

➤ Get the name, address, phone number, insurance company, and driver's license number of anyone who was involved.

➤ Get names and telephone numbers of anyone who witnessed the accident.

➤ Write down the details of the accident and notify your insurance company as soon as he gets home.

➤ Get a copy of the police report and save copies of everything.

Info Flash

Consider joining an auto club, which will provide your teen with an automatic "road support" system in case of emergency. If you join, be sure your teen has a membership card which lists the 800 number. Also consider giving your teen a gasoline credit card (only for use in emergencies).

Anyone can benefit from taking an auto repair course, but whether or not your teen has done so, store the following basic emergency equipment in the car. Even if she doesn't know how to use everything, having the items on hand may make it easier for a repair expert to get her going:

➤ An adjustable wrench for tightening and loosening bolts

➤ A jack and spare tire

➤ A light gauge wire to tie up muffler or tailpipe

➤ Three triangular reflectors in case of a breakdown

➤ A first-aid kit

➤ A flashlight (with fresh batteries)

➤ A piece of white cloth

Your teen should know the universal signals for help: Tying a white cloth to the antenna or propping the engine hood up. Your teen should also know what to do after creating the appropriate signal: Get back into the car, lock the doors, and wait for help. Tell your teen not to get out of the car until the police or state patrol arrives; if passersby offer to help, they should be asked to call the authorities.

Insurance: It's Going to Cost You Big Time

Call your insurance company as soon as your teen gets her permit or starts driver's education. After that, get prepared for the news you know is coming.

It's common to see insurance rates double—and even triple—upon adding a teen to the family insurance policy. Why? Because teen driving statistics are so poor. According to the Insurance Institute for Highway Safety, a teenage male driver's chances of having an accident are almost 100 percent, and while girls have slightly better driving histories, their records are deteriorating, too.

Though there's no way to avoid an increase, there are ways to minimize the damage to your pocketbook.

Shop around for the best rates. You may find someone who can write a policy for less than your current insurer. When you call, be aware of the following points—each one may cut your premium by 10 percent or more:

➤ The type of car you're insuring makes a big difference—you'll pay more if your teen drives a sports car or high-performance car.

➤ Add your teen to the policy as an occasional driver. (The family member who drives the car more than half the time is considered the principal driver; all other family members are considered occasional drivers.) If it's your teen's car or you've got more cars than parental drivers, then this isn't an option.

➤ If your teen is an honor roll student, you may be able to save. Good students tend to be good drivers, and insurance costs reflect that. Ask insurers how your teen can qualify.

➤ Some states offer premium discounts for young drivers who complete driving courses.

➤ Is your teen a nonresident? If your teen is at boarding school or college and has no car, discounts are usually available.

➤ Accept a higher deductible if you can afford it—you can save.

➤ Ask about insurance company client discounts. Some companies offer a discount for long-term customers or customers who have both home and auto coverage with the company. Or, families may get discounts for having all their cars on the same policy.

➤ Insurers may offer breaks for automatic safety belts, anti-lock breaks, and anti-theft devices.

➤ If your teen will be driving an older car, which would be damaged beyond repair in an accident, you might be able to forego collision insurance.

Under no circumstances should you skimp on your liability coverage. For bodily injury liability (medical expenses and legal fees arising from accidents you cause), carry at least $100,000 per person and $300,000 per accident. For property-damage liability, consider at least $50,000 coverage. For extra protection, you might also consider a $1 million umbrella liability policy. Check with your insurance agent.

Cruising Down Memory Lane

After this serious talk about envisioning your teen behind the wheel, it's time to give yourself a break. Close your eyes and remember the first time you took the family car out on your own, with the windows down and the radio blaring...What song do you remember most vividly from *your* first years on the road?

No parent wants to deny their child that wonderful sense of autonomy and freedom that comes with being a driver. Just remind your teen that (as the Beach Boys sang) he can "get around" and have just as much fun by driving at the speed limit with his seat belt on.

The Least You Need to Know

➤ Model responsible driving by obeying all traffic laws and wearing your seat belt.

➤ Provide your teen with lots of supervised driving practice both before and after she gets a license.

➤ Grant driving privileges slowly. Early on, your child should only drive alone, should not be allowed to drive at night or on major highways, and so on.

➤ Spell out family rules regarding car use. When is the car available? Who pays for gas? Who takes care of maintenance?

➤ Take precautions for emergencies. Consider a cellular phone and membership in an auto club and stock the car with appropriate emergency supplies.

➤ Call several insurance companies regarding adding a new driver to your policy. Prices vary greatly.

Part 5
Healthy Body, Healthy Mind

As the parent of a teenager, one of your most difficult tasks will be to help her navigate the teen years safely. This part is dedicated to being your guide.

Should you comment on your teen's four-bagel-a-day diet? Or late-night bedtime? The following chapters tell you. They also show you how to create an environment that promotes healthy living.

This section also provides critical information on everything from eating disorders and depression to sexually transmitted diseases and the dangers of drugs, alcohol, and smoking.

While some of the issues are frightening ones, this section is filled with advice on how to steer clear of the more dangerous teen health hazards. With time, thought, and care, you may get through all this with just a few ripples in the water.

Keeping Fit: Diet and Health

You need only spend one day with a teenager to realize that healthy eating and good sleeping habits are not high on any priority lists. Often teens rush out to school, gulping down whatever breakfast they can grab (like a sugar-slicked doughnut and soda). Lunch might be cheeseburger with the works and greasy fries, washed down with hefty swigs of soda. Maybe they grab a chunk of chocolate or a bag of chips as they rush off to sports practice or a part-time job. By the time they return home, they're famished for "real" food—ideally, pizza or a burger.

Mothers of boys say it's not unusual to open the refrigerator and find that all the food has been inhaled by a monster; mothers of girls note that the "damage" is more specific, but that large amounts of a particular food mysteriously disappear when their daughters come home.

Sleep, of course, comes last and late—after homework, television, and phone calls. Next morning comes far too early for your resident teen.

Just as you couldn't force your baby to eat strained carrots or take a nap if she didn't want to, there's not a lot you can do to change your teen's daily eating and sleeping patterns. However, you can get the facts and provide an environment that encourages your teen to take better care of himself.

You can start by pointing out that healthy eating, dental care, a good night's sleep, and exercise contribute to good looks (such as an ideal weight, healthy hair, skin, and nails), something that's crucial to most teens. Beyond that, read on for more teen health care tips.

"He Grew Overnight!": Your Teen's Nutritional Needs

The teen growth spurt is one of the most dramatic, rapid changes that the human body experiences; it's second only to the amazing growth that takes place during the first year of life. To support this major transition, the body requires increased calories and nutrients. During the year of the greatest growth in height (about age 12 in most girls and age 14 in most boys) the average female requires 2,400 calories per day and the average male needs between 2,800 and 3,000 calories per day.

"Oh, great," I can hear you saying. "My teen probably eats that many calories in bagels, burgers, cheese, pizza, and soda."

Not to worry (too much). If your child isn't obsessed with food (eating too much or not eating enough) and is getting good reports at regularly scheduled medical check-ups, then in all likelihood there's no cause for alarm.

The Good Eats Department

Hopefully, by the time your child is a teenager, you've laid the groundwork for good eating. (Food consumption during the teen years probably won't reflect the values you've taught; don't worry, she'll come back to them later on.) Ideally—unless *your* idea of a balanced meal is nachos and beer—your child has internalized some basic ideas about healthy eating:

➤ Meal time is a pleasant time when the family enjoys being together, and no one gets nagged about what they eat.

➤ Family members are encouraged to stop eating when they're full. No one is forced to "eat just a little more" or to clean their plate.

➤ Food is not a reward: A good grade on an English test doesn't warrant extra helpings of ice cream.

➤ Food isn't used as a substitute for comfort: If your teen didn't make the hockey team, going out for pizza is not the solution.

➤ Adult family members model good eating habits, and if they diet, they do it safely.

➤ The fridge is stocked with healthy foods and most meals are nutritionally balanced.

Info Flash

Teens don't know much about nutrition, so any time your teen expresses an interest in it, you should talk about healthy eating:

➤ Teach her that the foods closest to nature are also lowest in fat and sugar and highest in nutrients. If she eats fresh vegetables and fruits, whole grain breads, lean meats, chicken, fish, and low-fat dairy products, she's doing her body a favor.

➤ Show her how to read nutrition labels on boxes. You might point out that "fat-free" snacks are usually loaded with sugar and chemicals.

➤ Tell her the (sometimes shocking) calorie content of certain foods, such as two tablespoons of peanut butter equaling 180 calories. You can also point out that although one-half cup of cottage cheese is only 100 calories, most people eat more than half a cup.

By teaching nutrition basics early, you'll give your child a guide for a lifetime of healthy eating.

Happy Meals (Not the Kind You Get at McDonald's)

Though snagging family members to sit down and eat together can be daunting, you ought to make it a priority at least twice a week. (And if dinners are difficult, what about a family breakfast on Sundays?) A few tips to make the most of family meals:

➤ On nights when getting the entire family together is impossible, see who's available. If you eat only with your son, for example, he might tell you things you would never get to hear if the rest of the family was around.

➤ In addition to using meal time as a time to be together, a shared meal also offers you the opportunity to sneak some extra nutrition into your teen's diet. You don't have to mention the fact that your famous cheese lasagna is packed with calcium, but by preparing it, you're giving your teen some of the nutrients she needs to grow.

➤ Meal times also offer you an opportunity to introduce different foods (no need to produce a sliced mango or a baked tofu dish with a big flourish; just serve it and let your teen try what she wants).

➤ In addition to a basic dinner, always provide teenage-friendly filler foods such as bread or a bowl of pasta. That way even if your son doesn't like what's on his plate, he will stay at the table because there's something else that he'll eat. In addition, this "filler" food will help him reach the caloric intake he needs.

➤ Leave a meal in the fridge for times when you won't all be together. It offers the opportunity for her to have something healthy at the end of the day.

Short on time during the week? Everyone is, but there are still some ways to help the family eat healthy:

➤ Cook on the weekends, and freeze the food in appropriate portions.

➤ Teach you teen to cook—some healthy foods are simple to make. A grilled cheese sandwich provides calcium; a home-prepared hamburger is easy and nutritious; a quick baked potato topped with cheese, ham, or vegetables is microwavable; and pasta with sauce from a jar is fine, too. If your teen is an enthusiastic cook you may find yourself dining on a meal he's decided to prepare.

➤ Keep frozen pizza on hand. You'd hate to have to eat it every night, but no one ever died of having it once in awhile.

Snacking: "You'll Ruin Your Dinner!"

When your children were younger you may have had a very strict policy on when—and if—they could snack. By the teen years, your teen is in charge, and your job is to provide nutritious snacks and a flexible attitude.

Because they have high caloric needs, teens can't get all the calories they need in three meals a day, so it's natural and important for them to snack.

Keep nutritious and filling foods with lots of teen appeal within snacking distance, such as:

➤ Whole-grain crackers and a variety of low-fat cheeses

➤ Fluffy whole wheat bread and sandwich fixings (lean turkey, tuna packed in water, lettuce, and tomatoes)

➤ Colorful fruit (try plums, nectarines, bananas, kiwis, or a bowl of juicy mixed berries)

➤ Raw vegetables (precut carrots and celery store well kept in water in the refrigerator)

➤ Healthy munchies like low-fat, low-salt pretzels and light popcorn

➤ Yogurt

➤ Soup

"I Want to Lose Weight!"

To teenagers, appearance is all important. Most adolescent girls want to be rail-thin, like today's supermodels. And most adolescent boys want to be pumped-up and muscular like the sports heroes they idolize.

Our cultural bias for physical perfection means that teens who are overweight may get ridiculed and socially rejected by their peers. Not surprisingly, these experiences have a decidedly chilling effect on self-esteem and confidence.

It's worth listening if your daughter bemoans her weight. Talk about her feelings. How much does she want to lose and why does she want to lose it?

If she really is a few pounds overweight, you can offer to help her with weight loss. You must not support a desire to be "rail"-thin here—thanks to waif-like models and actresses, many girls have an unrealistic self-image. However, it's perfectly acceptable to help a child who's a little too plump for her height.

Info Flash
The number of overweight youngsters has doubled since the 1960s. One in five American children between the ages of 6 and 17 are overweight—20 percent of boys and 22 percent of girls. Two thirds of teenage girls try to lose weight.

Watch the Calories

If weight loss seems appropriate, you should first discuss *diet modification* (as opposed to full-fledged dieting). Active teens burn so many calories during the day that merely by cutting out desserts, switching to low-calorie snacks, and drinking skim milk or water instead of higher-calorie beverages can show results.

One nutritionist says she's seen teen patients lose weight simply by watching their beverage intake. She notes that teens tend to drink high-calorie beverages throughout the day, and all those Snapples and sodas add up. (An 8-ounce glass of orange juice contains 120 calories; a 16-oz bottle of Snapple has 220 calories; and a can of Coke has 150 calories).

Get Moving

Encourage your teen to get involved in physical activity. Kids today are more sedentary, thanks in part to computers, video games, and television. Simply being active for a minimum of 30–60 minutes each day will make a difference in how they look and feel.

The teen years are a great time to pick up sports that can develop into lifelong hobbies: bicycling, jogging, swimming, hiking, aerobics, or tennis are all wonderful activities that are enjoyed by people of all ages. (See Chapter 15 for more information about sports and exercise.)

Diet-Wise

If your child needs to lose more weight than diet modification and exercise alone will allow, then you should discuss a sensible weight loss plan with a nutritionist or doctor.

If a diet is to work, it must consider your teen's growth rate, stage of development, and energy expenditure. The goal should be *gradual* weight loss. (Warn your teen that healthy dieting won't make her thin overnight.) The nutritionist or doctor can talk to your teen about long-term healthy eating—the real secret to maintaining an ideal weight.

Helping and supporting your teen face a weight problem requires great sensitivity: You can't control what he eats, and if you try, you may end up sabotaging his weight loss program. Your best path is to provide him with the right information, including a consultation with an expert if necessary. Then stock the house with healthy foods, get rid of the junk, and back off. He'll be more successful if you do.

CAUTION

Danger Zone

Diet pills, laxatives, and diuretics are dangerous weight loss methods for teens. Fad diets are, too (remember the grapefruit diet?). A poorly planned diet can affect general health. If a doctor suggests any of the above methods for a teen, run—don't walk—to another professional for guidance.

If you discover that your teen is taking diet pills, or that she's on a diet that sounds nutty to you, talk to her about what she's doing. Check in with your pediatrician so you can give her the straight facts on why her weight-loss plan is harmful.

If you think it's OK for her to lose a little weight, offer to help her investigate a sensible weight-loss program instead.

Info Flash

Teens who are overweight run a very good chance of becoming overweight adults, and many medical studies show that overweight adults are at increased risk of diabetes, osteoarthritis, heart disease, and even some forms of cancer.

Danger Zone

Teens need an increased amount of all nutrients, but there are two that are most important to teen health:

Calcium. Calcium helps fortify bones, and teen intake of calcium has been shown to help prevent osteoporosis in old age. Teenagers need 1,200 milligrams of calcium a day—as much as pregnant women and nursing mothers! Healthy foods that are high in calcium include milk, buttermilk, yogurt, cheese, canned sardines and salmon, broccoli, tofu (processed with calcium lactate), cottage cheese, cheese pizza, and cheese lasagna.

Iron. Iron is an essential nutrient that helps the body manufacture red blood cells and transport oxygen to various parts of the body. Teens can get iron from iron-enriched or iron-fortified cereals and breads, lean red meat, poultry, fish, egg yolks, whole grains, and dried fruits such as raisins. Vitamin C increases the body's ability to absorb iron, so a serving of vitamin C-rich orange juice, tomatoes, or tomato sauce can make an "iron-enriched" meal more beneficial.

In addition, if you think your teen's diet is lacking in nutrients, you might suggest he take a multi-vitamin supplement.

"I Want to Be a Vegetarian, Mom!"

Vegetarianism is no longer a counterculture statement of shaggy hippies in Birkenstocks. It's a popular lifestyle choice for many people, including teens, who want to take control of their diets. Some see it as a way to eat healthily; others turn to it because they're animal rights activists who don't like the thought of animals being killed for people to eat. Professional trend-spotter Faith Popcorn predicts a greater number of people turning to vegetarianism in a permanent lifestyle shift. However, for your teen, it's more likely a fad—something she'll experiment with for a time before moving on.

The level of your teen's vegetarianism should dictate your level of concern over whether her body is being well-nourished. If she's kept dairy products in her diet, then she's probably getting all the nutrients she needs. If she's opted for a stricter regimen, talk to your doctor, consult a nutritionist, or investigate a book on vegetarianism such as *Diet for a Small Planet*. More creative food preparation will be necessary to be certain she gets what she needs.

It's possible to claim to be a vegetarian and subsist on a diet of sugary cereal and corn chips. If your teen has taken to this kind of vegetarian diet, you may want to guide her to more nutritious eating—with or without meat.

Eating Disorders

Eating disorders are psychological problems that require therapeutic intervention. These disorders make normal functioning difficult and can become chronic, life-threatening illnesses requiring hospitalization.

If you suspect your teen (male or female; boys suffer from eating disorders, too) has a problem, talk to your doctor. Don't attempt to correct the problem alone. Eating disorders stem from an underlying problem, and if you focus on food without dealing with the larger issue, you run the risk of making things worse. It's vital that you seek help. Research shows that early recognition and treatment of eating disorders provide the best chance for recovery.

Anorexia Nervosa

In this disorder, a preoccupation with dieting and thinness leads to excessive weight loss through self-starvation.

Info Flash
One percent of teenage girls in the United States develop anorexia nervosa; up to 10 percent of those who do may die as a result, according to information distributed by the American Anorexia/Bulimia Association.

Young adolescents who participate in sports such as dance or gymnastics where size and weight are important to success are especially prone to anorexia nervosa. (They're often told, "Be thin to win.") Young girls who entered puberty early, have low self-esteem, or have negative feelings about their bodies are also potentially at risk. Here are some warning signs to watch for:

➤ Losing a significant amount of weight (25 percent of normal body weight) when no diet plan is needed or has been discussed

➤ Distorted body image—the teenager feels "fat" even when she's very thin

➤ Continuing to diet even once she's thin

➤ Fear of weight gain

➤ Amenorrhea (losing monthly menstrual periods)

➤ Being preoccupied with food, calories, nutrition, and/or cooking

➤ Exercising compulsively

➤ Bingeing and purging

Bulimia Nervosa

This disorder involves frequent episodes of binge eating, almost always followed by purging (through vomiting, starvation, and laxatives) and intense feelings of guilt or shame about food. The bulimic feels out of control and recognizes that the behavior is not normal. Up to five percent of college women in the U.S. are bulimic, and one-third of bulimics have a history of being overweight. Here are some danger signs of bulimia:

➤ Bingeing or eating uncontrollably, often secretly

➤ Purging by strict dieting, fasting, vigorous exercise, vomiting, or abusing laxatives or diuretics in an effort to lose weight

➤ Using the bathroom frequently after meals

➤ Preoccupation with body weight

➤ Depression or mood swings

➤ Irregular periods

➤ Developing dental problems, swollen cheek glands, or bloating

If you notice any warning signs, be sure to consult your doctor.

Healthy Smiles

Unfortunately, a teen's need to eat frequently is not exactly the best prescription for maintaining good oral health. Because frequent snacking for teens is almost a given, you might emphasize the importance of good brushing for healthy teeth and fresh-smelling breath. Here are some other hints:

➤ Flossing and brushing the teeth, as well as brushing the tongue, are health care habits your teen should follow by now.

➤ Book regular visits to the dentist.

➤ Even if your child is going to an orthodontist, a checkup and cleaning by a hygienist is helpful.

➤ Ask your dentist whether your family is getting the right amount of fluoride. (In many communities it's added to the water supply.) Fluoride fights cavities, and your teen ought to benefit from it.

Bracing Your Teen for Braces

Braces are a rite of passage for many teens. If your child gets them at roughly the same time his friends do, the experience may be easier for him. But even then, it can be a difficult time. Many teens are reluctant to talk or smile for a period of time after they get braces because they feel so self-conscious.

A logical time for a trip to the orthodontist is related more to missing teeth than to chronological age. Your dentist will tell you when your child should see an orthodontist.

Unfortunately, orthodontic work is costly; the current average cost of braces runs about $3,500. To watch costs, shop around. Get recommendations of orthodontists your friends have used, and check your employee health plan. A recent study conducted by the American Association of Orthodontists shows that 71 percent of people covered by dental plans through large employers have orthodontia benefits.

Payments are usually spaced out over time, so you can probably arrange a workable payment plan with your orthodontist.

Info Flash
The "metal mouth" look for teens with braces can be avoided—at a cost. Ceramic (tooth-colored) braces are somewhat more expensive than the normal ones; and getting brackets on the back of the teeth will cost double.

If you have a dental school in your area, you might be able to get treatment through its orthodontia program (in which the work is performed by students under the supervision of professors) at half the normal cost. (This form of treatment may not be covered by your insurance, so check with your insurer first.)

Once your teen has braces, be certain to get him a mouth guard if he plays sports. (See Chapter 15 or check with your orthodontist.) And if your teen gets a removable bite-plate or retainer, talk to him about the importance of keeping track of it. Replacement is expensive.

The "Studious" Look?

You may notice your teen struggling with reading, rubbing her eyes, or having difficulty reading street signs that are far away. If so, you should have her eyes checked.

If her vision does need to be corrected, ask her what she'd like to do. In some teen groups, glasses are a sophisticated fashion accessory; in others, they're the hallmark of nerds. If you get the strong feeling that glasses will never come out of her backpack, you should look into contact lenses instead.

Sleeping Through the Snooze Alarm

You may blame morning sleepiness on too much late-night television. But today leading researchers agree that biology plays a large role. Recent research conducted at sleep disorder clinics indicates that during puberty, kids exhibit "delayed phase preference," meaning that they feel more active later in the day than early in the morning. (The clinicians could simply have interviewed parents to find that out!)

Teenagers who don't get enough sleep won't perform well all day; they may feel groggy in class, zone out on tests, and muddle through sports practice or gym class. Teens who lack sleep also tend to forget things and get confused.

The number of hours of sleep a teen needs varies, but averages between seven and nine hours a night. Teens going through growth spurts need even more, because as they sleep their growth cells are busy regenerating.

While napping can compensate, it's a rare teen who will lie down for a nap. Instead, you can hope that your teen will grab the extra sleep he needs on weekends. Don't bug him for sleeping late when he can—he needs it.

Otherwise, if you really think your teen is burning the candle at both ends, you might suggest that he drop or reschedule an activity so he can buy more time. Or, you may have luck with an "in your room and off the phone by 10 p.m." (or other pre-designated hour) rule on weeknights. Like adults, kids need the right inducements for going to sleep. By removing some of the stimuli around your teen, it may make it easier for him to get to bed at a reasonable hour.

The Wake-Up Call

Mornings are tough for everyone, no doubt about it. Yet by this age, your teen needs to take responsibility for getting himself going in the morning. If he's having a rough time, you might suggest the following strategies:

➤ Set the wake-up alarm earlier than necessary, so he can hit the snooze button once.

➤ Use a really annoying, loud alarm, and place the clock on the other side of the room so he has to get out of bed to shut it off.

➤ Make a deal: If he'll use the alarm to get going, you'll step into the room just to make sure he's up. (This works well if you have a pet who'll finish up the waking-up for you.)

➤ If he's always running late, tell him you expect him to start getting up earlier—that neither you nor the carpool or bus driver will wait for him, and you'll be upset if he's regularly late for school.

➤ Teach him to load his backpack, fix and refrigerate his lunch, and get his clothes ready the night before so he has as little as possible to do in the morning.

The Least You Need to Know

➤ Stock your kitchen with healthy foods and snacks so your teen is more inclined to eat them.

➤ Make meals a pleasant time, and try to plan dishes that supplement what your teen normally eats.

➤ Pay attention to your teen's comments about weight. She may be making a valid request for help with weight loss. If she seems obsessed with weight, consult your doctor.

➤ Schedule regular dental visits for your teen.

➤ If your teen is rubbing her eyes a lot or seems to be having difficulty reading, have her eyes examined.

➤ Encourage your teen to get to bed at a decent hour, and let him catch up on sleep when he needs it.

Chapter 18

Sex and Sexuality

> **In This Chapter**
>
> ➤ What to tell your teen about sex
>
> ➤ Taking appropriate precautions
>
> ➤ What your teen should know about sexually transmitted diseases

Well, now we've come to parenting's $64,000 question:

What are you going to tell your teen about sex?

If you're like most parents, you don't really know. A Planned Parenthood facilitator who runs workshops on this topic says, "Parents come saying, 'Tell me what's right; tell me what to say.' They want answers."

The fact is there is no single right answer. Coming up with what to tell your teen starts with *you*. Very confusing, isn't it? This chapter will provide you with the facts, and help you develop an opinion on how you feel about sex for your teenager.

So, What Do YOU Think About Sex?

How do you feel about sex and your teenager? Perhaps you hold a very strong religious or moral opinion on the issue. If so, then this is what you'll convey to your teen.

Or maybe you feel that expecting you teenager to wait until after marriage to have sex isn't realistic. Yet you want guidelines and suggestions on how to make your teen wait as long as possible and to take good care of himself or herself (physically and emotionally) in the process.

Or perhaps you don't really know. You may simply feel confused, or you may have issues in your own life (a bad experience in your past or a troubled relationship, for example) that hamper your ability to be clear on this issue with your teen. Don't blame yourself; it isn't an easy issue for anybody.

Info Flash

53 percent of high school students say they've had sex. This means that your teen may have sex, regardless of the values you've conveyed. It is vital to talk to your teen about safe sex.

If you're dead-set against sexual activity before marriage (or during the teen years), you can say, "I am opposed to sex for teenagers because I think that a sexual relationship should be saved for when you're older. However, I'm not an idiot, and I know you may disagree with me. If you should get to this point, please take precautions to prevent pregnancy or sexually transmitted infections." (You will, of course, have explained STIs and talked about "precautions" before this.)

Okay, let's add to your confusion (before giving your some answers). Consider the following questions:

➤ Do you believe it's okay for him to have pre-marital sex by the time he's in college?

➤ Well, if having sex at age 18 is okay, what's wrong with 16?

➤ How do you feel if he's had sex without protection?

➤ And if he becomes sexually active in middle adolescence, are you at all concerned with how many sexual partners he may have over the years?

And what if all the above pronouns were replaced with "she." Do you feel differently?

Even if you don't know exactly how you feel about your teen and sex, you surely have strong opinions about relationships. Talking to your teen about what constitutes a positive marriage or long-term liaison is a very important piece that needs to be conveyed to your teenager.

Having "The Talk"

If you've always been frank about anatomy, bodily functions, and sexuality with your child, talking about certain aspects of sex will be easier for you because you've always been open about these subjects.

In addition, if you maintain an easy, comfortable attitude when discussing all things sexual and anatomical when your child is younger, he is more likely to develop a positive attitude about sex. Sexual activity starts in early childhood (children learn early on what feels good, for example) and how you handle these issues early on will set the stage for his later development.

However, if you are still uncomfortable with having a more substantial discussion with your teen, "props" are generally a help, and there is a logical one for a discussion of sex: a book.

Buy your teen (preferably your young teen or pre-teen) a book about his or her body. Visit a bookstore or ask your pediatrician for recommendations. There are some excellent books about puberty for both sexes, and there are several other "issue" books written particularly for teenage girls.

Any of these resources may help your teenager, and when you present him with the book, it's a logical moment to mention your availability to talk about these issues. You might want to address anything your teen seems to be going through (such as the possibility of her period starting soon) or just simply open the door to future discussions.

After that, discussions come most easily if something introduces the topic. If you've just watched a television program about someone with AIDS, you might want to start a discussion about the disease; if neighbors have just adopted a baby that was born out of wedlock to teenage parents, this is an ideal opportunity to discuss whether teens should wait to have sex.

While you may have particular information you want to get across, your conversation will be more two-sided if you also solicit opinions from your teen. You might ask:

➤ "Is there a lot of pressure at school for kids to have sex?"

➤ "Are kids worried about AIDS?"

➤ "If teens are going to have sex, do they understand the importance of using protection?"

If you find these conversations awkward, your teen may have a good relationship with another adult who could cover the basics. (In addition, Chapter 5 stresses the importance of letting your teen establish her own relationship with the doctor.)

Remember, too, that sex and sexually related information should always be an acceptable topic of conversation between the two of you. Keep in communication, and stay tuned to when (and whether) new topics need to be introduced.

Modeling PDAs (Personal Displays of Affection)

Perhaps the strongest message you can convey to your teen has to do with sexuality and affection. If you are currently married or have a "significant other," think about what the two of you demonstrate about a relationship:

➤ Do you spend quality time talking?

➤ Do you make time for shared activities?

➤ What messages are you sending about what two people who care about one another do together? Don't be afraid to let them see you kissing or holding hands or indicating in other (discreet) ways that you have a satisfying, close relationship.

What you model in terms of a marital relationship will very likely be mimicked by your children. (If you've divorced, it doesn't mean they'll divorce. You may have a new "significant other" with whom you can demonstrate a positive relationship.)

If you're divorced, try to avoid dumping on your ex-spouse frequently. Criticizing your ex will have a big negative impact on your teen's view of relationships.

Single parents of teenagers have an additional burden—how can they date at the same time their children are dating? If you are in this situation, you should try to model proper dating decorum:

➤ It will be easier to tell your teen to hold off on sex if you don't bring someone home after only a few dates. (What you do elsewhere is your business, but you shouldn't confuse the issue at home.)

➤ You also need to hold your own counsel as you go through the ups and downs of a relationship. Your teen is your child; she should not become your confidante. Your relationship will be easier and stronger if you always remember that.

Tuning In

By introducing the concept that marital sex deepens and enriches a relationship and becomes more and more pleasurable because of the depth of the commitment and the pleasure of "being one" with someone, you'll accomplish two things:

1. You'll perk up your teen's curiosity. Maybe your sex life with your spouse didn't die right after the last baby was conceived.

2. You'll express the fact that there really is something terrific waiting for them that can only come later on.

Tuning In

Girls report that sometimes they agree to sex when a boy has paid expenses on the date, because they believe they owe it to him. Parents of both sons and daughters need to convey that sex is never "owed" to anyone, and that each individual should be able to decide when, where, how, and with whom to have sex without feeling pressured.

Additionally, parents of sons should instill in them a respect for women, so boys are not given the message that sex is some kind of required transaction or a mark of "stud-hood."

"But He Says He Loves Me"

Both partners have a right to feel safe in a physical or sexual relationship. When appropriate, talk to your teen (both sons and daughters) about asking the following questions before deciding to have sex:

➤ Do I respect this person?

➤ Does this person respect me, and do they understand when I set sexual limits?

➤ Do we trust each other?

➤ Do we talk *and* listen to each other?

➤ Is this person there for me when I need help?

➤ Do we share things other than sex?

➤ Can I discuss birth control and disease prevention with this person?

If any of the answers are no, your teen really ought to wait. Tell your teen it's perfectly okay to say no, and it's okay to say no even if you've said "yes" once.

How to Just Say No

➤ "You'd do it if you loved me."

➤ "Everyone's doing it."

➤ "Don't worry, nothing will happen."

Many girls still hear these age-old lines from their boyfriends—and they still don't know how to respond. Tell your daughter that if she doesn't want to have sex, she is allowed to tell her boyfriend "no" consistently and firmly. He should get the picture.

A good relationship consists of mutual respect, and if he doesn't listen to her "no" (or her "not yet"), a basic ingredient is missing. Tell her that sex won't be right for her if she isn't ready. Tell your teens that sex is never an emergency, and "I'm not ready" is a good enough reason.

Sex Without Consent

Unfortunately, there are a lot of stories about date rape out there, and it's a subject worth mentioning to your teen.

Info Flash
Young women who drink heavily are far more likely to be the victims of date rape or sexual assaults. They're also more likely to get pregnant or contract a sexually transmitted disease.

Tell your daughter that she can say "no" to any situation once she decides that enough is enough; at any level of sexual activity (from just kissing to anything else), she always has the right of first refusal. You might also tell her that the threat of date rape is a good reason for her to avoid drinking on dates; some boys will intentionally take advantage of a girl who has been drinking and isn't able to make responsible decisions.

Tell your son that if he is with a girl, and she tells him to stop, he should stop. The laws for date rape vary from state to state, and the consequences can be severe. And in any case, he shouldn't be doing anything against someone else's will.

Tuning In

Here's an analogy that you might appreciate. It demonstrates that as life changes, you may change, too.

Think back to when you were age 8 or 10. When you learned about sex, what did you think about it? "Yuck" was a term used by many kids then. Well, now you're 25 or 30 years older. How do you feel about it now?

So while you may feel that sex and your teenager is distasteful and inappropriate ("yucky") right now, keep an open mind. One day (I won't speculate as to when; when your kid is 50 might sound like a good age!) you may find out that your teen has "done it." At first you'll have very mixed feelings, but somehow, you'll understand.

Safe Sex

In earlier years, "safe sex" meant baby-free sex—sex with birth control. Today, safe sex means sex without worry of infection. Teenagers should have a full understanding of which methods are good for birth control and which are more likely to reduce disease.

Teenagers of both sexes should know the following facts:

➤ Protecting oneself and one's partner from disease and unwanted pregnancy is a personal responsibility that every sexually active person must bear.

Danger Zone
CAUTION
GET THE FACTS! Studies show that 75 percent of parents are misinformed about contraception, and 60 percent of adults have unplanned pregnancies. If you don't have the correct facts, your kids certainly won't. If you're confused, check with the doctor.

➤ Condoms, when properly used (which isn't always easy for teens), both prevent pregnancy and stop the spread of infection. Both boys and girls who are sexually active should take responsibility for buying, carrying, and knowing how to use condoms.

➤ The most reliable forms of birth control are the pill and the diaphragm. Both are used by females and have to be obtained through a physician. Depo-Provera, a shot given once every three months, is also available through a physician. But neither the pill, the diaphragm, nor Depo-Provera offer any protection against sexually transmitted infections.

➤ Vaginal sponges, chemical contraceptives (foams, jellies, suppositories, and cream), and condoms can all be purchased over the counter at a drugstore (and some supermarkets). All of these barrier forms of birth control must be used each time a couple has intercourse.

➤ Withdrawal is the least effective form of birth control, and it does nothing to prevent the spread of disease.

➤ A "morning-after" pill is available with a physician's prescription; it is quite reliable if taken within 72 hours of unprotected sex. In an emergency (rape or broken condom), it can be quite effective, but it should not be regarded as a regular form of birth control.

➤ Your son should be told that relying on a girl's opinion that she's "on the pill" or "not ovulating" is risky business. If she's missed a pill or miscalculated her period, they both may be in for an unwanted surprise.

➤ Though teens don't like to plan ahead to have sex, point out that it's the mature thing to do. If they don't have protection, they have to get some—or abstain.

Info Flash

Myth: Talking to your teen about sex will encourage him or her to have sex.

Reality: *Not* talking to your teen about sex is far more dangerous. Not talking about safe sex with your child is irresponsible, and if you neglect to convey your values (anything ranging from understanding to heartfelt disapproval), your teen has no way to know how you feel. Your message *will* have an effect.

Unexpectedly Expecting

What if your teen tells you she thinks she's pregnant? Your first act should be to confirm that she really is; many things can interrupt the regularity of a girl's menstrual cycle. Get her to a doctor to determine whether she's actually pregnant or not.

If you find that she is indeed pregnant, she has three options: she can have the baby and keep it; she can have the baby and arrange for an adoption; or she can have an abortion. Provide her with the information she will need to explore her options:

➤ If she wants to keep the baby, what kind of day-care programs are offered in the community? What will her financial situation be like? How will she continue her schooling?

➤ If she is interested in adoption, what kind of adoption services are available?

➤ If she's thinking of an abortion, she should talk to an abortion counselor and to women who have been through one before.

Difficult as it is, you must recognize that this is her decision—no matter how strong your opinion on the matter. If you try to railroad her into taking a particular path now, she could end up resenting you for the rest of her life.

If the boy who has gotten her pregnant wants to be included in the decision, she should be free to discuss it with him. But again, ultimately, the decision is hers.

In all likelihood, you won't be calm or happy during this time, and neither will she. You will both need plenty of space and the opportunity to talk to others (a counselor, trusted family member, or friend) while you sort things out.

Throughout this entire time, you should be letting her know you love her. Support her decision, and once it's been made, re-visit the topic of sexual responsibility. If she is going to continue to be sexually active, she has to learn to use both a contraceptive and a condom.

Sexually Transmitted Infections (STIs)

There are approximately 20 million new cases of sexually transmitted infections each year, and one quarter of these infections occur in teenagers who have not yet finished high school.

While AIDS is certainly the best known of the sexually transmitted diseases, it's very important that your teen know that there are other STIs that are highly communicable, including chlamydia, gonorrhea, genital herpes, pediculosis pubis (crabs), scabies, syphilis, trichomoniasis, and venereal warts.

Several of these infections can be extremely serious (some can eventually cause sterility in either males or females; others cause chronic pain and discomfort), and even life-threatening. What's more, several kinds of STIs, including herpes, syphilis, pharyngeal gonorrhea, and AIDS, can be contracted without having genital intercourse, as they can be spread orally.

Symptoms that may reflect STI in a sexually active person include:

➤ Painful, burning, or dark-colored urine

➤ Discharges from the vagina or penis that burn, itch, or have an unusual odor

➤ Soreness, sores, warts, redness, or a persistent pimple in the genital area

STIs can be totally avoided through abstinence or by having a mutually monogamous relationship with an unaffected person. Having multiple sex partners greatly increases the risk of contracting STIs.

If your teenager is sexually active, stress that a condom with spermicide is the best protection against STIs. Also stress that your teen should tell you or his doctor immediately if he notices any of the symptoms mentioned above.

What You Should Know About AIDS

Chances are your teen knows far more about AIDS (Acquired Immune Deficiency Syndrome) and its transmission than you do. In most school systems teachers have found innovative ways of conveying the seriousness of the spread of AIDS. Health classes cover how AIDS is spread and how it isn't.

The reality is grim. Studies show that because people with HIV (the virus that causes AIDS and AIDS-related complex) usually don't display symptoms for many years, many of the cases of AIDS that are appearing in people in their twenties were contracted while these individuals were teenagers. You (and your teen) should know the following about AIDS.

How AIDS Is Transmitted

AIDS is transmitted by an infected person in four ways:

➤ Through sexual contact

➤ By sharing needles while injecting drugs

➤ Through transfusion or injection of infected blood

➤ Through pregnancy—an infected pregnant woman can pass on the disease to her unborn baby

A person can be infected with HIV and not show any symptoms or seem to be ill in any way. However, even without symptoms the person can transmit the disease to others.

Though they can test for the hidden virus shortly after exposure (three to six months afterwards gives the most accurate results), few teens test for it, and even those who do *fail to inform their past or future sexual partners*. Even one sexual encounter can result in the transmission of AIDS, so it is vital that teens use adequate protection (condoms) for every sexual experience.

Stress to your teen that precautions for safe sex should be taken until both partners have been monogamous for a period of time and have tested negative for HIV.

How AIDS Is Not Transmitted

AIDS is not an air-born virus. It is transmitted through the blood, semen, and other bodily fluids, and is **not** spread by the following:

➤ Shaking hands, sharing meals, touching doorknobs, or using the same drinking fountains or toilet seats

➤ Social kissing, hugging, petting, or cuddling

➤ Coughing or sneezing

➤ Being close to an infected person (or having them serve food to you in a restaurant)

➤ Sharing anything from a swimming pool, bed linens, eating utensils, or office equipment, including the telephone

Whether or not AIDS is spread through saliva (such as in French kissing) is currently debated, but the general feeling is that it is unlikely.

"Is My Child Homosexual?"

Your teen needs your love and acceptance more than ever if she's beginning to wonder why she's not attracted to the opposite sex. (Some teens go through a period of same-sex sexual experimentation; others know that they really are "different.")

If you have concerns about your teen's sexual orientation, lay low. He may be going through an experimental period, and your interference or curiosity will be unwelcome and inappropriate. The best you can do is try to be open-minded and nonjudgmental (qualities you hopefully have modeled all along).

If your teen has a good relationship with her physician, you may want to make sure she has time alone to speak with the doctor when she goes for her annual visit. Connecting your teen with a person who can provide information, guidance, and support is the most loving thing you can do as a parent.

As many as one in 10 people are gay or lesbian, and if you're the parent of one, there is nothing to feel guilty about. Your adolescent didn't choose homosexuality, nor was there anything you could have done differently to change the pattern of things.

Accept him or her and be there to help him with any problems that arise. Gay and lesbian teens are frequent victims of name-calling, insults, jokes, and physical abuse because of the stigma attached to homosexuality.

Many teens in this situation are open to counseling as a way to sort things out. Make it available if you can. See the Resource Directory at the end of this book for groups that will provide additional information.

The Least You Need to Know

➤ Deciding what to tell your teen about sex first requires that you decide for yourself how you feel and what your values are.

➤ Even if you stress that you don't approve of teen sex, make it very clear that if your teen makes a different decision, it is vital that he practice safe sex.

➤ Condoms with spermicide should be used for every sexual encounter to reduce the possibility of the spread of disease.

➤ If you're in a relationship with a "significant other," model what you believe constitutes a positive relationship.

➤ Whenever you discuss issues such as sex be certain you have the facts straight.

Chapter 19

Living Dangerously: Alcohol, Smoking, and Drugs

> **In This Chapter**
>
> ➤ Establishing your position on substance abuse
>
> ➤ Setting limits for your teen
>
> ➤ Understanding why teens smoke
>
> ➤ The consequences of underage drinking
>
> ➤ Teenage drug abuse

Testing limits is part of growing up. One of the ways some teenagers choose to "push the envelope" is by experimenting with drugs or alcohol or by taking up smoking.

Many parents who grew up in the '60s find themselves wondering how to handle these issues: they remember throwing back some beers when they were still too young to drink legally; and many used pot and other drugs that were plentiful then. After considering their past and evaluating the present, parents usually come up with one of three responses:

➤ Experimentation is part of being a teenager.

➤ I want my teen to do as I say, not as I did.

➤ I'm not sure how to reconcile my past with my feelings about what I want my kids to do in the present.

Tuning In
One of the reasons kids turn to alcohol and smoking is to feel more grown up. If you give teens some control over family issues, they will feel more "adult" and may have less reason to abuse these substances.

So what's a parent to do?

You start by getting the facts. They will help you decide exactly what you want to communicate to your teen about drug, cigarette, and alcohol use.

These issues aren't easy ones. As all teens are tempted to "walk on the wild side," you have your work cut out for you, but with facts and vigilance you have a chance to make a difference. In this chapter, I'll give you the facts you need to know.

The Younger the Better

While some parents take the attitude that there's nothing wrong with a little experimentation, many more would prefer that their children stay away from cigarettes, drugs, and alcohol completely. If avoidance is part of your long-term plan, start establishing your beliefs early. (If your teen is already in his mid-teens, start talking about your beliefs anyway. It's late, but not too late.)

If you use alcohol, tobacco, or illicit drugs, your children are more likely to use them, too, so begin by being a good role model. Some parents use this as an opportunity to change their own habits. Your kids may have been nagging you to give up smoking for years, and reducing your alcohol consumption isn't a bad idea either. (If you're using illegal drugs, get professional help.)

Drinking in moderation at all times is important, and keeping it in context is, too. A parent who comes home from work announcing, "I had a bad day. I need a stiff drink," is showing a teen that alcohol will make him feel better and will also help "solve" the bad day.

Here are some other attitudes you should model:

➤ With smoking, you'd ideally like to invoke the two Ds: Dangerous (for your health) and Disgusting (to be around—who likes to have smoke blown in their face?). Even if a favorite grandmother smokes, the health dangers are clear, and she might even aid the cause by talking about how she would quit if she could.

➤ The dangers of drugs are also well known, and from the very beginning, your children should be taught that there is nothing acceptable about them.

➤ Drinking is a more difficult issue because it's so prevalent in our society. If you condemn teen drinking, what do you say if you want to have a beer with dinner one night? While there are additional tips concerning alcohol use later in the chapter, your best general approach is to say that drinking in moderation is acceptable for adults, and that *no one of any age should drink and drive.*

Because all three of these substances can lead to addiction, you should also point out to your kids that once you start, these habits are difficult to kick. (Statistics show that teens are more likely to start smoking or drinking if they believe that it's easy to stop.)

Keeping Communication Open

In addition to being a good role model, keep the avenues of communication between you and your teen open on these issues. Here are some ways to bring up the topic without sounding like you're about to give a lecture:

➤ Drinking and drugs are often a focus of some of the popular dramas kids follow on television. If you sometimes watch TV with your teen, then you may be able to use an appropriate television segment to discuss your teen's opinion on drinking or drugs, and to convey your opinion as well.

➤ If Uncle Steve "ties one on" at the family reunion and proceeds to dance around with a lampshade on his head, you have the perfect opportunity to talk about why one shouldn't drink to excess.

➤ The newspaper is, unfortunately, full of stories of drug overdoses and the consequences of drunk driving. You can use these stories as a basis for discussion. (A local story, or one your teen might identify with, is ideal.) You might also want to mention celebrities who have had problems with drinking or drug abuse.

When you talk, be matter of fact; don't lecture and don't use scare tactics, which are meaningless to teens. ("How do you know I'll get lung cancer when I'm old?" is a likely response from a 13-year-old.) Also, resist condemning your teen's friends whom you suspect may be smoking or involved in drinking or drugs. Negative comments immediately put a teen on the defensive; however, there's nothing wrong with reflecting appropriate concern.

Info Flash
Thirty-three percent of nearly 200,000 students surveyed in the PRIDE National Survey in 1995 (and reported in literature produced by Mothers Against Drunk Driving, or MADD), said that their parents often do not set clear rules. And half said they are not disciplined routinely when they break the rules.

Be sure to listen to your teen's comments. Her remarks may give you guidelines as to what educational gaps you need to fill (she may think one beer has no effect on her) or you may be relieved to find that she has little interest in these substances—at this point. (Keep checking in as interests change; it's good to tune in on this now and then.)

Reducing the Risks

Studies show that the most effective way to control teenage substance abuse are the following:

➤ Set limits and monitor your teen's whereabouts.

➤ Ask your teen to tell you his destination whenever he leaves home. (And he should call if his plans change.) If you don't like the sound of it, or if he sounds overly vague, ask for more specifics. And if you ever find that your teen didn't go where he said he was going—and he had no plausible explanation why—you should restrict his range for awhile. (One weekend with no evening privileges, for example.)

➤ Respect your relationship and maintain a good rapport with your teen.

➤ Remember that your teen is innocent until proven guilty. If you hear that she was at a keg party, ask her about it in a nonconfrontational manner: "Someone told me they saw you leaving the keg party the other night. What can you tell me about it?" By telling her you've been alerted but asking for her side of the story, you're still working within a relationship of trust. You may find that peer pressure got the better of her, and she's been feeling guilty about it (and she'll think twice before going again now that she knows that word travels fast). Or you may find that she actually stopped to try to convince a friend who had too much to drink to leave.

➤ Another way to keep teens safe is by banding together with other parents and presenting a unified front on drug and alcohol abuse. If none of the teens in your child's group have total freedom, the peer pressure will be reduced. (See Chapter 11 for additional suggestions on providing safe entertainment.)

Resisting Peer Pressure

Put yourself in your teen's shoes. Talk to him about what might help him resist peer pressure and save face when everyone around him is lighting up or swigging down a beer. "Just say no" wears a little thin by the teen years, but you might brainstorm tactics with him, starting with the following:

➤ "I don't drink because I just don't like the taste." (This could work with smoking, too.) The beauty of this excuse is that it shows your teen has a strong personality and has made up his mind. That's hard to argue with.

➤ "I'm not going to have a drink [take a smoke], because if the coach finds out, I'll be kicked off the team." Sports are important to most kids, and this will hold some credibility.

➤ "If my parents find out, I won't be able to use the car for a month." Again, another teen could understand that this is a high price to pay.

Some parents report success with holding out a reward: if the teen doesn't smoke, drink, or use drugs throughout high school, there is something wonderful waiting for her. Some families offer a car; others offer a lump sum of cash that fits within the family budget (it needn't be substantial—just an acknowledgment that she made it). If she can spread the word among her friends that she's not going to lose that prize, the peer pressure on her will be reduced.

What's a Parent to Do?

But what happens if your teen comes home drunk or is obviously high on something? Or you later learn that your teen experimented with something she shouldn't have?

Don't get into an argument while your teen is drunk or stoned. Your only issue at this point is safety. Your teen may require medical attention. (Alcohol poisoning can be a very real danger in teens whose bodies can't metabolize liquor as quickly as adults' bodies can.) Even a teen who seems only a little drunk when he comes home can move into a toxic state once he goes to sleep—a state that can result in permanent disability or death if it isn't treated. Don't let him sleep it off. Keep him up for awhile (walk him around the room if necessary), until the alcohol has metabolized out of his system. If your teen falls asleep and cannot be awakened, or becomes more groggy after being awakened, call your local emergency medical service.

When your teen has sobered up, talk to him. If it's his first transgression, express your disappointment and disapproval and require that it should not happen again. State what will happen if it does. Punishment should always fit the crime, and curtailing freedom to some degree will probably be appropriate in this case. (Don't make it excessive and try to listen to your teen's input, even on the punishment. He may be tougher on himself than you might expect.)

If your teen repeatedly abuses drugs or alcohol, or smokes, you should contact a drug or substance abuse counselor at school or through a community services agency. They can advise you on the next step.

Info Flash

The statistics on teenage drinking are nothing short of shocking:

➤ Of the 20 million junior and senior high school students in America, half drink monthly (source: Office of the Surgeon General).

➤ Approximately two-thirds of teenagers who drink report that they can buy their own alcohol (source: "Youth and Alcohol: A National Survey").

➤ The leading cause of injury and death among teenagers is auto crashes, and alcohol is involved in nearly half of these fatalities. Many of these deaths occurred during prom and graduation season (source: Mothers Against Drunk Driving and the Insurance Information Institute).

Bottoms Up?

In a national survey conducted recently by the University of Michigan's Institute for Social Research and the National Institute on Drug Abuse, 50,000 student in grades 8, 10, and 12 were interviewed on their drinking habits. Here's what they said:

➤ Fifty-five percent of the eighth graders surveyed said they had already had an alcoholic drink at some point in their lives.

➤ Of this group, nearly half had had a drink in the 30 days before the survey.

➤ One out of every seven eighth graders surveyed had had five or more drinks in a row in the prior two weeks.

So despite the fact that the legal drinking age in every state is 21, kids are obviously having their first taste of alcohol long before it's legal.

Drinking at Home

The way you treat alcohol in your home will make a big difference in how your teen handles the issue. Consider some steps you can take:

➤ Evaluate how your family uses alcohol. Daily, to relax? Only for special celebrations or for religious ones? Only when there's company? Are you comfortable with the message this conveys to your children?

➤ Don't involve your teenager in your drinking by asking her to bring you a beer or mix you a drink.

➤ Should you introduce alcohol to your teen at home so he can learn of its effects? Some parents do; others feel that serving alcohol at home reduces yet one more barrier to keeping him alcohol-free. (Also, most alcoholic drinks are an acquired taste; it may be advantageous if a teen isn't taught to like them.)

➤ Lock up your liquor. While motivated teens seem to have little trouble buying liquor, a good amount of what they drink comes from someone's home stock. If you lock it up, you don't have to worry about your teen (or her friends) getting hold of it.

Danger Zone

Here's what you should know about the legal aspects of serving liquor to minors:

➤ You can serve your own minor children in your home.

➤ You are responsible for any illegal behavior of your minor child, whether she has been under the influence of alcohol or not.

➤ Any person who delivers, sells, or gives liquor to a minor is liable to be punished under the law.

➤ If you serve minor children (other than your own) in your home, you can be held liable for any resulting problems.

Drunk Driving Equals No Driving

➤ "It's just one beer…"

➤ "I didn't drink the hard stuff…"

➤ "I can handle it…"

One beer in the system of an average-size teen is enough to push her alcohol level up to .02 blood alcohol level. That's high enough to result in a suspended driver's license in an increasing number of states.

Driving while intoxicated is particularly bad for teens because they're less experienced at both drinking and driving. They believe they can't have an accident—but they can.

And while many teens are cooperative about appointing a designated driver, this begs the point of whether you want teens drinking at all: if one agrees not to drink so she can drive, the rest now feel that they have permission to drink.

Sobriety Versus Safety

While talking about abstinence is all well and good, your teen may trip up at some point. Share your values, but stress what is really important to you: you don't want her to drink alcohol, but if she does, you want her to get home safely. She shouldn't drive herself if she's been drinking, nor should she ride with another driver who has been drinking. You'll come and get her.

By saying this, you're letting her know that transgressions can be forgiven, and that her life is what is most important to you.

Students Against Drunk Driving (SADD) offers an anti-drunk-driving contract that both teens and their parents can sign. By signing, the teen acknowledges the legal drinking age of 21 and promises to do his best to adhere to a substance-free existence. He also promises to never take a risk by coming home with someone whose abilities are impaired.

The parent is asked to promise to arrange safe transport for the teen, regardless of the circumstances. The parent also vows to seek safe transportation home if he or she is in a situation where no one is in a condition to drive.

See the Resource Directory at the end of this book for information on how to contact SADD for a sample copy of the contract.

"My Kid Smoking! You've Got to Be Kidding!"

Who isn't aware of the numerous health problems caused by smoking? And what addicted adult wouldn't do it over if he were given the chance never to have started?

Info Flash
Ninety-one percent of six-year-olds know who Joe Camel is and what he sells, according to studies conducted by the FDA.

That's why it's so surprising that teen smoking is on the rise. According to the Centers for Disease Control and Prevention, the number of smoking teens has risen from 27.5 percent in 1991 to 34.8 percent in 1995 (the most recent year for which statistics are available).

Info Flash

Tobacco use is the leading cause of preventable death in the U.S. Eighty-two percent of daily smokers began smoking before they were 18, and more than 3,000 young persons begin smoking each day. Of every 3,000 children who begin smoking each day, 1,000 will die a tobacco-related death.

Forty percent of teenagers who smoke daily have tried to quit and failed; 70 percent of adolescent smokers say they would not start if they could choose again.

Researchers have learned that there are several important factors that contribute to the likelihood of a teen starting to smoke:

➤ The strongest influence is what their peer group is doing. If they hang out with smokers, they're very likely to take it up themselves. (Girls whose friends are smokers are six times more likely to take up smoking; boys are eight times more likely to smoke if their friends do.)

➤ Another strong influence is how they perceive smoking. The impression that smoking will help them relax or combat stress may outweigh any risks they hear about. Risks like developing cancer are so far in the future that they take on an unreal quality to most teens

➤ Living with smokers will make a teen more likely to smoke.

➤ Finally, teens who think they could quit any time are almost twice as likely to smoke as teens who think they could not quit.

Info Flash
Young people who use tobacco are more likely than others to drink heavily later or use illicit drugs.

Reversing the Trend

Although virtually every state prohibits sales of cigarettes to teens under a certain age (usually 18), these laws are often only weakly enforced. Studies of communities that have launched enforcement campaigns, however, have found significant declines in teenage smoking.

Governmental support for curbing sales of cigarettes to minors has launched a movement for such measures as limiting advertising for tobacco products and banning vending machine and mail-order sales (where there can be no regulation of the age of the purchaser). The ultimate threat is that the FDA might find grounds to dictate acceptable levels of nicotine in cigarettes—or ban them altogether.

These are good ideas, but what can you say to your teen? The best ammunition are the factors that affect her today:

➤ Smoking makes you smell bad, and gives you bad breath: kissing a smoker is like kissing an ashtray.

➤ Smoking makes your fingers turn yellow, and gives you premature wrinkles.

➤ Smoking makes you short of breath (even those who have smoked for a short while will notice this). Your athletic skills will be impaired if you smoke.

Punishing your teen for smoking makes little sense because you have no way to monitor her moment-to-moment actions, and if you try the "sniff" test, she could be punished for not smoking but for being with people who do (her clothes will pick up the smoky smell if she's in a car or a room with smokers). Instead, use the tactics listed above to encourage her to quit, and lay out ground rules that seem appropriate to you. (You might stipulate no smoking in your house or car, for example.)

Where There's No Smoke There's Still Fire

If your son comes home telling you that the "chew" or the "snuff" or the "plug" he's got in his mouth isn't harmful, tell him the facts. Smokeless tobacco is not a safe alternative to cigarettes. It causes gum disease, tooth loss, and mouth cancer.

Give him the following facts:

➤ One can of snuff per day delivers as much nicotine as 60 cigarettes.

➤ Just like smokers, smokeless tobacco users have trouble quitting because of the addictive effect of nicotine.

➤ Long-term snuff users have a 50 percent greater risk of developing oral cancer than nonusers.

➤ Smokeless tobacco causes bad breath and yellow teeth; any thoughts that it provides sexual allure should be abandoned.

Info Flash

Though chewing tobacco has long been associated with sports stars, a recent report cited in literature put out by the American Dental Association says that seven out of ten major league baseball players *don't use* smokeless tobacco.

Athletes who are serious about their health and performance avoid nicotine because it can make users dizzy and it slows reaction time.

The survey found that of those players using the stuff, more than a third reported sores, white patches, or gum problems (which may be indicative of pre-cancerous lesions). Overall, 59 percent said they were seriously thinking about quitting.

Tuning In

If your teen wants to quit smoking, the biggest favor she can do herself is to tell a friend. Peers have the greatest influence at this age, so if she'll commit to quitting in front of a non-smoking peer, that will help.

Encourage her to keep busy and spend more time in places where smoking isn't permitted, such as the mall or the movies.

Quitting has to be something she accomplishes herself; however, no one said you couldn't add some incentive: Tell her if she kicks the habit and doesn't smoke for six months, you'll match the money she saves by not buying cigarettes during that time.

Drug Abuse

Illicit drug use is beginning to make a comeback among American young people, say researchers at the University of Michigan who have studied the topic. They note a sharp rise in marijuana use and significant increases in the number of teenagers using LSD, stimulants, and inhalants. One of the researchers also notes that the drug problem goes across race, ethnicity, gender, and geographical region. It's obvious that no one—parent or teenager—can afford to ignore this problem.

If your teen is using drugs, common signs to watch for include:

➤ Marked changed in behavior or friends

➤ Noticeable lack of interest in activities that used to provide pleasure, interest, or fun

➤ Sleeping too little (or too much)

➤ Changes in eating habits

➤ Combativeness or emotional distancing from family or friends

➤ Frequent sickness or signs of ill health such as nausea, headaches, bloodshot eyes, slurred speech, runny nose, and hangovers

➤ Problems at school

➤ Items of value missing around the house, indicating that your teen may be selling or pawning them to buy drugs

While marijuana is the most commonly used drug, some teens have also gotten into hallucinogens like PCP, LSD, cocaine, crack, and inhalants. In addition, Ritalin, commonly prescribed for Attention Deficit Disorder, has now made its way into the drug scene where kids use it to excess to get high.

The Legacy of Woodstock: "What Did You Do, Dad?"

"But Dad, you grew up in the '60s and went to Woodstock. Didn't everybody do drugs then?"

Many parents today are being confronted with questions about their past. Even if you did try or use drugs while growing up, it is still possible to convey an anti-drug message to your teen.

If you have fond memories of those days and the life you led, be certain not to talk too fondly of it or glamorize it.

If you're uncomfortable "telling all," you could answer most questions your teen poses completely by talking about your friends and providing your current opinion. "Back then a lot of people used pot, and we knew very little about it. This was before the very serious dangers of smoking were well known, and marijuana was generally viewed as just another form of tobacco."

Remember, too, that there is often a very big difference between experimenting with something once or twice and using it regularly, and you could tell this to your teen. "Yes, I tried pot a couple of times because my friends were doing it, but I stopped because I decided it wasn't a good thing to do."

Are you giving your teen permission to try drugs because you did? No. You might follow up with a comment that stresses belief in your child: "Now that we know what we do about each of these substances, I don't want you trying them. You are too valuable, and drugs, alcohol, and cigarettes don't solve anything—they don't make you popular, they won't help you grow up, and they certainly don't help your body or mind. You have too much to lose to mess around with that stuff."

Weed: Still Going Strong

If your teen is using drugs, chances are he's smoking marijuana. Marijuana is often called the "gateway" drug because it may lead people to other drugs as well. (A 1994 study by the Center on Addiction and Substance Abuse found that 43 percent of teens who use pot by age 18 move on to cocaine.)

Today, marijuana is openly promoted at concerts, on CDs, even on clothes—sending teens a message of social acceptance that alarms the experts. The government's National Household Survey on Drug Abuse last September found that the number of teens who smoked pot nearly doubled between 1992 and 1994.

While some parents dismiss pot-smoking as a "stage" teens go through, there are some facts you ought to know:

➤ Age of use is down. In the 1992 Adolescent Drug Survey, the average age of first-time marijuana users dropped to between 13 and 15 from 14–17 the year before.

➤ During the '60s and '70s, not much was known about the effects of marijuana. Now scientists have found that marijuana reduces coordination; slows reflexes; interferes with the ability to measure distance, speed, and time; and disrupts concentration and short-term memory. There are also cancer risks.

➤ Quantity is up. Kids today smoke larger amounts than their parents' generation did.

➤ Potency is up. The pot teens smoke today is stronger than what was around in the '60s, containing at least double quantities of THC (the primary psychoactive chemical).

Info Flash
The number of pot-smoking eighth graders has doubled since 1992, to 13 percent, according to a University of Michigan study. Among tenth graders, smoking jumped two-thirds to 25 percent; among seniors, it was 31 percent. The drug problem cuts across race, ethnic, gender, region, and size of city.

Inhalants: The Accessible High

Here's a new one: your kid may be getting high on a drug you keep right in your own home—an *inhalant*, like your paint thinner or spray fabric protector.

According to studies conducted by the University of Michigan, one in five eighth graders has sniffed inhalants in their life. Inhalants are particularly popular among young adolescents, and inhalant use decreases slightly as students get older and move on to hard drugs, according to the study.

Parents are usually totally oblivious to the problem of inhalants, and they are totally available to teens. One teen describes going around the house looking for all the products that had "do not inhale" warning labels; another talked of taking a spray with her to school and spraying and sniffing her sweater regularly. (It took months before anyone caught on, and it was her friends who eventually pointed out to her that she had a problem.)

Distressingly, inhalants are not child's play. According to the American Council for Drug Education, sniffing certain chemical products—even just one time—can lead to brain damage, kidney failure, loss of concentration, and death.

Here are some signs to watch for in your teen:

➤ Chemical smell

➤ Drunken appearance

➤ Flu-like symptoms (headache, nausea, runny nose)

➤ Lack of attention or difficulty staying awake

➤ Paraphernalia (soda cans, rags, plastic bags) that smell like chemicals

➤ Weight loss

➤ Rash or sores around the mouth

The Least You Need to Know

➤ Define the limits you intend to set for your teen on substance abuse, and begin communicating your feelings early.

➤ Work with facts, don't lecture, and solicit your teen's opinions on the topic. You may be pleasantly surprised to learn that she doesn't find drugs, cigarettes, or drinking enticing.

➤ If you suspect your teen has been to a party where there was drinking (or drugs), ask about it in a nonconfrontational way. An unjustified accusation of wrongdoing gives your teen little reason to be "good."

➤ Tell your teen that you'll pick her up anywhere, anytime, rather than have her ride with someone who has been drinking (or rather than have her try to drive home drunk).

➤ Smoking may seem like the lesser of the evils, but it's high addiction rate turns a third of teen smokers into lifelong smokers.

➤ If you serve liquor to minor children (other than your own) in your home, you can be held liable for any resulting problems.

Chapter 20

A Teen in Crisis

In This Chapter

➤ Distinguishing "the blues" from true depression

➤ Warning signs of suicide

➤ The truth about cults

➤ Helping a teen who's considering running away

➤ Getting help for your family and your teen

The teen years are turbulent ones, and problems can and do occur—even in the best of families. A death, divorce, parental unemployment, or illness in the family can catch a teenager at a particularly vulnerable time, causing stress-related problems or difficulties at home or at school.

Or sometimes emotional losses (parents divorcing or fighting, a bad relationship with parents, alcoholism and/or addiction in the family, abuse, or moving around frequently) that occurred when a child was younger can become magnified later. When kids become teenagers and are doing what they can to "find themselves," these early problems often lead to troubled times.

Yet "teen troubles" aren't always easy to catch. These are years of change, it's a time when family relationships are sometimes strained, and parents are often busy with their own lives. What's more, trouble sometimes brews in surprising places. The high school senior who has just been accepted to her first-choice college may still wind up with a serious case of depression, and the fun-loving, good-spirited football player may actually be hanging out with members of a cult who are working to recruit him. That's why you need to be particularly alert to some warning signs of trouble. These problems don't really "pop up out of nowhere," and if you're on the alert, you'll have some warning that there's trouble ahead.

In this chapter you will learn what some of those warning signs are, and what to do when you spot them.

(For information on eating disorders, refer to Chapter 17; information on drug and alcohol addiction is in Chapter 19; and Chapter 18 discusses sexual issues.)

> ### Tuning In
>
> If you think there's something wrong with your teen, chances are you're right. Don't ignore your instincts.
>
> While you should gather opinions from others who know your teen, don't let them dissuade you from looking for help if you're concerned. "What are you worried about? He's just a teenager..." is not an acceptable explanation for a teen who isn't acting like himself.

Just the Blues?

All kids get sad or upset about things now and then: being dateless for the prom, arguing with a best friend, not making the lacrosse team, getting an unexpectedly low grade on a science test. Temporary disappointment is not necessarily depression; it's probably just a case of the blues. However, you should treat your child's feelings of melancholy just as seriously as you would want your own sadness to be treated. Like adults, kids are often eager to shrug off or deny being upset, but even if the first response you get is "nothing's wrong," keep your antenna up. Your child may want to talk later.

If the two of you do talk, you may find that the problems are easily resolved: perhaps your son is just feeling stressed out about school work now that basketball practice is dominating so much of his time. A discussion and showing support and interest might be all the help he needs.

Some cases of serious blues (as opposed to true depression) can be solved simply by giving your child more support and attention. If your family has recently moved, or your teen has started a new school, you may find that a sympathetic ear and concrete suggestions for coping with the changes will do a lot to help her out.

Teens generally prefer to talk to friends when they feel down, so you might try to give your teen more time with her friends. Suggest that she invite a friend along on a family outing she's going to, or give her time with a relative you know she likes.

Talking it Through

If you're lucky, your teen may confide in you. Don't blow the connection; if he tells you he's depressed because his girlfriend dumped him, "You were too good for her anyway!" is not the right answer. Take him seriously. His self-image is shot, his free time is suddenly empty, and he hurts!

Tell him that his emotions are important and that you care how he feels. Basically, you want to walk him through the following steps:

1. Let him express his anger, frustration, and sadness. Getting it off his chest will help enormously.

2. Look to see if he can't begin to find a solution. (Don't push him to "solve" his problem too quickly; most people need a little time before they are ready for action.)

   He may not want to date anyone else yet, but you might point out that suddenly he has free time to shoot baskets with the guys again—something he missed when he was spending more time with her. Or if he's now dateless for the junior prom, you might point out that any of the girls with whom he is just friends might be delighted to go with him.

3. Encourage physical activity. Research shows that exercise can help alleviate depression.

4. Touch base with him a little more frequently than usual. He's feeling vulnerable, and even if he used to avoid your company, he might welcome it now. Try to fill in where you can until he's over this rough time.

If your teenager's sadness persists despite some initial efforts on your part (or if he's too depressed to exercise or participate in life as he usually does), consult the school counselor or his doctor for a referral to professional help.

Info Flash

In a study commissioned by *Seventeen* magazine and the Ms. Foundation for Women, girls reported feeling more depressed than boys. Sixty-seven percent of girls said they felt down a few times a month or more, compared with 51 percent of boys. In an alarming finding, 28 percent of girls said they feel depressed every day or at least a few times a week.

The girls said that problems with their friends, parents, and love lives are what depresses them most.

Beyond the Blues: Depression

Depression distinguishes itself from the "blues" because it's longer in duration and more intense in nature. In addition, it's an illness that can lead to some other serious problems discussed in this chapter (considering suicide, running away, joining a cult, and so on). Being aware of some of the warning signals of depression may help you spot a problem in time:

➤ *Changes in mood.* Sadness, dejection, listlessness, and hopelessness are signals of depression, as are a loss of pleasure or enthusiasm in activities your teen formerly enjoyed. Some teens may exhibit extreme mood swings.

➤ *Changes in behavior.* When you think of depression, you usually imagine someone who's very sad, but that isn't always the case. While dejection or hopelessness can certainly indicate depression in adolescents, there's also a strong likelihood that depression may be indicated by other types of behavior: rebellious behavior (by someone who usually doesn't rebel), or any type of defiant, antisocial behavior that isn't normal for your teen.

➤ *Changes in mental processes.* If your teen consistently displays an inability to concentrate, memory lapses, loss of self-esteem, guilt, paranoia, or unusual anxiety, look into it!

➤ *Changes in biological functions.* Not being hungry, or the opposite—overeating, seeming overly tired for the amount of physical activity, or sleep disturbances can also signal trouble.

➤ *School problems.* If your teen shows a sudden change in school performance, has recurring problems with teachers, or habitual truancy, these, too, are warning signs.

➤ *Psychosomatic health complaints.* While there may not be a physiological cause, your teen is, indeed, trying to tell you that "something hurts." Don't dismiss frequent medical complaints for lack of cause.

➤ *Self-medicating with drugs or alcohol.* Drug and alcohol use may come about for many reasons, but if you suspect your teen is abusing drugs or alcohol, get involved.

Tuning In

You really have to judge the "signs of depression" listed here against your teen's usual behavior. If your daredevil teen likes to experiment and take risks, that alone might not indicate a problem. But in a less adventurous teen, a sudden interest in experimentation might be something a parent or professional should take note of.

Suicide Threats

If any of the symptoms of depression listed in the previous section are also accompanied by suicidal talk or behavior, you're going to want to intervene. Fascination with death, dying, or suicide is a common feature of depression in adolescence and should not be taken lightly.

Info Flash

The suicide rate among adolescents has tripled in the last twenty-five years. It has grown so rapidly that suicide now ranks as the third leading cause of death among adolescents.

For every completed adolescent suicide, there are more than 60 unsuccessful adolescent attempts to end one's own life.

Some of the warning signs of suicide include:

➤ Seeming depressed; low energy level; loss of interest in things.

➤ Talking about suicide or discussing suicidal fantasies. Your teen may not discuss these issues with you, but you may get reports from siblings or even friends who are worried.

➤ Giving away treasured possessions.

➤ Writing about death in journals. A teen who wants you to know what he is thinking may actually leave a journal out around the house open to significant pages. (If he does, assume that it's supposed to be read.)

➤ Commenting, "I wish I were dead."

➤ Discussing or gathering information on suicide methods.

➤ Displaying a sudden mood lift following a period of depression without cause. (This may indicate that the teen feels elation and relief over finally deciding to take control of his problem—by committing suicide.)

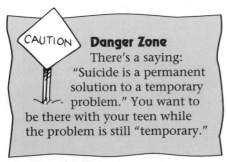

Danger Zone

There's a saying: "Suicide is a permanent solution to a temporary problem." You want to be there with your teen while the problem is still "temporary."

If you suspect that your teen is contemplating suicide, contact someone about your suspicions right away. Call your teen's doctor, the school psychologist (or your child's counselor), a suicide prevention center, a community mental health center, an emergency room, or a family service agency. Any of these places are prepared to help you or can refer you to the best place to get the help you need.

Cults: Fulfilling a Longing for Acceptance

While cults are not as prominent in the news as they were when the Unification Church ("Moonies") performed mass weddings or Jim Jones collected his followers in Guyana, they do still exist.

A *cult* is a group that's dominated by a charismatic leader, that uses deception in its recruitment process, and that tends to exert total control over its members' lives. Cults may be religious or political in their ideology.

To a teen who is depressed, who has poor self-esteem, or who feels "lost" for any reason (including simply having difficulty with a normal life transition), a cult offers the attraction of instant acceptance. New recruits are welcomed and approved uncritically, and prospective members sense that this group will solve all their problems—if they join.

Cults today have become mainstream and have become quite savvy about ways to locate future members. Today a wide variety of cults attract followers by offering programs that will appeal to their targeted group. It is not unusual to find a cult masquerading as an environmental group, a stress management support group, a business-opportunity organization, or offering study aid courses or Bible study sessions. And members of today's cults do not always live communally, making them seem more like "normal people" to your unsuspecting teen.

Cults are dangerous because they dull a teen's curiosity and desire to learn, because the cult's teaching methods rely heavily on repetition of doctrine. What's more, it's difficult for an individual to leave, for the cult will have cut him off from contact with his family and friends.

To decrease the likelihood that your teen will be the target of a cult, keep the communication channels open with your teen; pay attention to what's happening in his life and who he is hanging out with. The teen who feels good about who he is and feels he has a strong support system is less likely to be interested in dropping old friends to take up with new ones.

In addition:

➤ Talk to your teen and be available to your teen when problems arise. Cults promise "instant answers," and that can be intriguing to a teen who feels all alone in coping with a problem that arises.

➤ Help your teen feel included by a group of peers. Whether it's encouraging school activities, or linking her with the youth group of your church or synagogue, teens need to feel they belong somewhere. A religious affiliation may also fulfill a teen's need for finding "meaning in life," another benefit offered by cults. (Since many cults are religious in orientation, check out any that your teen finds on her own.)

➤ Don't pressure your kids. When teens feel overwhelmed by academic or parental demands, the new life being promised by the cult can look very inviting.

A teen who is being recruited by a cult may exhibit personality changes, a dramatic change in lifestyle, a change of goal, the need to separate from family and friends, start hanging out with new or different friends, and she may suddenly assume that the world must be viewed in black and white—with everything either good or bad. You also may notice that this new group of friends is requiring that your teen spend an inordinate amount of time with the group or on the group activities. At some point there may also be demands for contributing money to the group's cause.

If you are in tune with your teen and feel "funny" about her new group of friends or activities, you're probably right, and you'll want to move on the situation quickly.

Try phoning the organization or the individual who seems to have recruited your teen. A legitimate organization will be forthcoming about who they are and what they do; cult members will be more secretive and will try to quickly distance themselves from a family member of a new recruit.

Or you may prefer to contact an organization that can help you:

American Family Foundation
Box 2265
Bonita Springs, FL 34133
212-533-5420

International Cult Education Program
Box 1232
Gracie Station, NY 10028
212-533-5420

The Cult Hotline
212-633-4640

The Jewish Board of Family and Children's Services
120 W. 57th St.
New York, NY 10019

Maynard Bernstein Resource Center on Cults
6505 Wilshire Blvd.
Los Angeles, CA 90048
213-852-7864

If you're at all concerned, don't wait to get involved. Once cult brainwashing occurs, it will become more and more difficult to retrieve your child.

Running Away

The little girl who used to pack up animal crackers and threaten to "run away" under the dining room table is now a big girl whose threats need to be taken seriously.

Despite all appearances to the contrary, your teen is aware of what's happening in the family, and she does want to get along with you. If the family is experiencing problems right now, don't think for a minute that your teen is unaffected.

Take any threats of running away seriously. And if your teen has already disappeared for a day or two to a friend's home, you have all the more reason for concern. Next time she may not stay in the area.

Reach out to find friends and professionals who can offer the family the support it needs.

Getting Help

If you decide your teen needs more help than you are able to provide, your first call should be to someone *you* feel comfortable with. Call a trusted school counselor, teacher, or physician and ask for a referral.

The most important criteria you should look for—whether you choose a social worker or psychologist—is someone who sees lots of teens and has plenty of experience with this age group.

Help comes in all types of degrees (M.S.W., Ph.D., etc.). It may be helpful for you to know a little about the meaning of what they are:

➤ *School counselor.* The school counselor has a Master's Degree and counseling skills. If your school also has a school psychologist, that person should have a Ph.D., Ed.D., or a Psy.D. in psychology or counseling.

➤ *Psychologist.* A psychologist has a Doctoral Degree (Ph.D., Ed.D. or Psy.D.). To earn this degree, the psychologist must complete a rigorous program of academic courses, research assignments, supervised clinical practice, clerkships, field assignments, and a year-long supervised internship. Some psychologists are specially trained in counseling or therapy; others have a specialty in diagnostic testing which may be helpful in some circumstances.

➤ *Social worker.* Social workers have Master's Degrees in social work (M.S.W.) and have usually received supervised clinical experience as well. Because they are trained to analyze and work with emotional problems in a social context, they are sometimes particularly aware of family dynamics and peer group interaction. If you'll be using insurance to foot part of the bill, be certain that your social worker can sign insurance forms for you; some can't.

➤ *Family therapist.* A person specializing in family therapy has an advanced degree (a Master's Degree or a Doctorate), and is specially trained to treat family problems. A family therapist's work may focus on communications and relationship dynamics within the family.

➤ *Psychiatrist.* Psychiatrists are medical doctors who specialize in psychiatry. Some practice therapy and may combine it with use of medication to treat a particular condition. While all psychiatrists are able to prescribe medication, some prefer the use of therapeutic methods (such as psychotherapy) over the use of medication. In addition, psychiatrists can hospitalize a patient when necessary.

If you decide to use a specialist, you should begin by asking for referrals. Look for a person who is known for being terrific with teens or families. Then make sure he or she is a licensed practitioner.

Danger Zone

CAUTION

In addition to the specific warning signs of the conditions discussed in this chapter, professionals recommend that you seek help if your teen exhibits any of the following behaviors on a regular basis:

➤ Reclusive behavior

➤ Self-destructive behavior ranging from excessive dieting to threats of suicide

➤ Sudden changes in personality

➤ Noticeable drop in academic performance

➤ Compulsive behavior that interferes with daily functioning

➤ Fears or anxieties that are incapacitating

➤ Outbursts of violence or sadistic behavior

➤ Seemingly "out of touch" with reality

➤ Poor self-esteem

If you're worried about the cost of therapy, consider school counseling services. You might also look into university counseling services, clinics at psychological counseling training programs, and low-cost services offered at most state psychological associations. Otherwise, many individual practitioners offer sliding-scale plans, and public agencies will usually charge a rate based on what your family can afford. Your health insurance may offer some options, too.

Seeing a teen through a crisis is an extraordinarily draining experience, partly because a crisis-prone teen isn't likely to lead you into the woods once and let you come back out again. Once you realize your teen is battling demons bigger than a hard math test or not being invited to a party, you're likely going to need to be vigilant through the years.

As you go through a rough period with your teen, take a look at his or her siblings, too. One family member's problems will affect all of you. Check to see how everyone is coping. (And develop ways that you can give yourself a break as well.)

The gratifying part of this is that most teens desperately want to be helped. If you can recognize a crisis (or crises) and meet it head on, the odds are good that you'll slowly begin to make some progress. Every coping strategy or support system you can provide for her will be a gift that may help her re-build her life over the years.

The Least You Need to Know

➤ If your teen has a case of the blues, you may be able to provide enough additional attention to pull her out of a temporary slump.

➤ If symptoms of sadness or unusual behavior seem inexplicably intense and continue over a period of time, your teen may be suffering from true depression. You should seek professional help.

➤ Any discussion or symptoms of suicide should be taken seriously.

➤ A family doctor or member of the school staff can refer you to the best source for your particular needs. You might also look into community clinics, university counseling services, clinics at psychological counseling training programs, and low-cost services available at most state psychological associations.

Part 6
Practically Speaking

Did anyone ever teach you how to manage your money? Probably not. Most of us learned about cash flow the hard way—through trial and error. Yet, unless you're independently wealthy, chances are that you wish you'd learned a little more a little sooner. (And learning a lot more real early wouldn't have been bad either.)

So in this part of the book, you learn how to help your teen be practical. There are guidelines on everything from establishing his allowance to teaching him how to budget to encouraging him to invest for the future.

And what money issues do you worry about? If you're like most parents of teenagers, the answer is "paying for college." There's a lot to learn about financial aid and scholarships, and Chapter 23 tells you what you need to know.

Money for Today

Second only to sex, money management is one of the least talked about issues of family life. Yet how is a child supposed to become a financially responsible adult if no one teaches and guides him or her on the basics of cash management? Whether your teen earns money from a part-time job or an allowance, you need to provide him with hands-on experience in managing money.

What's more, teaching your teen about money offers a golden opportunity to communicate what's important to your family. You'll have a wealth of opportunities to discuss everything from why you felt a particular waitress deserved a 20 percent tip to what $100 designer jeans will do to a clothing budget. You can also convey vital life lessons about saving and giving.

Spending Money: Where Does it Come From?

Practically speaking, most young teens have limited employment opportunities. Savings from sporadic babysitting or summer lawn jobs probably do not provide enough cash to count on for a full year, so an allowance makes a lot of sense. As your teen gets older and begins to hold down steady employment, you may want to stipulate that his pay will be used to cover certain expenses. (A 17-year-old with a part-time job might absorb all car-related expenses, for example.)

Tuning In

If you pay an allowance, follow these guidelines:

➤ Choose a time to pay it and adhere to that schedule. Just as your salary should be paid on time, so should an allowance. Young teens will do best with a weekly allowance; older teens should be expected to manage their money for a longer period of time, so gradually switch to monthly payments.

➤ Once you've given them their allowance and they've abided by your savings guidelines (see "The Art of Saving" section later in this chapter), it's theirs to spend as they see fit. Resist criticizing when they "waste" money (that's how they'll learn), and don't borrow from them without permission.

➤ Let them learn from experience. If your teen blows his allowance early in the week or loses the new baseball hat he just bought with his savings, let him deal with it (within reason, of course). If you bail him out once, you'll probably end up doing it regularly. What about an advance on his allowance? You can agree to it occasionally, but don't let it become habitual. If you feel it's been necessary one too many times, charge interest on the next loan.

➤ Have an annual allowance review. Tell your teen that if she wants an increase, she'll need to make a case for it by demonstrating her added expenses.

➤ Your boss doesn't withdraw your salary because you were late or because you were out sick or did something wrong, and you shouldn't withdraw your teen's allowance as a form of punishment, either. His allowance is designated for specific expenses that he needs to pay, and if his income source is cut off, you've put him in a real bind with no warning.

Whether or not you pay an allowance largely depends on how you feel about his holding an outside job during the school year (if you want him to focus on school work, you may be more generous with his allowance), and how profitable his summer employment was. Some families have their kids draw on summer earnings to support themselves through the winter months; others want that money saved for college.

If you have not paid a regular allowance before now, this is a fine time to start. You may think that providing your teen with money on an "as needed" basis works just fine and lets you watch her expenditures, but in reality, it's probably costing you more money. Think about it. If someone offered to give you lunch money every day, wouldn't you always buy lunch? Now suppose that the money is yours to manage. It wouldn't take you long to figure out that by packing a lunch several days a week, you could save up money for that new CD you'd been wanting.

That's what money management is all about, and this is a good time for your teen to learn about it—before minor financial mistakes become major ones.

How Much Is Enough? How Much Is Too Much?

So that brings us to a logical question: "How much?" You can't rely on statistics. A 1993 survey conducted by Youth Monitor discovered that teens were paid the following average weekly allowances:

>Ages 12–13: $5.82
>
>Ages 14–15: $9.68
>
>Ages 16–17: $10.80

Yet figures gathered by Teenage Research Unlimited reported that teen boys have an average weekly income of $76 and teen girls have $48 (these figures include money from outside employment). Without knowing more about how these figures were derived, it's hard to make them meaningful for your household. For that reason, you're not going to get your answer from national statistics.

And you can't listen to your neighbors. Unless you know what the other kids are expected to pay for, you can't give much weight to the allowance they receive.

Your teen, however, will likely insist on reeling off the allowances of the best-paid kids in the class. Enlightening though it may be, assure her that what another teen gets has nothing to do with what you're going to pay, because the two of you are going to establish an allowance that is uniquely suited to *her* and her individual expenses.

Adding Up Expenses

What expenses would you like your teen to assume? Consider the following checklist, and check off what you feel should be a teen responsibility.

Teen Expenses Checklist

_____Gifts for the family

_____Gifts for friends

_____Lunch money

_____Haircuts and treatments

_____School supplies

_____School fees (field trips, team expenses)

_____Club dues and uniforms

_____After-school snacks

_____Toiletries (above and beyond the family supply)

Entertainment costs:

_____Film and film processing

_____CDs

_____Books

_____Hobby-related expenses

_____Computer games

_____Videotapes (purchase and rental)

_____Movies

_____Misc.

(Clothing expenses will be discussed later in the chapter.)

If the school year is underway, sit down with your teen to look back over one month's worth of expenses. This is a great learning experience for both parents and teen. (If the year is just getting started, give your teen money as needed for a "test run" during September. Then do an analysis.) How much does she need for the following categories?

Teen Spending Budget

Lunch and/or snack money   _____

Transportation   _____

School supplies and fees   _____

Entertainment   _____

Other   _____

Within each of these categories, there is a lot of latitude for parental guidance. For example, you may want your teen to take a homemade lunch; he may feel that brown-bagging it is too nerdy and would rather buy it. Consider a compromise. Budget generously for lunch for two or three days, leaving your child with a choice: He can buy a more expensive lunch for two of the days and pack a lunch for the remainder of the week, or he can eat less expensively and manage to make his lunch money last for the full week. These opportunities represent personal money management at its best.

Entertainment is a difficult category. If the school or community has an ice rink or a hangout that charges $2–$3 admission, that's an easy one to budget for regularly. It becomes more problematic to estimate the cost of something like movies, a relatively expensive form of entertainment for a teen to enjoy weekly (unless she is covering some expenses through an outside job). Consider writing in some money each week that can be saved for movies, sporting events, concert tickets, and CDs, so your teen can afford these treats occasionally.

You might also consider funding your teen's hobbies. If your daughter is great at amateur photography or playing the drums, her hobby may provide her with a "fall-back" position when other things in her life aren't going so well. (If her friends close her out temporarily, for example, she'll draw strength from her other interests.) By giving her money to save for a new zoom lens or set of sticks, you express your approval of the activity—a great booster to a teen who is changing in so many ways.

Once you have determined how much money your teen needs to cover expenses each week, you have the first part of the Allowance Equation pinned down.

Tuning In

Does an allowance come with strings or no strings? (Chores or no chores?) Since your priority is teaching your teen to manage money, the answer is "no strings." But that's not to say that your teen isn't an active, contributing member of the family. As discussed in Chapter 3, your teen should carry a share of the family burden when it comes to household responsibilities; that's just being a "good citizen." But should the allowance "pay" for those chores? No.

As outlined in Chapter 3, there are occasions when parents may "hire" their own teen for chores above and beyond regular family responsibilities. Extra work, like raking the entire yard in the fall or cleaning out the garage, may merit extra pay. This type of work and the resulting pay have nothing to do with allowance or regular family chores.

That said, there's no reason not to pay for extraneous chores. If you need the garage cleaned out, the entire yard raked, or the silver polished, then make a "fee for services" deal with your teen. You get the job done, and he can pick up some extra income while learning a "real life" lesson about how earning money requires hard work.

The Allowance Equation

To arrive at a reasonable allowance, consider the following formula:

A = Spending money; weekly amount needed to cover expenses

B = Agreed-upon sum to be set aside for savings

C = Agreed-upon sum to be set aside for giving

A + B + C = New allowance

The Art of Saving

Perhaps the single greatest benefit to paying an allowance is that in paying it, you are given the right to earmark a portion of it. This earmarking demonstrates to your child your value system, and, if you're consistent, it sets him or her on the path for the habit of lifelong savings.

A part of you may be asking, "Why should I give my teenager money for savings? I could just as easily put it in the bank myself!"

The reason to pay your teen directly is because this is a "teachable moment," and in this day and age, it's vital that everyone learns to save. If you do the saving, your child is denied the opportunity to learn. Your risk by not doing the saving, of course, is that on occasion the money will be mismanaged—a lesson that is also important for your teen to learn.

Set Goals for Savings

Savings programs fail when the "why" of putting money in the bank is lost. Even adults have difficulty with the concept of saving for a rainy day if what constitutes a rainy day is never defined. For that reason, teach your teen that the first step in savings is to establish goals. (If you're not a saver, this process may help you, too.) Ask:

➤ What is your long-term goal?

➤ What is your short-term goal?

For most teens, saving for college (or for life after high school) is the most important long-term goal. Setting aside money regularly for this is vital in most families. (See Chapter 23 for more information on what you should be doing to plan for college.)

Short-term goals are what keep the savings program going. Does your 13-year-old want a mountain bike? A new CD player? A modem for the computer? Does your 17-year-old want to purchase his cousin's used car? (In many families, saving for a car may not be a realistic goal; however, "buying" use of the family car by paying for gas and covering additional insurance costs may be.)

Some families stipulate that a percentage of a child's regular allowance should be set aside for savings. Other families like to specify a certain dollar amount.

Long-term savings and short-term savings should not be placed in one savings account, or the first thing you know, your teen's college fund will be spent on a mountain bike. Short-term savings can be placed in a regular savings account. The next chapter will tell you about better places to park long-term savings. You and your teen should discuss how savings should be split between the two accounts.

Though most parents place more value on long-term savings, remember that short-term goals are the carrot that will entice your teen to save. Don't short-circuit your "importance of saving" message by being too hard-hearted about putting money away.

Tuning In

There are three ways to assure a successful savings program:

➤ Let your teen set goals that are meaningful to her.

➤ Teach your teen how small amounts add up to big savings. Collecting loose change in a jar or piggy bank, for example, can mean a deposit of $25–$50 periodically.

➤ Match what she saves. This is a sure-fire motivator. You can match dollar-for-dollar or develop any system that works for you (such as promising $25 for every $250 saved). And matching money in the college fund isn't a bad way to remind you to keep setting money aside.

The Art of Giving

When it comes to "goodwill," what does your teen care about? Teenagers can be very self-involved, so providing them with a reason to look beyond their immediate lives can be a positive experience for the whole family.

If your teen is not sure where to donate money, you could suggest that she give money to your local church, synagogue, or other religious institution. Or you can suggest that your teen pick another group or organization (an environmental group like Greenpeace, a political cause like Amnesty International, or a local institution like the ASPCA, for example) worthy of a donation. If he wants to talk about his choices, be helpful, but eventually turn the reins over to him. You may be pleasantly surprised to learn what appeals to your teen.

Info Flash
Remind your teen that a good budget enables you to pay for what you need and save up for what you want.

Like savings, you can either set a figure for donations that is based on a percentage of allowance (5–15 percent), or you can agree on a specific dollar figure. For safekeeping, you may want to agree on where this earmarked money will be held.

Gotta Have It: Spending on Clothing

To teens, what they wear is a statement about who they are. This "thread-by-thread" search for self can get expensive, and that's where the clothing allowance comes in.

Though some boys and the majority of very young teens may be content to wear what you buy them, once they start wanting to make their selections, watch out:

"I don't have anything to wear to the concert."

"The team warm-up jacket looks stupid without the matching pants."

"I know those sneakers are $110. So?"

Setting a clothing allowance for your teen provides you with the opportunity to hang on to your wallet and your sanity at the same time. If she wants to blow one-quarter of her clothing budget on an expensive jacket, it's no longer your problem—or your decision. (Don't worry; eventually she really will learn how to make responsible purchases.)

Establish a System

If your family is like most families, you probably reinvest in clothing about twice a year—in the fall as school starts, and again in the spring when you realize that your teen has sprouted up a few inches since you last bought spring/summer clothing. However, to save your teen from himself, you're going to pay clothing money quarterly. That way, if he spends almost everything on one or two items, you'll be doling out some more cash again in a few months and the season won't be lost.

To arrive at your quarterly figure, estimate what you spent on your teen's clothing last year, or come up with a figure you're comfortable spending this year. (Advertisers say average annual spending per teen on clothing is approximately $650.) Estimate on the low side as you're still going to cover a few of her expenses.

Divide that amount into fifths: three-fifths should be paid out in two payments in the fall (perhaps September 1 and December 1); and two-fifths should be paid out in the spring (March 1 and June 1). This formula allows for the fact that winter clothing tends to be more expensive than spring and summer items.

"I can see it now," you're saying. "She won't own a winter coat or a decent nightgown, but she'll have the most expensive jeans in town! What a good deal."

That's why you've got to outwit your teen. Your teen's clothing allowance should cover his daily clothing needs; he'll soon learn that by shopping wisely for some things, he can afford to splurge on others, like a great pair of sneakers.

This is where the Parental Wallet comes in. You're going to pay for a winter coat, one dress-up outfit (for formal occasions), underwear, and a single pair of shoes, as needed. (You'll probably need to purchase new shoes in fall and spring, and if your child's feet grow a great deal, you may need to buy additional pairs to be certain he has shoes that fit year-round.) You might also offer to pay for any school- or team-related uniform expenses.

By covering these basics, you've provided for the fact that your child won't be shivering, barefoot in the cold. Nor will he suffer censure because he didn't have enough clothing allowance left over for a new band uniform.

Upping the Responsibility

As your teen becomes skilled at managing her clothing allowance, you may want to make a few changes:

➤ Consider providing a little more money and letting her cover *all* clothing expenses; you'll let her be fully in charge.

➤ Make payments twice a year instead of four times. Ultimately, a teen should be able to manage a budget for a full season's wardrobe.

By the time your teen graduates high school, she may need to be capable of managing a budget for food, rent, clothing, and living expenses. Taking charge of a clothing budget is an exercise you can begin with a young teen that will teach her the benefits of smart shopping and balancing needs and wants.

Tuning In

Open a discussion about whether or not your teen has experienced age discrimination in a store. Chances are you'll get an earful—stories of being short-changed and tales of salespeople ignoring him in order to help an adult first. These experiences are irritating and discouraging to a teenager who is beginning to spend like an adult and desperately wants to be perceived as something other than a "kid."

After validating his feelings, you might suggest strategies such as staying at the counter until he's counted his change so that he can't be accused of lying; or speaking up, politely, when he's been waiting in line to make a purchase longer than an adult. You might also add, "If I'm ever in the store and you need me, I'd be glad to help out." Your services probably won't be wanted, but your offer will be accepted with goodwill.

Their Budget, Their Choice?

By having covered the fact that your child will own one decent outfit, a coat, and shoes (the clothes you're going to buy), you should try to let your teen make as many of his own clothing choices as possible. While you can certainly limit where he wears the T-shirt with the logo of his favorite band, the Bleeding Skulls (not to his sister's recital, not out to dinner with Grandma, etc.), you probably shouldn't prohibit him from buying it.

The less you confront a teen about issues such as articles of clothing, the less likely it is he will buy items that shock you.

Help Your Teen Become a Wise Consumer

While the nature of teenhood involves endless trips to the mall with lots of money dropped on makeup or at the video arcade, when it comes to major purchases, your teen wants to get the most "bang for the buck," just as you do. You can help him learn the art of wise shopping:

➤ Preach against carrying a lot of cash. This guards against catastrophic loss and also teaches Good Consumer Tip #1: Resist buying on impulse.

➤ Teach her to consider the life span of everything from a sweater set to a used car. "Is this really worth the money?" "Will it last?" And when appropriate: "Is it durable?" "How much trouble will it be to take care of?" "Will it shrink?"

➤ Teach about comparison shopping for a better price and a better product.

➤ Encourage him to benefit from the experience of others by talking to people who own what they are shopping for: Do they like it? Did they have any problems?

➤ Help non-drivers get to sales. They'll love being able to afford more because they're paying less!

➤ Owning "label" items is a rite of passage for teens who are trying to carve out an identity for themselves. Tampering with this compulsion is likely to bring on a fight that you'd rather avoid. If a certain make of jeans or sneakers is a "must," you might mention the premium that is charged for the label (don't nag, just offer a point of information), and point out other areas where your teen—who may now be running low on funds—might buy off-brands and save.

Info Flash
According to a 1994 study conducted by Teenage Research Unlimited, teens have real spending power. They spend nearly $100 billion a year ($63 billion of it their own money). Teen boys spend an average of $44 per week of their own money, while girls spend $34.

➤ Discuss the costs of things, not in terms of dollars but in energy spent: Are new rollerblades worth 40 hours of babysitting or six lawn jobs? They may look at purchases in a new light when viewed in this way.

➤ *Zillions* magazine is a kid-version of *Consumer Reports*. The magazine rates everything from best frozen pizza and toothpaste to computer games and boom boxes. Ask to see a copy at your library.

➤ Any teen making a major purchase (electronics gear? computer accessories? CD player?) should know about *Consumer Reports*, also available at your local library. By teaching your teen the art of doing homework before making major purchases, you'll be giving her a gift that will last a lifetime.

The Least You Need to Know

➤ To learn money management, your teen needs to assume responsibility for covering agreed-upon expenses via an allowance or earning from an outside job.

➤ Earmark part of a teen's allowance for savings and donations, and help your teen establish both short- and long-term savings goals.

➤ Once a teen has set aside money for saving and giving, she should be permitted to spend her allowance as she sees fit.

➤ Providing a clothing allowance will save your sanity and protect your wallet. Come up with an annual figure and pay it quarterly.

➤ Talk about "real-world" expenses so that your teen will gain an understanding of what life costs.

➤ Teach your teen to be a savvy consumer by demonstrating how you research and evaluate the worth of a product.

Chapter 22

Money Management for Tomorrow

In This Chapter

➤ Setting up a bank account

➤ Credit cards for teens

➤ The art of teen investing

Once you've convinced your teen of the wisdom of being the ant (who stored something away) rather than the grasshopper (who played all summer long, and saved nothing), you need to help him or her learn more about long-term money management.

In preparation for life after high school, you should help your teen open up a savings and checking account, and older teens should be introduced to the dangers and advantages of credit cards. They'll fare better than their counterparts who have no experience with "plastic."

You also ought to seriously consider exposing your teen to the world of investing. (It can be a great family activity!) As baby boomers are learning somewhat belatedly, saving and investing wisely for the future is more important than ever. If you can get your teen started now, she'll have an easier time making her money grow.

If you're among those who have failed to save, a grim peek at how soon you'll have to start paying for college (and then fund your retirement) should set you on the road to reform. It is *never* too late to start saving. And if you've never tried investing in the stock market, why not make it something you learn about with your teen? By working with only a small percentage of your savings, you can get your feet wet without taking a full plunge.

Setting Up a Bank Account

Remember the pleasure of watching the numbers in your passbook grow as your savings and interest mounted? That kind of tangible savings is now gone in most places. Today's bank customers (kids included) work with monthly statements and automatic teller machines (ATMs), and the world you're preparing them for will rely on electronic banking via phones and personal computers. (Then your teen can turn around and help *you* through the intricacies of banking!)

You'll need to shop around for the best bank for a teen account—some banks have minimum-balance requirements or stiff service charges on small balances that can eat up what's been deposited. If your teen is 15 or older, ask about setting up two accounts: a savings account and a checking account. Your teen is only a few years away from living independently, and now is the time to start showing him how to write checks and reconcile bank statements.

First take your teen to your own bank. Many banks will link accounts and you may get some breaks on fees through this linkage. Your teen should inquire about the following:

➤ How much money is needed to open a savings account? And a checking account?

➤ What fees will I encounter with these accounts?

➤ Are fees deducted automatically?

➤ How often will I receive statements? How can I learn my balance in between statements?

➤ Can I withdraw money at any time?

➤ How much interest does the bank pay, and when is it paid?

You'll also need to know the bank's rules concerning parents and co-signing. Many banks offer the choice of a joint account (in which both of you can conduct transactions independently) or a custodial account (in which you have to sign off on every transaction). Because the point of this is to teach your child independence, the joint account is preferable.

To open an account, you'll both need proper identification (if you're at a new bank), and your teen's social security number. This number should be used as the tax identification number on the account (even if you're required to co-sign). That way, interest earned will be treated as your child's income for tax purposes.

When Does What Goes in Come Out?

As money goes into a savings account, the family will need to come to an agreement on how and when the money comes out. Can the money be used to pay for a short-term goal?

Yes, ideally, this savings account should be for short-term goals. This will increase your teen's enthusiasm for saving. As she acquires more money, some of it should be moved into a higher-interest savings instrument or invested (keep reading for more information on investments).

Ask your bank for information on the different savings vehicles it offers. Banks may offer certificates of deposit that could be timed to pay out around the time your child graduates from high school. That money will be very welcome when your daughter is calculating tuition, setting up a dorm room or apartment, or contemplating how she'll pay for a badly needed car.

Info Flash

Earning money on your money—and then earning money on the money you've earned (interest accrues on interest, if it's left in the bank)—is a valuable lesson for teens.

A simple savings account will spew out some interest; if your child has a good-sized chunk of money, you might also investigate earning more interest on it by depositing it in a certificate of deposit or a money market fund.

While comparing interest rates is instructive, you can also teach your teen the *Rule of 72*. By dividing 72 by the interest rate you're earning, you'll get a rough idea of how long it will take to double your money. The thought of doubling one's money just by letting it sit there is an impressive one, and making this point will help persuade your teen to get that baby-sitting or lawn-cutting money into the bank regularly.

Checks and Balances: Opening a Checking Account

No teenager should be sent off into the world without learning to write a check and manage the account. A checking account also offers teens an additional measure of independence (they, too, can now order from catalogs; and their charitable donations will accurately reflect who's doing the giving because the check comes directly from them).

Spend a few minutes with your teen to make sure he knows how to use and manage his checking account:

➤ Show him how to fill out a check properly.

➤ Show him deposit slips so he knows how to make a deposit into his account. (This is particularly important because teens often can't get to the bank during banking hours and will be making deposits at the cash machine.)

➤ Point out that for every check written, there must be enough money in the account to cover the check.

➤ Stress the importance of *writing down every single deposit or withdrawal* so your teen knows what her balance is at all times. (Point out that ATM activity must be recorded as well.)

➤ As bank statements arrive, show your teen how to reconcile the statement with the check register, label the statement, and file it away.

➤ Set up a small filing system for her so she'll be independent from you on these financial matters.

➤ There are some terrific money management programs for the computer, including online banking (for certain banks), and software like Quicken. Your teen might find these packages interesting, and since computerized banking and electronic bill-paying are the way of the future, one day you may find yourself asking *her* questions about how to use them.

ATM (Always Taking Money?)

In all likelihood, your teen will get an ATM card along with her account. While the thought of your daughter having instant access to her money at the mall ATM may give you pause, remember that learning to manage money on a broader scale is the point of this exercise. Better that she blow $60 on a pair of jeans while she's living at home than blowing $600 when she'll need that money for next month's rent.

Be sure to ask the bank about ATM charges. While ATMs offer greater teen convenience (because banks are generally closed by the time students finish with school and after-school activities), you'll need to be aware of what this convenience costs.

Danger Zone

An ATM card is almost as valuable to a teen as a credit card—and almost as dangerous. Teach your teen to:

➤ Record all transactions conducted through the ATM.

➤ Keep the card somewhere safe, and never loan it to anyone (or tell them the Personal Identification Number—PIN).

➤ Be alert when entering an ATM area. Don't patronize poorly lit ATM areas, and don't enter one if someone is hanging out nearby.

Info Flash

No sense in wasting a "teachable" moment. As you select a bank, tell your teen that banks don't take care of money and pay interest out of the goodness of their hearts. Banks are for-profit businesses, and they make money by using customers' deposits to lend money to other people. Those borrowers must pay back the loan with interest—some of which is paid to you for the service your money performed. The rest of it goes to the bank in the form of profit. (You can also assure your teen that her money will always be there when she needs it.)

Credit Card Mania

Imagine life without your credit card...Impossible thought, isn't it? Now imagine your teenager *with* a credit card...A nightmare, yes? Despite your angst, it's better that she learn now (most credit cards offered to teens have relatively low limits) than later (when the risks are greater). So buckle in. If you believe in credit cards and want your teen to have one for emergencies, it's time to let an older teen give it a try.

Start Slow: Store Credit Cards

Particularly if your teen can successfully manage her clothing budget, consider getting her a department store credit card first. With a store card, she can pay by card rather than cash (but not charge dinner at the diner for the entire soccer team on her Visa card). Because she knows how to watch her costs (and that she's liable for her expenses), she will probably have a successful experience with a store card.

Rather than adding her to your account (so you continue receiving the bill), talk to the department store about setting up a separate account for her (you'll likely have to co-sign). The learning isn't in whipping out the plastic at the store; the learning is in managing the bill responsibly, so you want that experience to be on her shoulders.

Here's what your teen should know about credit cards:

➤ A credit card is a privilege, not a right, and because a credit card is a form of short-term loan (buy now, pay later), anyone using a credit card has to be very aware of how they will pay the bill.

➤ Because interest is charged on any unpaid balance each month, this inflates the cost of the purchases. (Point out that a 19.8 percent interest rate means paying an extra $20 on every unpaid $100.)

➤ Don't charge anything you can't pay for that month—unless you're in a true emergency.

➤ Warn your teen of the danger of charging something for her friends and expecting them to pay her back in cash. Somehow, the money she'll owe at the end of the month will never end up in the bank.

➤ Just because the bank gave her a certain credit limit, it doesn't mean she should spend to that level.

Make your attitude toward a "bail out" known. Specify that any bailing out will eventually be fully repaid by her—with high interest.

When the account is set up, work with her so she'll learn to:

➤ Save receipts from purchases to compare against the invoice.

➤ Note her billing due date, and decide with her on what date she will mail the check. *You will want to stay involved with this.*

Danger Zone

CAUTION

A credit card is serious business. Your teen is building a credit history that will follow him for years. A black mark on his credit could prevent him from renting an apartment, create difficulty at a job interview, or keep him from buying a car. If he handles it irresponsibly, he stands the chance of bringing down your credit rating (as his co-signer or just as his parent). Impress upon him the necessity of treating this experience responsibly. That's why it's worth supervising his bill-paying schedule, and providing him with the experience before he's in college, where credit cards are easy to obtain.

The Next Step: Getting a Bank Card

Of course, you can't charge travel or an emergency car repair on a department store credit card, so after a successful year of experience, you may want to let your teen graduate to a bank card. This can be a "high risk" experience, so before doing so, consider your teen's spending habits. Is he reasonable and responsible and likely to handle it wisely?

Some families start with a "secured" card. The card holder pays a set amount as a deposit (perhaps $500) and then he can charge up to that limit.

Your best bet for obtaining a credit card will be stopping at your own bank. If you and your teen both bank there and your teen has a part-time job of some type, the bank will probably issue him a credit card of some type. (You may still have to co-sign.) You can do some card-shopping, and look for a card with a lower interest rate or no annual fee, but the card may be more difficult to get.

Some kids use credit approval for one card as a means to qualify for other cards—a recipe for disaster. Before they leave home, try to impress upon them that splurging on a trip they can't afford for spring break is a problem that will come home to roost in the form of a bad credit rating, something they'll have to live with for a very long time.

Introduce the "Real World"

Because money is often a taboo subject, many teens leave the family nest without a clue as to how much it costs to rent an apartment or how much typical telephone and utilities bills are.

Sitting down for a formal lecture is useless, of course, but you should mention costs that affect your teen. What did you pay the telephone company last month? How much was the online bill? And include your teen in the cost of day-to-day experiences. When he goes with you to the grocery store, remark on how much the final charge was. Tell him how much the movie with popcorn and soda costs. If you're having lunch together, let him handle the check, complete with figuring out what the tip should be.

As your teen gets older and starts thinking about how she can't wait to have her own apartment, be supportive (or she'll be back in her old bedroom at age 22) but instructional. Pull out the paper one Sunday morning, and show her the apartment ads. A quick glance will give the two of you a general idea of apartment costs.

The Art of Teen Investing

Like all other aspects of money management, the more you can expose your teenager to during these years, the better off she'll be. If you've instilled in your teen the habit of saving, then it's time to introduce her to the world of investing.

For anyone young (who can afford to wait before withdrawing the money), the stock market is well worth investigating. Historically, stocks have outpaced bonds and "safe" investments, like certificates of deposit (CDs), money market funds, and U.S. Treasury bills. (Your biggest market risk is if you have to pull out your money unexpectedly, when the market is low.)

Info Flash

From 1926 through 1995, stocks returned an average of 10.5 percent per year, compared with 5.2 percent from long-term government bonds and 3.7 percent from U.S. Treasury bills. Inflation over that same period averaged 3.1 percent a year—meaning that after taxes, only stocks have significantly enhanced purchasing power.

Creating a Portfolio

When it comes to money, you never put all your eggs in one basket, so diversification is the first rule to teach your teen. The two of you should talk about how much she has in her savings account and decide how much to pull out for investing; you might suggest that 20 percent is a good amount. This leaves the majority of her savings in an accessible, guaranteed instrument (her savings account) and takes only a portion to put into the higher promise but higher risk of the stock market.

Now comes the fun part. In what company would your teen like to invest? You're in relatively safe hands here, try to relax. If she's permitted to "buy what she knows," she's likely to choose Coca-Cola, McDonald's, Disney—all good solid "blue chip" stocks.

Info Flash

If your teen has ever played poker, she'll know the derivation of the term "blue chip." Like the more valuable blue chips used in poker, this market term is used to describe the stocks of the largest, most consistently profitable companies.

After your teen expresses an interest in a particular stock, more research is necessary. She may love a particular type of computer and want to buy that stock, but if the company is having difficulty in its foreign division or other performance problems, you'll want to learn that now. Show her the steps you can take to check out a company:

➤ Call the company for a copy of the annual report; it will tell her about what goals the company has set and how well it has met them.

➤ Visit the library and take a look at *Value Line Investment Survey, Moody's Handbook of Common Stocks,* or *S & P Reports,* any of which will provide some insight into the company's track record and how the analysts feel about it.

➤ The online services (such as the World Wide Web, the Internet, or America Online) also offer a wealth of financial information. If you subscribe to one, investigate what information is available to you online.

If there doesn't seem to be any bad news the company is sweeping under the carpet, then go for it!

Info Flash

Explain to your teen the basic concept of the stock market—that it was created so the general public could invest money in companies in which it believed (and possibly gain financially as a result), while the companies benefited by having additional cash to invest in their business.

The price of stock rises and falls based on supply and demand. When demand is high (for example, when a company announces good news), shares of stocks can command a higher price because they're harder to come by; when demand is low (based on bad news), the prices drop.

Opening a Brokerage Account

Whether you deal with your own broker, contact a discount broker, or purchase stock through one of the new online services, you will need to set up an account with your teen. The process is much like opening a bank account.

Until your teen is 18 or 21 (depending on your state of residence), any brokerage account you set up must be a custodial one. Though you'll conduct all transactions, you can set up the account using her social security number for tax purposes. (Remember, too, that legally she'll have access to this money the moment she turns legal age, so don't use the account to stash anything you don't want her to have when she's 18 or 21.)

When you make your stock purchase, ask the broker for how the company is listed and on which exchange (if you haven't already picked up that information in your research).

And if the commissions (the amount charged by the firm that buys or sells the stock for you) seem high compared to the size of the investment, chalk it up to "education." If you're fortunate, the money will grow and the commissions will seem smaller as the account grows bigger.

Following the Stock

With luck, charting your teen's market investment can become as involving as following your favorite baseball team throughout a season. A benefit of "buying what you know" is that either of you may read articles about the company, and you can check the newspaper daily to see how the stock reacts to various news (like a new product announcement or a poor retail Christmas season).

If you have a home computer with an online service, your teen can set up a customized portfolio to follow his own investments. It makes investing more "real" and more fun.

What do you tell your teen as his $500 investment becomes $475 after the company announces bad news? That's part of the risk and part of the benefit of not needing to sell under pressure. If he hangs in there, history is on his side—the stock will come back up again, and he'll see a profit.

Translating the Financial Pages

To follow the stock, you'll need to show your teen how to read the stock listings. The sample stock listing shown on the next page illustrates what to show him.

| | | | A | B | C | | | | | |
| | | | \| | \| | \| | | | | | |

52-Week				Yld		Sales				
High	Low	Stock	Div	%	P/E	100s	High	Low	Last	Chg
					A					
$16^1/_4$	$9^3/_4$	A Plus	...	...	dd	393	$13^3/_8$	13	13	$- \ ^3/_8$
$10^1/_2$	$4^3/_8$	AAON	...	...	13	36	$5^1/_8$	$4^3/_8$	$4^1/_2$	$+ \ ^1/_8$
15	10	ABC Bc s	.40	2.8	11	443	15	$14^1/_2$	$14^1/_2$	$- \ ^1/_4$
$27^5/_8$	$17^1/_8$	ABC Rail	...	...	19	4	$24^3/_4$	$24^1/_2$	$24^1/_2$	$+ \ ^1/_4$
55	$10^5/_8$^	ABR Int s	...	...	cc	1824	$53^1/_4$	$53^3/_4$	55	$+ \ ^7/_8$
$19^3/_4$	12	ABT Bld	...	...	14	194	$19^1/_4$	$18^1/_2$	$19^1/_4$	...
$30^1/_4$	13	ACC Cp	...	...	dd	1971	$29^7/_8$	$28^5/_8$	$29^5/_8$	$+ 1^1/_8$
$19^3/_4$	$9^1/_8$	ACT MI	...	...	93	175	$13^7/_8$	$13^1/_2$	$13^7/_8$	$+ \ ^1/_8$
$27^1/_2$	$5^3/_4$	ACT Net n	...	...	dd	2733	24	$22^1/_4$	$23^7/_8$	$+ 1^1/_4$

Show your teen a sample stock listing and explain the basics of reading it.

The figures in the far left columns report the high and low of the stock price for the previous 52 weeks.

The figures on the far right show the market activity for the stock price for that day. Prices are reported in $^1/_8$ -point increments ($^1/_8$ of a dollar is 0.125 cents). The following list describes the other elements in the figure:

(A) *Dividend.* This reflects the latest annual dividend paid by that stock on each share owned.

(B) *Yield.* This is the stock's latest annual dividend expressed as a percentage of that day's price.

(C) *Price/earnings ratio.* This is the price of the stock divided by the earnings reported by the company for the latest four quarters.

Another Possibility: Mutual Funds

Though buying shares of a specific company is fun, some people prefer investing in mutual funds. Buying mutual funds is like letting someone else select your stock portfolio: You buy shares in the mutual fund and the fund managers worry about buying and selling the stocks in which the fund has chosen to invest.

The initial mutual fund investment can be as low as $100–$500, and later purchases can generally be in any amount you desire. Like stocks, mutual fund track records can be researched by contacting the fund directly for information; you can also ask a broker or look for information at the library.

Mutual funds are known for their specialty. "Growth" funds take on greater risk with the hope of long-term reward. "Income" funds select stocks for their capability to pay good dividends. Other funds specialize in certain industries, such as utilities or the entertainment industry.

Recently, the Stein Roe Family of Funds has created a Young Investors Fund, which specializes in stocks that appeal to young people. Their financial goal is one of long-term growth, and investors receive teen-oriented information about money management and investing.

Tuning In

You might consider forming a Family Investment Club. Family members can "buy into" a percentage of the club. Each club member can participate by researching various stocks or mutual funds, and the family decides together how the pooled money should be invested.

If you decide to do this, consider seeding the club with a fair—but not overly generous—amount, so you can relax and take a back seat. If you try to coerce any decisions, your kids will sense it immediately and will become disinterested.

The key to any type of learning experience is giving your kids as much "rope" as you can without letting them hang themselves.

The Least You Need to Know

➤ Help your teen open a savings account, and consider letting an older teen open a checking account.

➤ Ask at your own bank if family accounts can be linked to reduce the bank fees charged against your teen's account.

➤ If your teen gets an ATM card, caution him about keeping it in a safe place, not revealing the PIN number, and using ATM areas cautiously.

➤ Give your teen experience at handling a credit card by starting out with one for a clothing or department store.

➤ Supervise payments to be certain that this experience doesn't damage anyone's credit rating.

➤ Introduce your teen to investing by encouraging her to buy a few shares of stock with some of her savings.

Chapter 23

College Money: Savings, Financial Aid, and Scholarships

> MY FINANCIAL AID CAME THROUGH!

Are you sitting down? You'd better be when you learn what college costs today. Public universities currently cost between $5,000 and $12,000 per year; and top-tier private colleges can run as high as $30,000 (if you add up tuition, room and board, books, transportation, and other expenses). What's more, college costs increase 4 to 10 percent annually—a figure that substantially exceeds the rate of inflation.

Though this kind of money is impossible for most parents to fathom, there are ways to manage it by artfully linking financial aid, scholarships (yes, they're out there), and savings.

The key is to plan ahead and to act fast. Delaying anything—from setting up a savings account to filling out financial aid forms—can cost you big bucks at a time when you can least afford it.

Here's what you can do to take the sting out of your teen's step into higher learning.

Info Flash

There are two important guidelines to keep in mind as you seek financial aid:

Always look for the most current information available. Don't rely solely on books (even this one) because the information on financial aid changes all the time. (For example, this year, for the first time, some schools tied their financial aid awards to a minimum score on the SATs.)

As your teen looks at colleges, always investigate costs. You can be a good consumer with colleges just as you can with any other item. A high price tag shouldn't deter your teen from applying to a particular school, but she should also apply to one or two schools you *can* afford. That way if the financial aid package at a particular school isn't what you hoped for, you'll still have an affordable school where she can begin her college education.

Sock It Away Early

Time is your best ally when it comes to saving for college. You natural savers out there may have started tucking money away for college the day your baby was born. If you did, the power of compound interest has probably given you a nice nest egg to pay for a college education. But what if you didn't?

Whatever age your children are, start putting away money now. It's not too late.

Also, contact your state department of education and ask about college savings programs. Many states offer prepaid college tuition plans for schools in the state that lock in tuition prices (and protect you from inflation and rising costs). If your teen is interested in a school in a different state, contact that state's department of education for any programs for which you might be eligible.

Under Your Mattress Isn't Good Enough

As you tuck away money, consider where you're stashing it—savings account interest is so low right now that it's about as profitable as putting your money under your mattress. Talk to your banker, a broker, or a financial planner about where else you might invest college savings.

If you have pre-teens who are still several years away from college, consider putting as much as two-thirds of your savings in high-growth investments; financial experts recommend stock mutual funds. These investments will help your money keep pace with inflation and rising tuition costs.

If you're investing more than $1,000, you'll want to diversify by investing in more than one mutual fund. Look for funds that emphasize growth rather than income. Consult a financial advisor on fund picks, or buy a few personal finance magazines and read their recommendations. Then call the funds themselves for more information.

The remaining college money should be placed in safe, fixed-income instruments such as certificates of deposit or zero-coupon government bonds.

As your teen gets closer to entering college (two to three years away), begin moving your money out of growth investments and into safer instruments, such as CDs where you can lock in the value. By planning early, you won't have to cash in your mutual funds if the market is down; you'll have time on your side to wait for the best opportunity to sell.

Keeping It Yours to Keep It Safe

Holding savings in your child's name may affect your family's eligibility for financial aid. The federal formula for determining financial need weighs students' assets more heavily than their parents'. If you're going to apply for financial aid, you should not keep major savings in your child's name.

Tuning In
Are your teen's grandparents looking for a great way to mark Sweet Sixteen or some other special occasion? Ask them to devote money to your child's college savings.

If you've already transferred money to your child in some type of irrevocable savings program (such as establishing a custodial account for your teenager), use that money for first-year expenses. Then when you file for financial aid in subsequent years, you'll be eligible for increased aid because the money will have already been spent.

Financial Aid: Getting the Buck to Stop at Your House

Most financial aid packages are made up of any combination of four general types of aid.

➤ *Scholarships and grants* are the most desirable because you don't have to pay them back.

➤ *Work study programs* allow your teen to work at a campus-related job. They're good for covering school expenses like book costs.

➤ *Government loans* are, without a doubt, the largest and most frequently offered type of financial aid.

The amount of financial aid you receive is based on the college cost and your ability to pay. Financial aid officers stress that it's worth applying for financial aid, regardless of your income. Every family's situation is different. (Unfortunately, financial aid offices don't always view "financial need" the way families do, but it's always worth trying.)

Middle- and upper-income families will have more difficulty qualifying for need-based financial aid, but they can still look into funds given out on the basis of merit, such as academic and athletic scholarships.

Empty Pockets: How to Qualify for the Money You Need

To qualify for federal aid, you must fill out a FAFSA (Free Application for Federal Student Aid) form. This form is also used by many colleges, though some require a second aid application as well.

The FAFSA requests information about family income, savings, assets, and the number of children presently in college. See your child's guidance counselor for a copy.

The FAFSA is used to assess how much your family can contribute to the cost of college. The standard government formula requires that 35 percent of a student's assets be used for college education, but only about 6 percent of a parent's. Therefore, the lower your assets, the more likely you are to qualify for more financial aid.

The college then assembles a financial aid package that may or may not fully fill the gap between college costs (including tuition, books, housing, food, and transportation) and your ability to pay. The package is usually a conglomeration of scholarships, grants, loans, and work-study arrangements.

Bridging the Gap

If there is a gap, you have a few possible solutions: If your child gets a better financial offer from another school, see if you can negotiate a better deal. Or, consider whether you're comfortable borrowing from family members or taking out a loan.

Info Flash
According to *The Chronicle of Higher Education*, only 14 percent of today's college students complete their degrees in a traditional four-year span.

Loans range from low-cost federally guaranteed student loans to higher-cost but virtually unlimited loans for parents. As long as a student does well, more loans are generally offered each year. Though helpful, remember that graduating with several thousand dollars of loans to pay off isn't fun.

On the bright side, students who handle these loans wisely establish a good credit rating that will make it easier for them to qualify for credit cards and mortgages later on.

If you're still strapped, you should investigate some creative options. More and more students are completing a four-year curriculum in five or more years so they can work to pay some of their own expenses. Others are attending less expensive community colleges for two years before transferring to a larger institution.

> **Danger Zone**
> If you're separated or divorced, talk to your former spouse now about your teen's college plans. You'll want to begin negotiating who's going to pay what and how. Also check on current laws regarding which parent(s) will be reporting income on the financial aid form.

First Come, First Serve

"Early Bird Gets the Loot" trumpeted one headline on an article about financial aid, and you should remember that as you go through the lprocess. Delays will cost you. Remember this advice when applying for aid:

➤ *Learn all you can about the process.* Attend any financial aid seminars in your community, and stop by the financial aid office of any colleges you visit with your teen. You may learn a great deal through an in-person visit.

➤ *Apply early.* The process starts on January 1, and money is given out on a first-come, first-serve basis. The longer you wait, the lower the money supply. If you can't calculate your taxes before the end of the year, base your figures on estimates, and mail in your FAFSA as soon as possible after January 1. You'll have an opportunity to enter corrections later in the process.

➤ *Plan where your money is.* Your previous year's income and assets will be used to determine your financial need, so delaying income (such as bonuses) or accelerating or postponing the sale of assets may be wise.

➤ *Check on your credit rating.* To be a good credit risk for any type of loan, you don't want to have a total debt of more than 37 percent of your gross income before taxes.

Danger Zone

Myths swirl around the anxiety-laden subject of paying for college. Don't believe everything you hear—like these myths:

We can't afford college. Many colleges have adopted something called the "100 percent need" formula which means that *no one* will be turned away for lack of money.

There's little financial aid available. Not true. There is 35 billion dollars per year available through various programs.

You must be poor to receive financial aid. Many middle-income families qualify. It depends on your family's situation.

Scholarships are easier to get than financial aid. While scholarships are certainly worth investigating, there's actually more money available through financial aid; because more money is available, it's somewhat easier to get.

My child should only apply to state institutions; we'll never to able to afford a private school. Because many private colleges have large endowments (money used for financial aid), they may actually offer your teen a competitive financial package. Just remember to protect your teen by having him also apply to a school you know you can afford.

Scholarships: Best Bang for the Buck

Enterprising students may be able to snatch thousands of additional dollars in scholarship money—the more you look, the more you'll find.

To find out what scholarships and grants are out there, talk to your child's guidance counselor and college financial aid officers. Also go to a local or school library to check out directories on the subject.

Here are a few worthwhile places to start hunting for scholarships:

➤ Many companies offer scholarships for qualified children of employees. Check with your Human Resources department.

➤ Many fraternal groups or industry associations give money to worthy students.

Many scholarships go unclaimed each year because students don't seek them out. Start looking in your teen's sophomore or junior year—and watch deadlines.

Sometimes, scholarships and grants reduce the total aid package your child receives from the school, but it's worth this tradeoff. Scholarships confer special achievement and will look impressive on your teen's resume; and remember, they don't have to be paid off.

Sports Scholarships

There's no central resource to keep track of how much money is available through sports scholarships, but the Women's Sports Foundation estimates that $179 million in athletic scholarships is available for women each year and another $350 million is available for men.

> **Info Flash**
> There are computerized search services that promise to find scholarships your teen might be eligible for, for a fee. Save yourself the money. You can find the scholarships yourself in directories on the computer or in your local library.

If your teen is looking for a sports scholarship, keep the following in mind:

➤ There are scholarships for many sports, not just football, baseball, and basketball. Though those three sports do generate a large pool of money, there's also a great deal of competition for it. There are lots of scholarships for other sports ranging from soccer to archery.

➤ Your teen doesn't need to immerse herself in one sport. Proficiency in more than one sport increases scholarship opportunities and impresses admission committees.

➤ To find local sources of scholarship money, talk to coaches, college administrators, and staff at regional sports camps and clubs.

➤ Most sports scholarships require students to display a degree of academic proficiency as well as athletic ability.

Some schools, such as Ivy Leagues and all NCAA Division III schools, don't offer athletic scholarships; but some do offer merit scholarships, grants, or other forms of financial aid.

Money for Kids of All Types

When you start looking, you'll discover some interesting categories of scholarships based on, shall we say, unusual categories. Take a look at the following:

➤ In Georgia, students with a family income under $100,000 and a 3.0 grade point average are entitled to free tuition at any Georgia public institution, courtesy of the state lottery.

➤ The University of Colorado in Boulder has just instituted First Generation, a scholarship program for state students who are the first in their families to attend college.

➤ One specialized fund offers up to $1,000 to needy left-handed students attending Juniata College in Huntingdon, Pennsylvania.

➤ The Asparagus Club of Paramus, New Jersey, gives $1,000 scholarships each year to financially needy students who intend to work in the food industry.

➤ David Letterman has a scholarship at Indiana's Ball State University that is awarded to C students "like him" (whatever that means!).

Apply Yourself: Going After Financial Aid

Here are the tasks you and your teen will need to take care of during his senior year. (Expect him to do as much as possible; it's a great way to learn the way the world works.)

➤ Call the financial aid offices at each college your teen is interested in. Ask for a packet of financial aid information, and find out what deadlines you must meet.

➤ If your teen is considering applying for early decision, ask the college whether you can get early financial aid estimates. If not, and financial aid is crucial, your teen will just have to apply as a regular applicant so he'll be able to apply to several places and compare offers from different schools.

➤ Request a FAFSA form from the guidance office, and plan to fill it out in December. You'll want to mail it shortly after the first of January.

➤ Start gathering the personal information you'll need to fill out financial aid applications. The type of information is very similar to an income tax form. You'll need:

Your last paycheck stub

Bank statements, including checking and savings accounts, money market funds, certificates of deposit

Investment statements from brokers, mutual funds, partnerships or other income sources

Property records showing the purchase price, value, and outstanding debt on second homes or other real estate (the value of your primary residence is not part of the financial need calculation)

Business or farm records to establish value and debt levels

➤ Fill out the form and photocopy it for your records before mailing it.

➤ After processing, a Student Aid Report will be sent to you. *Check it carefully for accuracy.* If it's inaccurate, follow the instructions provided for making corrections. After you have a correct form in hand, send it to the appropriate colleges.

➤ Most colleges will want a copy of your federal tax return, and some may want state tax returns, medical and dental expense records, or other documents as well.

For Further Info

The financial aid process can be intimidating and confusing to the best of parents. Luckily, there are several resources you can turn to for help:

➤ If your teen's high school has a financial aid counselor on staff, you're very fortunate. He or she can advise you on the best packages possible and can help you navigate through the intricacies of getting financial aid.

➤ In some schools, your teen's guidance counselor is the right person to contact.

➤ For more specific information, phone the admissions office, financial aid office, or academic counselor at your teen's target schools. (Save yourself time by drawing up a list of questions you want to ask before you make the call.)

The Least You Need to Know

➤ As college nears, shift savings into safer, more liquid investments.

➤ Apply for financial aid early.

➤ Look for scholarships and unique sources of funding.

➤ Encourage your teen to keep her grades up and to try a variety of extracurricular activities to keep open the possibility of academic or specialty scholarships.

➤ If the financial aid package doesn't meet your needs, negotiate. You've got a particularly strong case if your teen has been offered a better package elsewhere.

Teen for Hire: Working Hard for a Living

Having work experience—from baby-sitting to landscaping to clerking at the local video store—is an invaluable experience for teens. Among other things, they learn:

➤ How to present themselves professionally

➤ Self-discipline

➤ Responsibility

➤ The value of money (how long *did* it take to earn those new rollerblades?)

They also learn what skills they enjoy and what tasks they loathe. Do they absolutely hate waiting on cranky customers, or do they thrive on human interaction? Is shelving books in a quiet library enjoyable, or would they rather work among the bustle of a busy restaurant?

Their work experience will introduce them to a broader world and will prepare them for the future. But when should you let them start, and how much should they do? Here's what you need to know when your teen starts pounding the pavement.

Retiring the Lemonade Stand: Your Teen's First Job

Occasional work such as baby-sitting, lawn mowing, pet-sitting, and snow shoveling tend to be jobs taken by young teens. These are excellent "first job" experiences and teach the importance of reliability and dependability.

In all likelihood, your teen will consider you a consultant as he searches for employment. When you discuss his work, promote the merits of professionalism:

➤ Anyone who works should set a fee for their services. "Oh, pay me whatever you want..." isn't the right response to "What do you charge?" Have your child do a little research (for example, find out what rival leaf-rakers charge) and set his price accordingly.

➤ If your child has to cancel out on a scheduled job, stress that she must try to find a substitute.

➤ Know your young teen's whereabouts. If she's shoveling snow, what area will she cover? If he's baby-sitting, he should leave the family name and telephone number with you.

➤ During work time, your teen must put the job first. If she's baby-sitting, she can't spend hours on the phone while the kids are awake, and she should limit herself to a brief call or two after they're in bed. If she's raking leaves, her friends shouldn't hang out "to keep her company." A job is a job.

➤ Point out various ways your teen can advertise his services. There's nothing wrong with picking up the phone and saying, "Mrs. Smith, would you like me to rake your leaves?" Or "If you ever need a baby-sitter, I'm available on weekends." He can also post flyers in neighborhood stores.

➤ Watch the time commitment. You may not want your teen baby-sitting at all on school nights, or perhaps you'll feel okay limiting it to jobs that end by 9:30 p.m. It's your job to help your teen manage her job.

Info Flash

In most states, adolescents (14 or over) who want a job need work permits. Your teen can obtain working papers from the school guidance office. To apply, he will need your permission and some proof of age (such as a birth certificate). In states where permits are not issued, employers require proof of age before hiring adolescents to be sure they comply with child labor laws.

In addition, federal child-labor laws limit the number of hours a 14- or 15-year old can work:

➤ No more than three hours on a school day or 18 hours in a school week.

➤ No more than eight hours on a non-school day or 40 hours in a non-school week.

➤ Not before 7 a.m. or after 7 p.m. (except during the summer, when they can work until 9 p.m.).

Superteen: Juggling Job and School

Whether your teen is 13 or 17, she already has a full-time job: school. As you discuss whether your teen can (or should) get a job during the school year, remember that she'll be "moonlighting." Making decisions will be much easier for both of you if you keep that in mind.

If your teen is thinking of taking a job during the school year, here are some questions to consider:

➤ *Will the demands of the job threaten or enhance your child's commitment to school?* Some working students take fewer challenging courses or cut corners on homework; others rise to the challenge because the job teaches them to become more efficient.

Info Flash
A recent study by researchers at Stanford and Temple Universities found that students who worked more than 20 hours per week did less well in school, were more detached from their parents, and had a higher rate of drug and alcohol use (in part because they had more discretionary income).

➤ *Will there still be time for extracurricular activities?* Have your teen ask her employer if she can work around soccer practice, play rehearsals, or saxophone lessons.

➤ *Will he have less time with the family?* Relationship-building with a teenager is hard work at best, and if the two of you don't cross paths often, it will become all the more difficult.

In addition, encourage your teen to make academic concerns his top priority. He may need to be creative to find study time but with your encouragement, he'll know that you still think school takes precedence over his job.

Three months or so after your teen starts her job, evaluate how it's going. Is homework getting done? How are her grades? Is she enjoying her position? Does she have enough time flexibility for activities and family responsibilities?

If you're not thrilled with the situation, encourage her to look around again. A little work experience may open up additional job possibilities, and she may get more flexibility or better working conditions in a new job.

Tuning In
Even a teen's first job should be something that holds some appeal (even if it's primarily financial). The better the teen feels about the job, the more successful he will be.

If she really feels committed to maintaining her job and doesn't want to look for something else, talk to her about your concerns. Perhaps you wouldn't worry about her if she could bring her C in English up to a B or a B- in the next marking period, or maybe you'd find the situation more palatable if she can get different hours so that she could have dinner with you twice a week. If she's truly committed to the job, that's a great quality, and you certainly don't want to dampen her enthusiasm. Just let her know what her other obligations are.

"Summertime and the Livin' Is Easy..."

Summer employment offers your teen an opportunity to earn money, shoulder responsibility, and learn about the world of work—all without the burden of having to worry about school.

Info Flash
According to a recent survey, nearly half of teens between ages 16 and 19 work.

Advise your teen to start hunting for summer employment early. To teenagers, starting to look once school is out makes perfect sense—that's when they're free to work. Adults, of course, know that employers plan ahead.

Looking for a Job in All the Right Places

No matter what kind of job your teen decides to apply for—whether it's folding sweaters at the Gap or monitoring the waves as a lifeguard—there are certain basic steps she should follow:

➤ *Where to apply.* Classified ads, local newspapers, or the town recreation department will have information on camp counselor or lifeguard jobs. (Private area day camps and clubs are also fruitful sources of employment.)

Your teen can also walk through the neighborhood and check in at local stores that may need teen-age help: video stores, movie theaters, ice cream parlors, restaurants, and clothes shops are all popular possibilities.

Encourage your teen to apply in more than one place. Your son might think that putting in a single application to be a lifeguard is more than enough effort on his part, but you should remind him to apply for several jobs.

➤ *What to wear.* Even if the job he's after requires nothing more stylish than a shiny blue polyester uniform, your teen will need to wear decent clothes when he applies. Clean slacks and an unwrinkled shirt are fine for both boys and girls; punk jewelry, torn flannel, and anything fishnet should be left at home.

➤ *What to do.* In many places, picking up an application is the first step. Your teen should go in alone. (If you go in with her, it looks like it's your idea; if she takes a friend, it looks like she isn't serious about getting work.)

Unless the application must be filled out on-site, tell her to bring it home and photocopy it so she can fill out a "scratch" copy before filling out the original.

➤ *How to interview.* If the employer requires an interview, your teen should dress neatly, be on time, be prepared to talk about why she wants the job, and express interest in the business ("I love the clothes you sell here." "I know all about guitars, so I'd make a great salesperson for your music shop."). This is a fairly sophisticated thought for most teens.

If your teen is nervous about the interview, offer to role-play with her. When you do, point out that a good handshake and strong eye contact will serve her well.

Tell your teen it's okay to ask about pay and hours...subjects that many job applicants (not just teens) are uncomfortable talking about.

Tools of the Trade: The Resume and Letters of Recommendation

Some jobs require a resume. While your teen may not have much work experience to include, she can still arrange a neat, professional-looking document (see the sample resume on the next page).

Info Flash
Teenagers who get fired from their first job often fail because they don't know the importance of punctuality, proper dress, poise, and strong communication skills.

Tell her not to be afraid to spell out accomplishments such as being class president or head of the French club. Positions of leadership show an employer responsibility and the ability to take charge.

In addition, suggest that she collect two or three letters of recommendation from teachers, counselors, family friends, or former employers (if she's already held a job). Ready references may clinch a job for a teen.

Finally, remind your teen to send a thank-you note for the interview.

Rebounding from Rejection

The local pool hired 15 kids (including three of his close friends), and he wasn't one of them. She wanted to work at the Gap more than anything, but she didn't get the job.

What can you say when your teen is turned down? Be encouraging. The job market for young people is tough, and many who want employment don't get it.

One or two blatant rejections shouldn't knock him out of the job-hunting market, though. Tell him that getting a job takes persistence.

If the summer arrives and there's still no job in sight, try to help him out. Do you have a friend or relative who might be able to use his services? Can he go back to some of the lawn jobs he had when he was younger? Once he finds some type of income-paying job, you might suggest that he select a place where he can do volunteer work. He can then list his volunteer work on a resume or future job application as work experience, and it may give him an advantage in lining up work for next summer.

Sally Smith
13 Oak Lane
White Falls, OH 12345
(555) 123-4567

EDUCATION	**GRADE POINT AVERAGE**
White Falls High School	3.2

WORK EXPERIENCE

Sales clerk, Vinny's Video	9/95 to present

Assist customers, use register, and clean store after closing.

Baby-sitting	1992 to present

Occasional child-care work for three families. Prepare meals, play games, help with homework, and handle bedtime.

VOLUNTEER ACTIVITIES

English tutor	9/95 to present

Stay after school twice a week to help an ESL student learn how to speak and write English.

AWARDS, SKILLS, ACTIVITIES

Yearbook photo editor	1994, 1995
MVP, White Falls JV Field Hockey	1995
Speak fluent Spanish	

REFERENCES AVAILABLE ON REQUEST

Sample teen resume.

The Road to Head Honcho: Being a Great Employee

Once your teen has a job, there are several simple steps he can take to make sure he keeps it for as long as he wants it:

➤ Always dress appropriately for the job.

➤ Arrive on time.

➤ Be respectful to employers, coworkers, and customers.

➤ If he needs to call in sick or take time off, he should give as much advance notice as possible.

➤ Work at assigned tasks cheerfully and willingly. (Many adults know how annoying it is to try to get service from a surly, bored, or monosyllabic employee.)

➤ Take criticism and/or instruction with good will.

Info Flash
According to the U.S. Department of Labor, 75 percent of Americans report that they don't like their jobs. That's why it's important to encourage your teen to explore many possibilities.

If your teen gets fired, talk to her about what happened. You may learn that it was nothing personal, the store just didn't need an extra clerk anymore.

But if you think that something your teen did caused her to lose the job—for example, if she was late for every shift—you may not find out from her. (She might say, "Oh, the boss was a jerk.") In that case, you might discuss the punctuality issue. No sense harping on it; she'll learn as she suffers the consequences of lost income. (She'll learn her lesson best if you don't bail her out financially.)

If your teen complains about her job, listen up. Teens are sometimes taken advantage of in the workplace. Here's what you can do:

➤ Contact the superintendent's office in your school district or call your state labor department to get information on the laws governing the employment of minors. (Most states have a booklet about it.)

➤ Visit your child's workplace from time to time. Sometimes teens are asked to do hazardous jobs—which are illegal for them to do.

➤ If your teen has a personality conflict with a boss or coworker, discuss strategies: Can your teen switch to a different shift? Would apologizing (with or without cause) and offering to start out on a new foot win this person over?

➤ Your teen should be told that there are two forms of sexual harassment. The first involves any situation where it is communicated (openly or implicitly) that sexual favors will be required if a person wants to keep a job or get a raise. The second form of harassment is when unwelcome or demeaning sexual comments are made, which creates a hostile work environment. Your teen shouldn't put up with either kind.

A worker of any age has the right to a decent work environment, and your teen should know that.

Spending Versus Saving

Some teens love working because it means they can afford stuff—gassing up the car, a leather jacket, new CDs, high-tech sneakers, and so on. You may want to stipulate that a certain percentage (25-50 percent?) of all her earnings must go into savings, and that major purchases of over $100 are to be discussed with you. This will discourage most teens from working as many hours as possible to live a newly affluent lifestyle.

The Great World Beyond

Many teens think that by the time they leave high school, they ought to know what they're going to do "when they grow up." Of course, this isn't true. Reassure your teen that she'll be able to explore one, two, or even three careers during her lifetime.

That said, it doesn't hurt for teens to discover areas of possible interest. The teen who's interested in marine biology but can't stand the sight of blood, for example, ought to know that marine biologists frequently have to deal with blood. This may strengthen her resolve to overcome her fear, or convince her to switch to another interest.

Here are some other ways you can encourage your teen to explore the world of work:

➤ If your teen has a particular interest (taking care of animals, working in the fashion industry), encourage her to go to some of the local establishments where she can learn more about her career interest. She may even want to investigate whether there's an opportunity to "shadow" someone in the job (follow the person around for a work day).

➤ Is career exploration more important at this stage than income? If so, your teen could take on a volunteer responsibility that interests him.

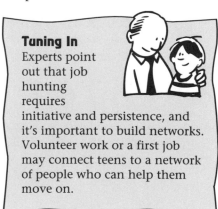

Tuning In
Experts point out that job hunting requires initiative and persistence, and it's important to build networks. Volunteer work or a first job may connect teens to a network of people who can help them move on.

➤ Serve as your teen's cheerleader. You may begin to notice that he's very good at articulating complex thoughts or that he has a "head for figures." When he does something well, point it out. It may help him focus on a career direction.

➤ The job market should affect your teen's thinking, but not control it. Suggest that your teen look up possible careers in the *Occupational Outlook Handbook* (available in the library), which is published by the U.S. Department of Labor. The book describes a wide variety of occupations and covers everything from needed qualifications to working conditions to the outlook for the future.

The Least You Need to Know

➤ Talk to young teens about professionalism: setting a fee, working diligently, and soliciting work in a professional manner.

➤ Limit the number of hours your teen can work during the school year, and tell him you expect a percentage of his income to go into savings.

➤ Teens seeking summer employment should be reminded that the hiring process often starts long before the weather warms up; they should apply early.

➤ Suggest that your teen look for work or volunteer experiences to help better understand what she might like to do one day.

Forging a New Bond

Parenting would be so much easier if babies came with notes. They could warn that a parent's tour of duty will include many night shifts—walking them when they are infants; sitting by their bedside when they suffer from nightmares or fevers; and worrying about them and their late-night whereabouts when they are teens.

The notes could also explain that this is the most difficult—and potentially most rewarding—job you will ever undertake. To acquire this less-than-ten-pound being and have the honor of raising him or her to adulthood is truly an awesome responsibility! (I mean *awesome* in the true sense of the word; not the way teens currently use it.)

As you parent your teen through his or her adolescence, you will inevitably hit some rocky times—all parents do. You will gradually be handing more and more responsibility to your teen. Celebrating when he handles it well and suffering when he goofs up will be a given part of the process. But with intelligence and a sense of humor, you can make it through.

As time goes by, you'll see that you have created a person who possesses self-confidence and is truly incredible at many things—from writing the most gracious thank-you notes to playing a great game of tennis! And chances are excellent that wonderful being who is now fully grown is going to truly appreciate you (maybe not quite yet, but soon—I promise).

You've laid the groundwork for the next stage of both of your lives—relating not as parent and child, but as best friends. Enjoy it—and get some sleep.

Resource Directory

The following organizations are good sources of information, publications, referrals, and support.

Attention Deficit (Hyperactivity) Disorder (ADD & ADHD)

Attention Deficit Information Network, Inc.
475 Hillside Ave.
Needham, MA 02194
617-455-9895

Children and Adults with ADD (CHADD)
499 NW 70th Ave., #308
Plantation, FL 33317
305-587-3700

Eating Disorders

American Anorexic/Bulimia Association, Inc.
293 Central Park West, #1R
New York, NY 10024
201-501-8351

American Dietetic Association, NCNC-Eating Disorders
216 W. Jackson Blvd.
Chicago, IL 60606
800-366-1655

National Anorexic Aid Society
445 E. Granville Rd.
Worthington, OH 43085
614-436-1112

National Association of Anorexia Nervosa and Associated Disorders
Box 7
Highland Park, IL 60035
708-831-3438

Health Issues

American Academy of Orthopaedic Surgeons
P.O. Box 2058
Des Plaines, IL 60017

American Dental Association, Division of Communications
211 E. Chicago Ave.
Chicago, IL 60611

Center for Disease Control National AIDS Clearinghouse
P.O. Box 6003
Rockville, MD 20849-6003
800-232-1311

National Black Child Development Institute
463 Rhode Island Avenue, NW
Washington, DC 20005
202-387-1281

National Coalition of Hispanic Health and Human Services Org.
1501 16th St. NW
Washington, DC 20005
202-387-5000

Learning Disabilities

Council for Exceptional Children—Division of Learning Disabilities
1920 Association Drive
Reston, VA 22091-1589
800-328-0272

Learning Disabilities Association of America
4156 Library Road
Pittsburgh, PA 15234
412-341-1515

National Center for Learning Disabilities
381 Park Avenue South, #1420
New York, NY 10016
212-545-7510

Orton Dyslexia Society
8600 LaSalle Road, #382
Baltimore, MD 21204
410-296-0232

Parents of Gifted/LD Children, Inc.
2420 Eccleston St.
Bethesda, MD 20902

Mental Health

American Psychiatric Association
1400 K Street NW
Washington, DC 20005
202-682-6000

American Psychological Association
1200 17th Street NW
Washington, DC 20036
202-955-7600

Clearinghouse on Family Violence Information
P.O. Box 1182
Washington, DC 20013
703-385-7565

National Association of Social Workers
7981 Eastern Avenue
Silver Spring, MD 20910
301-565-0333

National Domestic Violence Hotline
800-333-SAFE

National Institute of Mental Health
Public Information Office
5600 Fishers Lane
Rockville, MD 20857
301-443-4536

National Network of Runaway and Youth Services, Inc.
1400 Eye Street, NW, Suite 330
Washington, DC 20004
202-783-7949

Sexuality

Center for Population Options
1025 Vermont Ave. NW
Washington, DC 20005
202-347-5700

National Gay and Lesbian Task Force
666 Broadway, #410
New York, NY 10012
212-529-1600

Parents and Friends of Lesbians and Gays (PFLAG)
1101 14th St. NW, #1030
Washington, DC 20005
202-638-4200

Planned Parenthood Federation of America
810 Seventh Ave.
New York, NY 10019
212-541-7800

Sexuality Information and Education Council of the United States (SEICUS)
130 W. 42nd St., #350
New York, NY 10036
212-819-9770

Substance Abuse

Al-Anon/Alateen Family Group Headquarters
P.O. Box 862
Midtown Station
New York, NY 10018-0862
800-344-2666

Drug Abuse Resistance Education (DARE)
P.O. Box 2090
Los Angeles, CA 90051
800-223-DARE

"Just Say No" International
1777 N. California Blvd. #210
Walnut Creek, CA 94596
510-939-6666

Mothers Against Drunk Driving (MADD)
511 E. John Carpenter Freeway, #700
Irving, TX 75062
800-GET-MADD
214-744-6233

Nar-Anon Family Groups
P.O. Box 2562
Palos Verdes Peninsula, CA 90274
213-547-5800

Narcotics Anonymous
P.O. Box 9999
Van Nuys, CA 91409
818-780-3951

National Association for Children of Alcoholics
11462 Rockville Pike, #100
Rockville, MD 20852
301-468-0985

National Clearinghouse for Alcohol and Drug Information
P.O. Box 2345
Rockville, MD 20847-2345
800-729-6686
800-487-4889

National Council on Alcoholism and Drug Dependence, Inc.
12 W. 21st Street, 7th Floor
NY, NY 10017
800-NCA-CALL
212-206-6770

National PTA Drug and Alcohol Abuse Prevention Project
330 N. Wabash Ave., Suite 2100
Chicago, IL 60611-3690
312-670-6782

Parents' Resource Institute for Drug Education, Inc. (PRIDE)
50 Hut Plaza, Suite 210
Atlanta, GA 30303
800-677-7433
404-577-4500

Students Against Driving Drunk (SADD)
200 Pleasant St.
Marlboro, MA 01752
508-481-3568

Index

C

automobiles, 173-174
  financial considerations,
    170-171
  sharing, 170-171
educational courses,
    167-168
emergency equipment, 172
learner's permits, 167
licenses, applying for, 167
punishing, 169
SADD, 208
safety, 168-169, 171
  cellular telephones, 171
  passengers, 166-167
  seat belts, 166
  staged licensing, 169
drugs, 202, 211-212
  communicating, 203-204
  confronting substance
    abuse, 205-206
  depression, 221
  inhalants, 214
  marijuana, 213
  parental use, 212-213
  peer pressure, 204-205
  reducing abuse, 204
  symptoms, 212
dying intestate (dying without
  a will), 19
dysgraphia, 106
dyslexia, 105

E

earnings issues (teen
  employment), 273
eating disorders, 184-185
  anorexia nervosa, 184-185
  athletics, 156
  bulimia nervosa, 185
eating habits
  healthy, 178-179
  vegetarianism, 183-184
education
  computers as educational
    tools, 149
  driver's education, 167-168
  Freedom of Information Act,
    96
  learning disabilities
    defined, 100

facts, 100
  warning signs, 101-105
online services as resources,
    149-151
parental involvement, 95-96
substance abuse, 203-204
see also academics
electrolysis, 50
electronic media (video games,
  rating systems), 148
emergencies
  driving equipment, 172
  driving accidents, 172-173
emotional growth
  adolescence, 59-61
    peer interaction, 60
    rebellion, 60
    self-esteem, 61
    sexuality, 59-60
  body image, 57, 59
  depression, 220-221
  early adolescence, 56-59
  establishing independence,
    58
  expressing, 8
  mood swings, 58-59
  peer communication, 57-58
emotions, 219-220
employment for teens
  after-school jobs, 267-268
  career exploration,
    encouraging, 273-274
  coping with conflicts in
    workplace, 272-273
  coping with rejection, 270
  earnings issues, 273
  federal child-labor laws, 267
  guidelines for employee
    behavior, 272-273
  guidelines for finding, 269
    letters of recommenda-
      tion, 270
    resumes, 270
  professionalism, 266-267
  summer, 268
  work permits, 267
entertainment (allowances),
    235
entrance exams (college),
  preparing, 125-126
essay section (college
  applications), 127

etiquette (telephone calls),
    141-142
exercise (depression), 219
expectations, defining, 22-23
  checklists for household
    chores, 23-24
expenses (allowances), 234-236
experimentation (teen)
  appearance, 66-67
  clothing styles, 70-71
  cosmetic application, 70
  supporting, 67
extracurricular activities
  (sports)
  injuries, 155-156
  safety, 154-156

F

FAFSA (Free Application for
  Federal Student Aid), 258
families, building self-esteem,
    76-77
family activities
  communication via, 5-6
  reasons for, 14
  television viewing
    (guidelines for), 143-144
  vacations, planning, 15
family therapists (depression),
    225
federal child-labor laws, 267
feelings, 219-220
  depression, 218-221
    suicide, 221-222
  girls (sexual issues), 193
females, *see* girls
financial aid
  application process, 262-263
  college expenses, 256
  loans, 258-259
  myths, 260
  packages, 257-258
  qualifying for, 258
  resources, 263
  scholarships
    seeking, 260-262
    sports, 261
    unusual categories,
      261-262

287

Q

R

When You're Smart Enough to Know That You Don't Know It All

For all the ups and downs you're sure to encounter in life, The Complete Idiot's Guides give you down-to-earth answers and practical solutions.

Personal Business

The Complete Idiot's Guide to Terrific Business Writing
ISBN: 0-02-861097-0 ▪ $16.95

The Complete Idiot's Guide to Getting the Job You Want
ISBN: 1-56761-608-9 ▪ $24.95

The Complete Idiot's Guide to Managing Your Time
ISBN: 0-02-861039-3 ▪ $14.95

The Complete Idiot's Guide to Speaking in Public with Confidence
ISBN: 0-02-861038-5 ▪ $16.95

The Complete Idiot's Guide to Winning Through Negotiation
ISBN: 0-02-861037-7 ▪ $16.95

The Complete Idiot's Guide to Managing People
ISBN: 0-02-861036-9 ▪ $18.95

The Complete Idiot's Guide to a Great Retirement
ISBN: 1-56761-601-1 ▪ $16.95

The Complete Idiot's Guide to Starting Your Own Business
ISBN: 1-56761-529-5 ▪ $16.99

The Complete Idiot's Guide to Protecting Yourself From Everyday Legal Hassles
ISBN: 1-56761-602-X ▪ $16.99

The Complete Idiot's Guide to Surviving Divorce
ISBN: 0-02-861101-2 ▪ $16.95

You can handle it!

The Complete Idiot's Guide to Learning French on Your Own
ISBN: 0-02-861043-1 ▪ $16.95

The Complete Idiot's Guide to Dating
ISBN: 0-02-861052-0 ▪ $14.95

The Complete Idiot's Guide to Hiking and Camping
ISBN: 0-02-861100-4 ▪ $16.95

The Complete Idiot's Guide to Cooking Basics
ISBN: 1-56761-523-6 ▪ $16.99

The Complete Idiot's Guide to Learning Spanish on Your Own
ISBN: 0-02-861040-7 ▪ $16.95

The Complete Idiot's Guide to Gambling Like a Pro
ISBN: 0-02-861102-0 ▪ $16.95

The Complete Idiot's Guide to Choosing, Training, and Raising a Dog
ISBN: 0-02-861098-9 ▪ $16.95

The Complete Idiot's Guide to Trouble-Free Car Care
ISBN: 0-02-861041-5 ▪ $16.95

The Complete Idiot's Guide to the Perfect Wedding
ISBN: 1-56761-532-5 ▪ $16.99

The Complete Idiot's Guide to Getting and Keeping Your Perfect Body
ISBN: 0-286105122 ▪ $16.99

The Complete Idiot's Guide to First Aid Basics
ISBN: 0-02-861099-7 ▪ $16.95

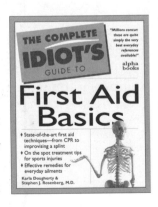

The Complete Idiot's Guide to the Perfect Vacation
ISBN: 1-56761-531-7 ▪ $14.99

The Complete Idiot's Guide to Trouble-Free Home Repair
ISBN: 0-02-861042-3 ▪ $16.95

The Complete Idiot's Guide to Getting into College
ISBN: 1-56761-508-2 ▪ $14.95